PERFORMANCE AND PROTEST

Cover photo by William A. Robinson and Alfred J. Roe, Kenn Harper Collection

From left to right, back row: unknown, Julia Hedwig Lucy, Tomasi Lucy, John Lucy, Simon Lucy, Abraha Lucy, Jonas Palliser, Jonasi Lucy, unknown, Zacharius, Peter Palliser, unknown; **middle row**: Katerina Lucy, Susan Palliser, Christopher Palliser, Esther, Nanji, Helena, Naimi, Tabia, Justina (standing); **front row**: Susan Palliser, Lucy Palliser, unknown, unknown, unknown.

PERFORMANCE AND PROTEST

Inuit of Labrador and the World's Columbian Exposition, 1893

NIGEL MARKHAM

Library and Archives Canada Cataloguing in Publication
Title: Performance and protest : Inuit of Labrador and the World's Columbian Exposition, 1893 / Nigel Markham.
Names: Markham, Nigel, author
Description: Includes bibliographical references and index.
Identifiers: Canadiana (print) 20250225719 | Canadiana (ebook) 20250225751 | ISBN 9781990445286 (softcover) | ISBN 9781990445293 (EPUB) | ISBN 9781990445309 (PDF)
Subjects: LCSH: World's Columbian Exposition (1893 : Chicago, Ill.) | LCSH: Inuit—Newfoundland and Labrador—Labrador—History—19th century. | LCSH: Inuit—Illinois—Chicago—History—19th century.
Classification: LCC E99.E7 M37 2025 | DDC 971.8/20049712—dc23

Copy editing: Rebecca Roberts
Cover design: Randy Drover
Page design and layout: Alison Carr

Published by Memorial University Press
Memorial University of Newfoundland and Labrador
P.O. Box 4200
St. John's, NL A1C 5S7
www.memorialuniversitypress.ca

Printed in Canada

30 29 28 27 26 25 1 2 3 4 5 6 7 8

Funded by the Government of Canada | Financé par le gouvernement du Canada

for Carol Brice-Bennett

Esther and Nancy, Lucy and Susan Palliser.
World's Columbian Exposition, 1893
(Photo: William A. Robinson and Alfred J. Roe,
Kenn Harper Collection).

In the summer of 1892, an American company, J.W. Skiles & Co, of Spokane Washington, chartered a schooner to travel to Labrador to recruit Inuit for the "Esquimaux Village," an ethnological exhibit to be presented the following year at the World's Columbian Exposition in Chicago. When the vessel arrived in Boston with its cargo of Inuit, dogs and artifacts, R.G. Taber, one of the agents for the company, announced to the American press: "Our trip has been successful, and we have with us some of the best specimens of the race to be found in their country."

—"Esquimaux Here," *Boston Daily Globe*, October 14, 1892

"Esquimaux Village," World's Columbian Exposition, 1893 (Photo: William A. Robinson and Alfred J. Roe, Kenn Harper Collection).

Contents

Acknowledgements | xi
Notes to the Reader | xv

Introduction: Christmas in Chicago | 1
Maps | 6
Chapter 1 The Voyage of the *Evelena* 1892 Part 1: Aiviktok | 11
Chapter 2 The Voyage of the *Evelena* 1892 Part 2: The Moravian Coast | 23
Chapter 3 The Voyage of the *Evelena* 1892 Part 3: Nachvak | 37
Chapter 4 Chicago and the World's Columbian Exposition | 55
Chapter 5 Ethnology and the Fair | 63
Chapter 6 The "Esquimaux Village" | 77
Chapter 7 After Chicago | 119
Chapter 8 Aftermath | 141
Postscript | 159

Appendix 1 Passenger List of the *Evelena* | 165
Appendix 2 Revised Passenger List of the *Evelena* | 168
Appendix 3 The "Esquimaux Village" and the Stoney Avenue Exhibit | 171
Appendix 4 After the World's Columbian Exposition | 173
Appendix 5 Imagining "Esquimaux" at the World's Fair | 175

Notes | 179
Bibliography | 209
Index | 219

Acknowledgements

Any book is a journey which cannot be completed without the help of many people. I would like to thank all those who have encouraged and helped me throughout this undertaking. Without Tom Gordon, former director of Traditions and Transitions, the joint research project of the Nunatsiavut Government and Memorial University of Newfoundland, I would never have embarked on this project, and I am grateful to him for his early encouragement and enthusiasm. I am also grateful to Traditions and Transitions for financial support and to its subsequent director Lisa Rankin for her assistance.

I would like to thank my MA thesis supervisor, Kurt Korneski, for his insights, critiques, and continued interest throughout the process, and my good friend and colleague Anne Budgell who read and re-read the manuscript and whose suggestions always resulted in improvements. In the same spirit, I received valuable criticism and advice from my friends Angela Baker and Bev Brown.

This story is international in its scope, and I have relied heavily on the work of Canadian and American scholars for guidance, insight, and understanding. The field of academic research on Labrador has many luminaries who have contributed to the writing of Inuit history. Among those who informed and influenced this work are: J.K. Hiller, Susan Kaplan, Carol Brice-Bennett, J. Garth Taylor, Marianne P. Stopp, David Zimmerly, Hans Rollmann, Kurt Korneski, William Fitzhugh, Lisa Rankin, and Peter Whitridge. I am further indebted to Hans Rollmann for his generosity and patience in translating several important Moravian documents on my behalf and to Christina Petterson of Skriveriet/Villagescribe for additional translations. I would also like to thank Patty Way for sharing with me her deep knowledge of Labrador genealogy, Joyce Allen for information on the Lucy family, Joan Dicker for advice on Inuktitut linguistics and spellings, and Aimie Chaulk for access to the resources of *Them Days* magazine and its unique oral history archive.

My perspective on the history of Chicago, the World's Columbian Exposition, nineteenth-century anthropology, and ethnological exhibits in general was shaped by numerous American scholars and writers, including Rodney Reid Badger, William Cronon, Curtis M. Hinsley, Robert Rydell, Gertrude Scott, and Bessie Louise Smith. I am particularly indebted to Curtis Hinsley whose work on Frederic Putnam and the organization of anthropology at the fair was essential to my understanding of the ideological and intellectual environment in which Labrador Inuit found themselves. While undertaking research in the US, I received valuable assistance from Christopher Pollock, Historian-in-Residence at the San Francisco Recreation and Park Department, without whom I would have been unable to access the Raymond Clary papers relating to Inuit participation in the 1894 San Francisco Midwinter Fair. I would also like to thank Kenn Harper who shares my interest in this story and with whom I have had many enjoyable conversations and valuable exchanges of information.

At Memorial University Press I would thank my editor Fiona Polack for her guidance through a long process that I did not always understand or appreciate, Vicki Hallet who helped me finish that process, Alison Carr, MUP's managing editor, for her diligence and patience, Randy Drover for his artful cover design, and the helpful and patient staff at the Centre for Newfoundland Studies at Memorial University, particularly Colleen Field, Glenda Dawe, and Jackie Hillier, who guided me through their archives and helped locate sources I might otherwise have overlooked. I would also like to thank keen-eyed copyeditor Rebecca Roberts for helping to polish the text and David Mercer who carefully created the maps used in this publication.

My time in Labrador and particularly my time on the north coast many years ago first stimulated my interest in Labrador, its people, and their histories and I will be forever grateful for the kindness and hospitality shown to me by the people I had the privilege to meet there. They gave generously of their time, tolerated my questions, and shared with me their stories. Sadly, most of these individuals have now passed but I remain indebted to Bill and Mary

Andersen, Ted and Gladis Andersen, Toby Andersen, Gus Bennett, Boas and Kitora Boase, John and Hulda Dicker, Bill Edmunds, John Edmunds, George and Andrea Flowers, Chesley and Jesse Flowers, Job Flowers, Manasse Fox, Johannes Green, John Jararuse, Titus and Martha Joshua, William Kalleo, Jacko and Emma Kaujautsiak, Apa Kojak, Johannes Lampe, George Lane, Abel and Bella Leo, Eugene and Hulda Lidd, Sam and Bella Lyall, Mabel Manak, Rupert and Peace McNeil, Jacko and Minnie Merkuratsuk, Amelia Merkuratsuk, Julius and Naeme Merkuratsuk, Levi Nochasak, Joshua Obed, Martin Sillett, Jerry Sillett, Clara Voisey, and Fran Williams. Without these people, and others I have failed to mention, my love of Labrador would never have taken hold, and this book would never have been written.

Finally, I would like to thank my partner Mary Sexton whose love and support over the years has helped make this project possible.

Notes to the Reader

The term "Inuit" is generally used in this book when discussing the people from Labrador who attended the World's Columbian Exposition in 1893. It means "the people" and includes the article. The term "Esquimaux" or "Eskimo" was commonly used in the period under consideration. It is considered derogatory today but is retained in this text and used with direct quotations when citing contemporary reports or historical texts from the time under discussion.

Inuit nomenclature is varied in historical records and evolving in current practice, so it is often difficult to establish definitive spellings for personal names and place names. Historical usage is particularly variable as the writer was rarely Inuit and often had a limited understanding of Inuktitut. A case in point is the passenger list of the schooner *Evelena* which forms the primary record for identifying Inuit who attended the fair.[1] This was likely written by a crew member and was subject to his interpretation of what he heard and how he thought it should be written. For the most part I have used spellings as they occur in Moravian or Hudson's Bay Company records because these were a more common usage. Geographical place names, however, have been updated where possible to conform to current usage.

Traditionally, Inuit in Labrador did not use surnames. Inuit north of the Moravian mission communities, called "Northlanders" by the Moravians, identified themselves with a single name. Inuit associated with Moravian communities did not use surnames at the time of the World's Columbian Exposition but began the practice, at the instigation of the missionaries, shortly after the fair.[2] To avoid confusion when two people had the same name, a person was identified by his or her association with their spouse. Thus Âpili was known as Âpili-Heleneup and conversely Helene was known as Helene-Âpiliup; "iup" is a form of the possessive in Inuktitut, the "i" being dropped if preceded by a vowel.[3] Inuit living south of Moravian communities, called "Southlanders" by the Moravians, had, through their association with European traders, adopted the use of surnames earlier in the nineteenth century.

I have attached several short appendices following the text. These may be particularly helpful for those interested in tracking the movements of individuals or families in the time covered by the narrative. Appendix 1 is the original passenger list of the *Evelena* referred to above. It includes all the people who attended the World's Columbian Exposition as part of the original "Esquimaux Village." However, the document can be confusing. Both the spelling of names and the family groupings can be misleading. Appendix 2, which is based on further research, reflects more common spellings, contains more accurate family groupings, and identifies the region in Labrador from which each family came.

During their time in the United States, the original group splintered and reformed several times. All were part of the "Esquimaux Village" until the rebellion, when the group split, with some remaining with the original concession and some leaving to establish a second exhibit outside the fairgrounds. After the World's Columbian Exposition, some people went back to Labrador while others remained. Some of these attended the Midwinter Exposition in San Francisco the following year while others undertook a tour of dime museums in the eastern United States. Nearly all Inuit returned to Labrador in the summer of 1894, although one family stayed until 1896, and a few individuals did not return at all, apparently choosing to remain in the US. Appendix 3 helps clarify who participated in each exhibit at the World's Columbian Exposition while Appendix 4 provides information on all the subsequent movements of individuals before their return to Labrador.

INTRODUCTION

Christmas in Chicago

On 20 December 1892, while Chicago was in the grip of winter and construction of the much-anticipated World's Columbian Exposition was being hampered by snow and freezing temperatures, a small delegation of Inuit set out from their makeshift homes on the fairground to do some Christmas shopping. They were part of a contingent of sixty Inuit who had arrived in Chicago the previous October, having been recruited in Labrador for an ethnological exhibit at the fair called the "Esquimaux Village." A correspondent from the *Chicago Tribune* witnessed the shopping expedition and filed a newspaper report the following day. He noted: "Curiosity, amazement, in fact all the feelings of extreme satisfaction, shone in their round countenances as they gazed at the brilliantly coloured toys and painted things on the counters. It was fairy land to them."[1]

Inuit were accompanied on this trip by one of the exhibit's agents who told the startled store clerks to let the shoppers have whatever they wanted. The clerks hardly knew what to do. A hurried consultation assigned two of them to attend to the group and for over two hours a chaotic shopping spree ensued, bringing to a halt all other transactions. Within an hour, "the sides of the store were lined with spectators and the center of the room seemed turned into a stage with the Esquimaux and the clerks as actors."[2] Much to the consternation of the clerks, their customers touched and handled everything, from delicate fabrics to fragile bottles of perfume. First, they purchased dolls, next perfume, and then toys: "Someone wound up a bug and let it run on the floor. The sight astonished and delighted the Esquimaux and they ordered a dozen. The same result followed the order of jumping jacks, kicking mules and walking alligators."[3]

At this point the owner of the store arrived and demanded to know what was going on. After being assured that it was legitimate business, he was reported to have declared: "Go ahead. Sell them the whole store if they will buy it!" They didn't buy the store but they did purchase ornamental boxes, bells and Christmas decorations, half a dozen silk tassels, thirty dolls, three boxes of fancy soap, four yards of muslin, two yards of coloured beads, a half peck of perfumery in fancy bottles, a dozen jumping jacks, a dozen handkerchiefs, four toy donkeys, all the automatic flies and crocodiles in the store, six toy horses, three revolving chimes, two boxes of building blocks, one music box, five yards of coloured ribbon, several toy sheep, coloured calico, cheese cloth, and cotton flannel.[4] Its mission accomplished, the delegation headed back to the fairgrounds to distribute the gifts among the families living in the "Esquimaux Village." As a result, their first Christmas away from home was likely a happy and festive occasion.

This book tells the story of a small and diverse group of Inuit who left their lives as hunters and fishers in Labrador to attend the World's Columbian Exposition as part of the ethnological exhibit called the "Esquimaux Village." The concession opened for business upon their arrival in Chicago, seven months ahead of the official opening of the fair, and it immediately generated widespread public interest and press attention. Yet from the beginning, there were misconceptions about the concession's inhabitants. Newspapers described them as "survivors of the stone age and the glacial epoch,"[5] "blubber-eaters,"[6] "children of the far north,"[7] "ice-dwellers from the land of the midnight sun,"[8] and people "unsullied by the touch of civilization."[9] There was little understanding of who they really were and less interest in finding out. Prevailing scientific and racist ideologies permeating European and American societies at the time contributed to the misrepresentations, as did the interests of the exhibit's promoters, the Exposition's administrators and their scientific advisors, the American press, and the public at large.[10] In general, they were perceived as "exotic curiosities" and promoted as living examples of "primitive" people.

Traditional Inuit society with its governance practices, belief systems, and unique material culture, ingeniously adapted for survival in harsh northern environments, was far from "primitive" and Labrador Inuit were neither "stone-age" nor "untouched by civilization." They had been among the first North American Indigenous people to have contact with Europeans and shared with them a history in Labrador extending as far back as the sixteenth century. By the time of the World's Columbian Exposition, most were living near European trading establishments and had converted to Christianity, some could speak English, many could read and write, most had business relations with European organizations, and some could play European musical instruments. Over the years, they had adapted to the presence of colonizers living in their territories and devised their own strategies for dealing with them. This experience, knowledge, and resourcefulness would defy the stereotypes and prove useful in Chicago.

I first became interested in the story of Inuit at the World's Columbian Exposition after reading Jim Zwick's *Inuit Entertainers in the United States*.[11] This book is a brief sketch of Labrador Inuit participation in various ethnological exhibits from 1892–1903. What is absent from Zwick's work, apart from detail, is any discussion of Labrador and who these "entertainers" were in the context of their homeland and history. I was by this time fairly familiar with Inuit history in Labrador, having developed an interest when I lived there while working for the CBC, the Labrador Inuit Association, and *Them Days* magazine. I subsequently made several films in Labrador, the first of which was *The Last Days of Okak*, a film about the devastating impact of the Spanish Influenza of 1918 on the largest Inuit community in Labrador, which I made with my friend and colleague Anne Budgell. Research for this project was my first dive into the Moravian archives, a vast and fascinating record of Inuit-Moravian relations spanning more than two hundred years. My research of Inuit at the World's Columbian Exposition was meant to be the basis for another documentary film; however, I was unable to secure the necessary funding. With the support of Traditions and Transitions, the Nunatsiavut Government and Memorial University of Newfoundland's multi-faceted research project, I transformed my research through the master's program in the Department of History at Memorial University of Newfoundland. This book is essentially a reworking of my MA thesis.

The book begins with the story of Inuit recruitment in Labrador by the American company that won the right to stage an "Esquimaux" exhibit at the World's Fair. These early chapters describe Inuit life in Labrador at the end of the nineteenth century, identify the individuals who travelled to Chicago, and discuss the distinct histories of the various regions from which they came. This is significant as Inuit who attended the fair were not a single homogenous entity but instead represented distinct groups from different regions of Labrador, each of whom had developed unique identities.

The story then turns to Chicago and the World's Columbian Exposition itself, providing background to the origin of the fair and the ideological context in which it took place. A further chapter recounts the history of ethnological exhibits and the development of scientific theories that sustained exhibits such as the "Esquimaux Village," providing them with apparent scientific legitimacy.

The next chapter describes the specific experiences of Labrador Inuit at the World's Columbian Exposition and their struggles with the pressures and daily demands of being exhibition "Esquimaux." The initial curiosity, excitement, and interest Inuit displayed at the beginning of the enterprise dissolves as conditions at the "Esquimaux Village" deteriorate and relations with their employers become increasingly contentious. Inuit grievances would end up in the courts and the resulting judgment would dramatically redefine the relationships with the exhibit's owners, the press, and the public at large. Most Labrador Inuit remained in the United States after the Chicago fair for another year and the following section of the book describes their activities in subsequent exhibits in California and on the east coast of the United States.

The final chapter tells the tale of events that occurred in Labrador after most of the people returned home in 1894. That summer, an epidemic of typhoid fever devastated the Inuit community at Nain, killing a third of its population. Blame for the outbreak settled on the Inuit families returning from the United States. These dubious allegations were later used by colonial agencies to pass legislation restricting all Inuit movement outside the colony, a law that remained on the books until after Newfoundland's confederation with Canada in 1949. A brief postscript ends the book, describing, as well as possible, what I have been able to discover of the subsequent lives of those Inuit who attended the fair.

During my research for this book, I was continually impressed by how Inuit were able to navigate the difficult challenges they encountered throughout their time in the United States. They continually faced discrimination and prejudice based on their race, class, and culture and yet despite limited resources in an alien and often hostile environment, they responded with resilience and ingenuity, resisting injustice, subverting preconceptions and stereotypes, and eventually transforming relationships with both their employers and audiences.

Unfortunately, there are few indications of how Inuit viewed the experience. No one left behind any written account and no in-depth interviews were ever recorded. Instead, we are dependent on the writings of others to understand what happened but the observations of journalists, missionaries, and traders often reveal more about the observer than the observed. Inuit are mostly viewed through a lens distorted by preconceived tropes or racial prejudice. Only rarely do sympathetic writers engage their subject with a pertinent question that provides a momentary insight into what people are thinking or feeling.[12] Such is the nature of the historic record and the limitations of the material used to reconstruct this story.

I have tried to demonstrate that the Inuit response to the challenges they faced in the United States was based on self-reliance and an independence of mind firmly rooted in their lives in Labrador, and that their strategies for dealing with problems reflect their experiences with local colonial institutions accumulated over a considerable period of time. As such this book not only tells the story of Inuit involvement with ethnological exhibits in the United States but also provides some general insight into the history and experience of Labrador Inuit at the end of the nineteenth century.

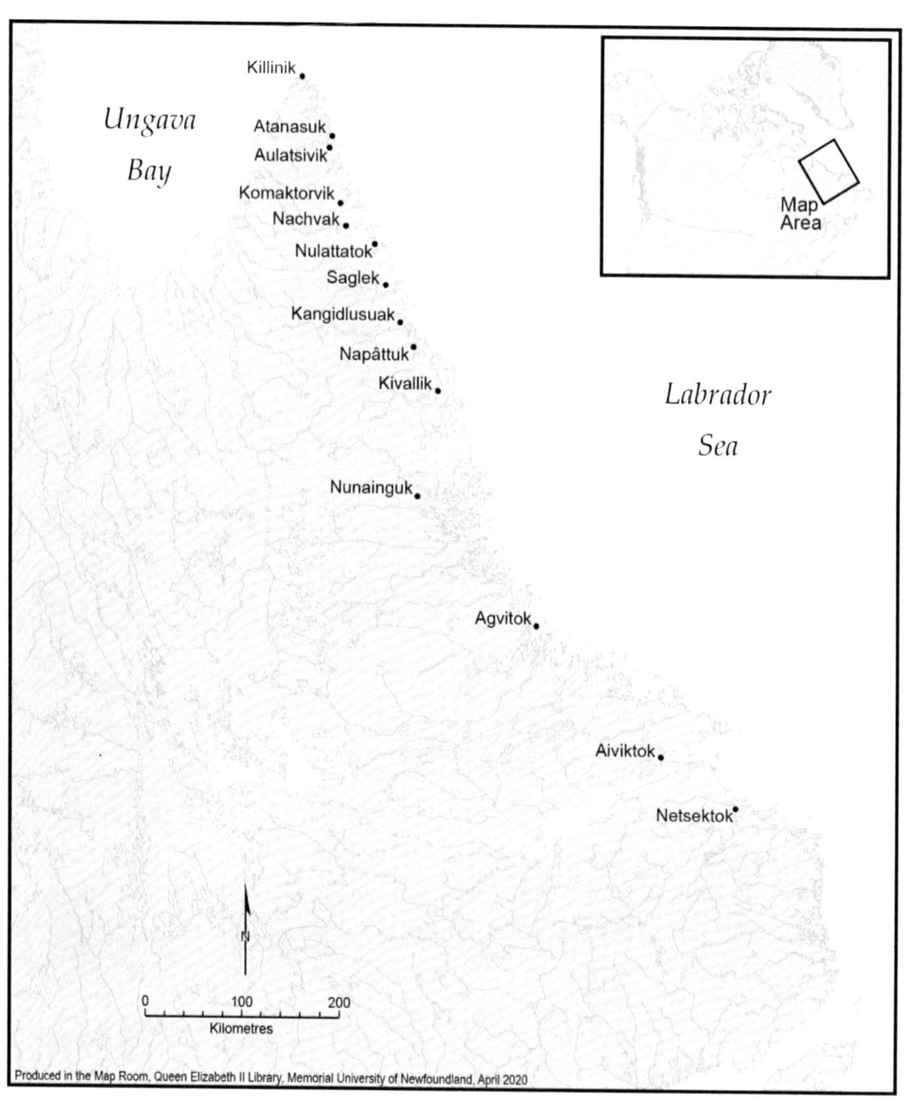

Map 1 Inuit Communities, circa 1771

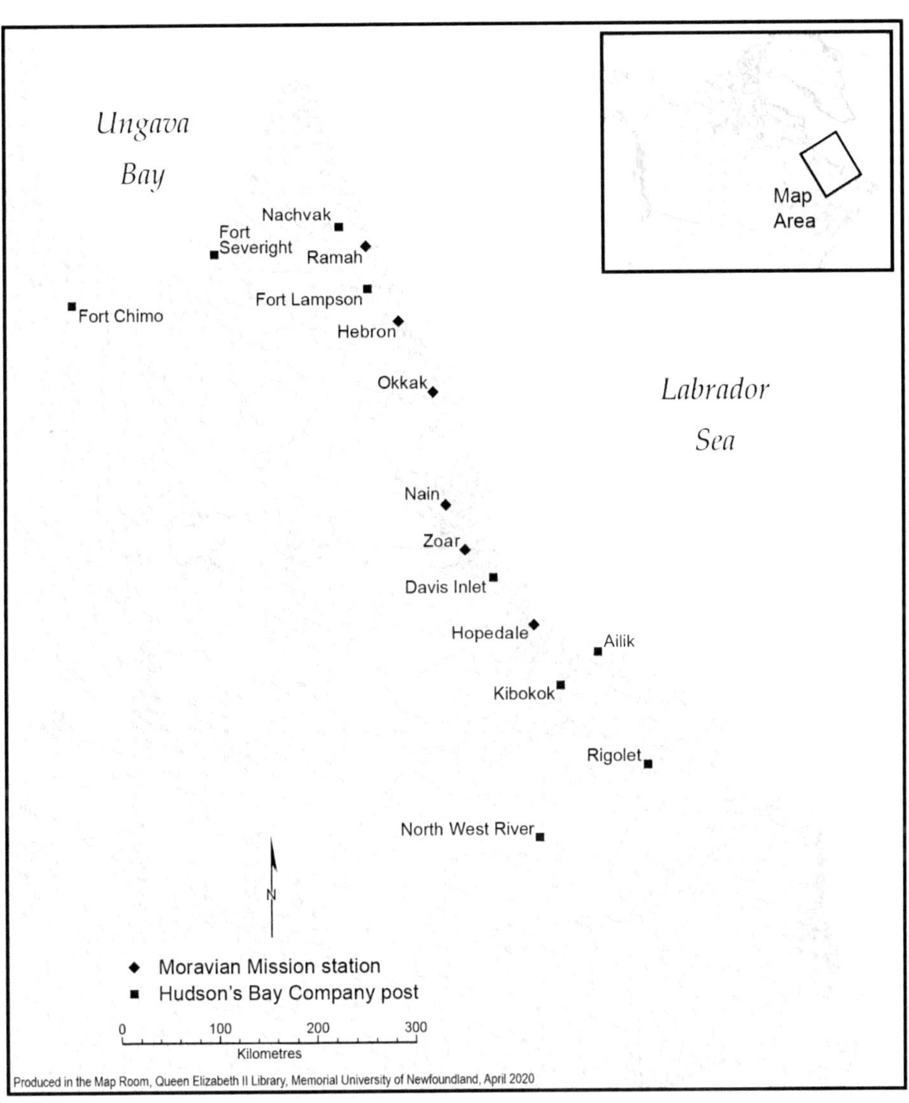

Map 2 Moravian Mission Stations and Hudson's Bay Company Posts, 1771–1904

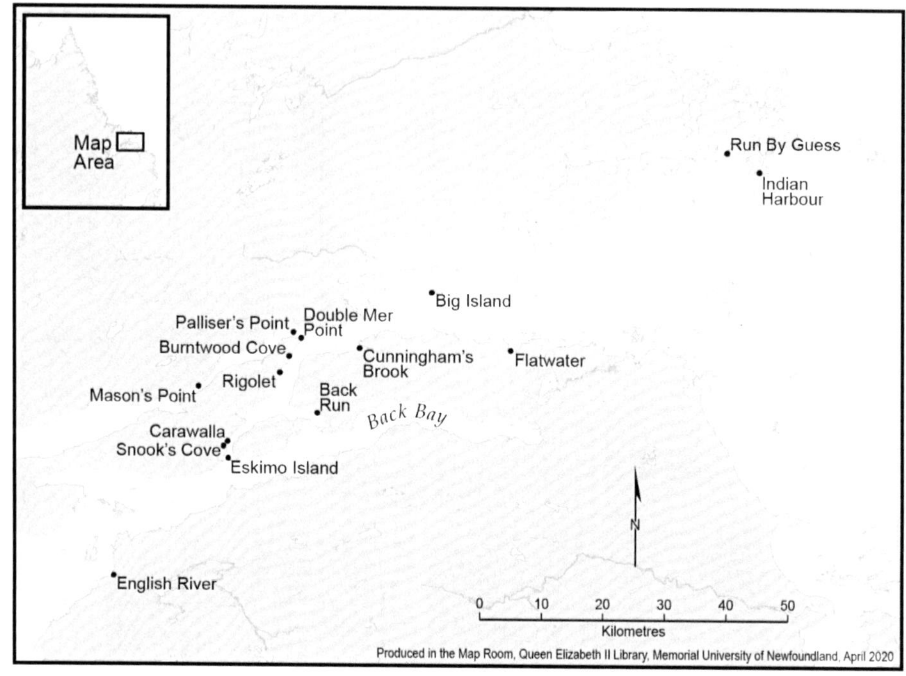

Map 3 Aiviktok/Esquimaux Bay

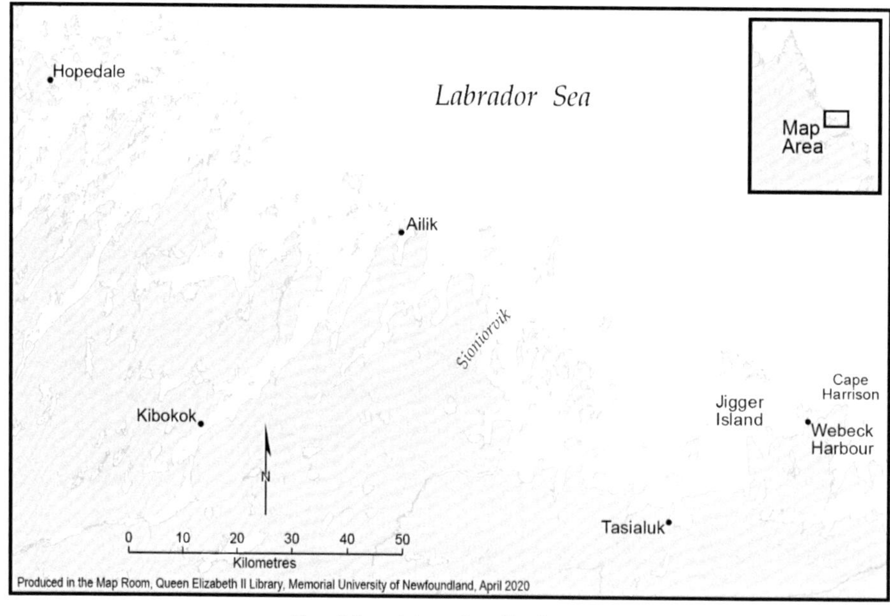

Map 4 Hopedale to Cape Harrison

Zoar
Map
Area
Opatik
Bay
Notakwanon R
N
Moravian Mission station
Hudson's Bay Company post
Ukkusiksalik
HBC Davis Inlet
0
10
20
30
Kilometres
Produced in the Map Room, Queen Elizabeth II Library, Memorial University of Newfoundland, April 2020

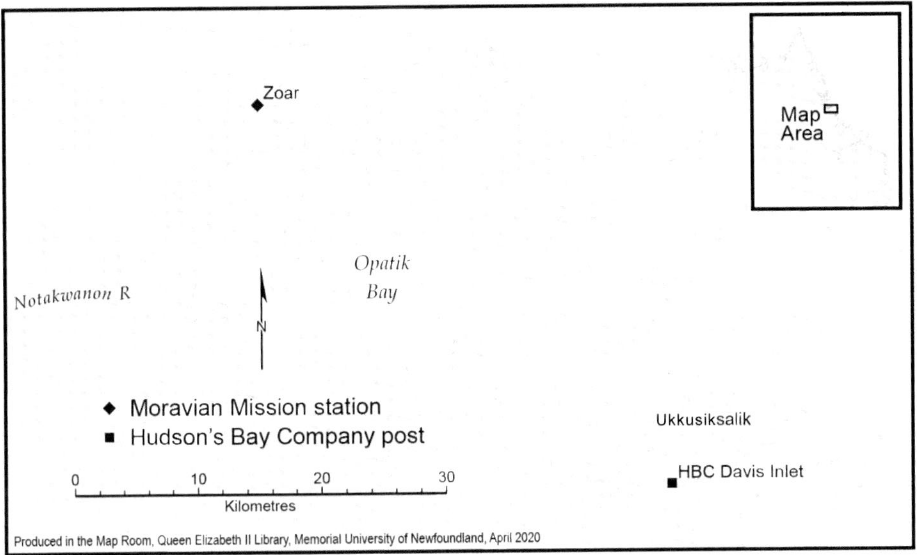

Map 5 Zoar, Ukkusiksalik, and Davis Inlet

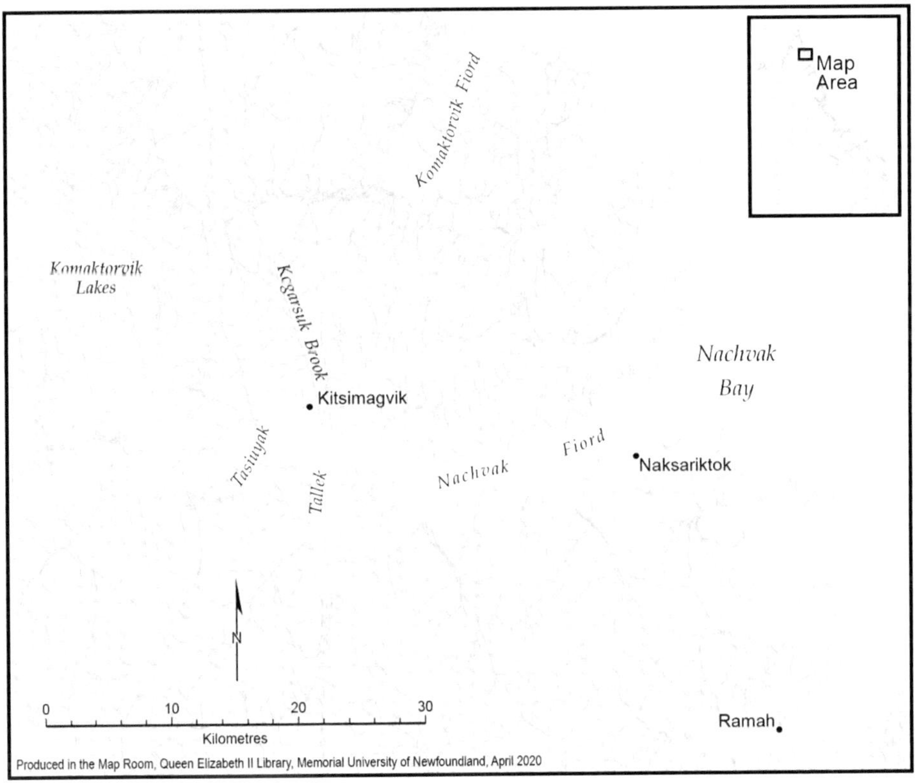

Map
Area
Komaktorvik Fiord
Komaktorvik
Lakes
Kegarsuk Brook
Nachvak
Bay
Kitsimagvik
Tasiuyak
Tallek
Nachvak
Fiord
Naksariktok
N
0
10
20
30
Kilometres
Ramah
Produced in the Map Room, Queen Elizabeth II Library, Memorial University of Newfoundland, April 2020

Map 6 Nachvak Fiord

CHAPTER 1

The Voyage Of The *Evelena* 1892

"The Esquimaux secured (from Labrador) were selected from various points on the northern coast and include representatives from the partially civilized tribes at the Hudson's Bay Company posts, converts from the Moravian mission stations and heathen aborigines from Cape Chidley and the shores of Ungava."[1]

PART 1: AIVIKTOK

In June 1892, the schooner *Evelena* set sail from Halifax, Nova Scotia, bound for the Labrador coast. It had been chartered by J.W. Skiles & Co., based in Spokane, Washington, a private enterprise which had been granted a concession from the World's Columbian Exposition to present an ethnological exhibit of Inuit at the fair to be called the "Esquimaux Village." On board the *Evelena* were two representatives of the company, William David Vincent and Ralph Graham Taber. Their mission was to find prospective recruits for the village and to acquire Inuit artifacts such as hunting equipment, sleds, kayaks, and clothing. Vincent and Taber were not scientists and had no previous experience organizing ethnological exhibits. They were aspiring businessmen, agents for a company that had seized an opportunity to stage a potentially lucrative venture at what promised to be one of the greatest public spectacles of the century.

Creating the "Esquimaux Village"

The World's Columbian Exposition was conceived as a commemoration of the 400th anniversary of the landing of Christopher Columbus in the Americas and a showcase of American cultural and industrial achievement. At the urging of Harvard professor Frederic Putnam, the organisers of the fair had been persuaded to include "a comprehensive exhibition of people from all over the Americas," representing the Indigenous cultures already present when Columbus arrived.[2] The idea of an Inuit exhibit likely originated as part of Putnam's plan. A press report in 1892 suggests that Putnam's assistant, Franz Boas, who had previously conducted fieldwork among Inuit at Cumberland Sound on Baffin Island in 1883–84, intended to return there to recruit families for an exhibit.[3] Boas, however, dropped the idea in favour of showcasing the Kwakwaka'wakw (Kwakiutil)[4] of British Columbia and the task of creating an Inuit exhibit passed into the hands of private enterprise.[5]

On 9 March 1892, the Ways and Means Committee of the World's Columbian Exposition granted J.W. Skiles and Co. exclusive right to establish an "Esquimaux Village and Labrador Trading Post" at the fair. The Company promised to provide not less than fifty natives from "Labrador, Greenland, and the Northeast Territory," with their "household utensils and furniture, wearing apparel, and sledges, canoes, musical instruments and weapons of the chase."[6] They also agreed to erect "a true and life-like representation of an Eskimo village and Labrador Trading Post, with its houses, including log cabins as is used by the Hudson's Bay Company... a Moravian Mission chapel, Eskimo huts, dogs and deer corrals."[7] Inuit were expected to provide entertainments, demonstrations of their hunting skills with kayaks and dog-sledges, musical performances, and Moravian church services. In exchange, the company was granted a parcel of land within the exhibition grounds, permission to enclose it, and the right to charge admission. The only clause in the contract relating to the welfare of the people stated that the company should furnish their employees "such sleeping accommodations as they have been accustomed to in their own country and supply them with such food as they usually eat."[8] As with all concessions, the company was expected to pay a percentage of revenues to the Exposition. With the agreement secured, the company now faced the challenge of finding some bona fide Inuit willing to participate.

Why a company based in Washington State should choose to travel to Labrador to recruit Inuit is a mystery. Alaskan Inuit were readily accessible through established trade routes and whaling companies, but most likely it was a case of convenience and cost as Labrador Inuit, the most southerly Inuit in the hemisphere, lived closer to Chicago. Labrador, however, was not without its own difficulties. Sea-ice, forming in December and lasting as late as June, made the territory inaccessible to shipping for much of the year. This meant the company would need to move quickly. If there were to be Inuit in time for the fair, they would have to be hired in the summer of 1892, almost a full year before the exposition's official opening scheduled for May 1893.

According to a later account by William Forbush published in his book *Prince Pomiuk: A Prince of Labrador*, J.W. Skiles & Co. made its initial contact with Labrador through a business associate who had once travelled to the Labrador coast with a missionary, Rev. Charles Carroll Carpenter.[9] The businessman contacted Carpenter for advice and Carpenter put him in touch with the Nova Scotia schooner captain and trader William McConnell who had business interests in Labrador and was familiar with the region and its people.[10] The company and McConnell came to terms and Vincent and Taber, the company's agents, joined McConnell in Halifax and sailed for Labrador under his guidance.

Vincent and Taber had no knowledge of Labrador and no understanding of the people who lived there. Their notions of Inuit were likely no different than those of the general public, shaped principally by popular newspaper accounts of the exploits of Arctic explorers. However, the people they would meet in Labrador would bear scant resemblance to popular stereotypes. This would frustrate Vincent and Taber during their voyage along the coast and later confuse those attending the fair.

Labrador Inuit

Inuit are thought to have first appeared along the Labrador coast sometime after 1400 CE, following sea mammals, such as whales, walruses, and seals, as they moved out of Davis Strait on their southern migrations. While some Inuit attached themselves to resource rich areas in the north, others continued to follow game south, eventually travelling as far as the Strait of Belle Isle, the north shore of the St. Lawrence River, and the north-east and west coast of the island of Newfoundland.[11] With the coming of Basque whalers to southern Labrador in the sixteenth century, and later French fishing enterprises, Labrador Inuit began a complex and unpredictable relationship with Europeans. Both groups were interested in trade, but the relationship was complicated and characterized by mutual suspicion and fear and by competition for marine resources, such as whales and seals. Encounters were frequently violent. Despite this, the appetite for trade persisted on both sides and over time an extensive trade network developed between northern Inuit communities and southern European traders facilitated by Inuit middlemen who exchanged supplies of whale baleen and oil for coveted European trade goods.[12]

Confrontations continued, however, even after the British assumed responsibility for the territory following the Treaty of Paris in 1763. A particularly egregious incident occurred in 1766 when Inuit, in an apparent reprisal for earlier killings, attacked and destroyed British fishing premises at Cape Charles. The British responded in kind, killing about twenty Inuit men, and capturing women and children.[13] To pacify Inuit and make the territory safe for merchants, the British government supported the proposal of a German evangelical organization called the Unitas Fratrum, or more commonly, the Moravian Mission, to convert Inuit to Christianity. The British gave the missionaries a series of land grants and a trading concession in the hope that they could contain Inuit in the north. As a result, the missionaries established their first outpost in Labrador at Nain in 1771.[14] Over time, they would expand their mission along the north coast attracting many Inuit to their settlements. However, not all Inuit in Labrador became Moravian. By the nineteenth century, the missionaries themselves identified three groups of Inuit within the Labrador territory. These were the Mission Inuit: those who lived part of their lives in Moravian settlements and held accounts in mission stores; those the Moravians called Southlanders who lived south of the southernmost mission station of Hopedale, some of whom had resisted or rejected mission overtures and chose instead to associate themselves with southern traders; and those the missionaries called Northlanders or "heathen" who lived beyond the reach of the mission in the most northern part of the Labrador peninsula.[15] Regardless of where they lived, by the end of the nineteenth century, Labrador Inuit had engaged with European traders, Government agents, and religious organizations for almost two hundred years and had acquired a good deal of knowledge and understanding of European beliefs, behaviour, and practices.

Recruitment

McConnell's vessel took three weeks to travel from Halifax to Rigolet in central Labrador. Rigolet was the site of a Hudson's Bay Company trading post, located just inside the narrows at the beginning of a long bay that cuts 150 kilometres into the interior of the Labrador Peninsula. The region had been called Baye Kessessakiou as well as Baie St. Louis and Baye Esquimaux by early French traders, and Esquimaux Bay by British traders, before it was renamed Hamilton Inlet by British colonial authorities in 1821. To Inuit it was known as Aiviktok, the place of the walrus, also spelled Ivuktoke on some eighteenth-century charts.[16]

Inuit had occupied Aiviktok at least as early as the seventeenth century, finding the region at the mouth of the estuary a haven against intruders and an area rich with fish, marine mammals, and birds.[17] With the coming of Europeans to Labrador, it became a convenient base for Inuit traders, who were middlemen between European merchants in the south and Inuit whale hunters in the north. They had become wealthy exchanging whale baleen and oil for manufactured goods such as muskets, knives, pots, fishhooks, and axes.[18]

By the mid-eighteenth century, European traders began to move into Aiviktok, harvesting the fish and furs of the region and trading with the Inuit population.[19] The French visited the region in the mid-1700s, and in the 1740s had established a trade post in the Rigolet area.[20] They maintained a presence in the region until the British assumed authority after 1763.

While the Moravians began to build their mission and trading posts in the north, English merchants in the south continued to court Inuit trade. One such merchant was George Cartwright who arrived in Labrador in 1770. His engagement with Inuit would prove particularly consequential for Aiviktok Inuit.

Cartwright established his business at Cape Charles in southern Labrador and was keen to develop trade with Indigenous Peoples. To that end, he persuaded an Inuit family from the Hopedale area to live and work with him. In 1772, he took a number of these people to England to help promote his business interests.[21] It would be a fateful voyage. In England, all Inuit contracted smallpox and only one woman, Caubvick, survived. When they returned to Cape Charles in the summer of 1773, they were met by "the whole of three of the southernmost tribes of Esquimaux," amounting to "five hundred souls," all eager to greet their family and friends on their return from Europe, only to be told that all but Caubvick had perished. After this gathering, Inuit returned north. Those travelling to Aiviktok took Caubvick, and smallpox, with them.[22] It would be two years before Cartwright learned of their fate:

> A little to the northward of this place is a bay, separated from Sandwich Bay by a neck of land of no great breadth, and runs forty or fifty leagues into the country, having many large rivers emptying into it; this place is called by the Esquimaux, Iboucktoke (sic), and upon an island near the mouth of it was one of their settlements. A planter from Newfoundland went there last year in winter, and upon the island found an Eskimeau town with all the inhabitants dead, their boats thwarted up, and all their goods left in their houses and tents... from which I conclude that after they left me they reached that place in safety and intended spending the winter there, and that (from) some of the infection of the smallpox remaining in Caubvick's cloathes, they caught that dreadful distemper and all died of it.[23]

The smallpox epidemic decimated the Inuit population of Aiviktok and most likely helped facilitate European occupation and settlement of the area. A short time after the outbreak, British merchants established their own operations inside the narrows at Rigolet, Carawalla, Kenemish, and North West River. As a result of this increasing activity, a growing number of European planters settled in the territory, marrying Inuit women, raising families, and working as independent trappers and fishermen.[24] The Hudson's Bay Company established itself in the region in 1836 and immediately began buying out its competitors, taking over the trading posts at Rigolet, Kenimish, and North West River, as well as the post at Kaipokok, on the Labrador coast south of the Moravian settlement of Hopedale. By the end of the nineteenth century, the Hudson's Bay Company was the dominant economic force in the region, providing the only year-round trading establishments where Inuit and planters alike could sell their produce, buy supplies, and find employment.

By the time the *Evelena* arrived in Aiviktok in the summer of 1892, Inuit were rapidly becoming a minority in their homeland and were finding it increasingly difficult to compete for the resources in the region.[25] A Methodist missionary, who lived in the district a short time later, claimed the decline was principally due to Inuit women marrying white men.[26] The number of Inuit in the district in 1890 consisted of only seven to ten families, numbering about seventy people.[27]

The *Evelena* arrived at Rigolet during the summer salmon fishery, the most important economic activity of the year in the region. Both Inuit and planters depended on this fishery, setting nets along the shores to intercept the migration of salmon as they moved from the Atlantic Ocean through the narrows to spawn in the rivers further up the bay. Some fishermen returned year after year to traditional berths selling their catch to the HBC or itinerant traders while others worked directly for the Company, which had, over time, bought up numerous berths and assigned them annually to local residents to fish on their behalf, usually for a fifty-fifty share of the catch, with the company supplying nets and gear.[28] Many Inuit fell into this category, including most of those who would be recruited for the world's fair.[29] For Inuit, the commercial salmon fishery and the seal hunt were the principal means to a livelihood. Seals were their main food resource, and provided additional products for trade: seal pelts, seal fat, and skin boots. The failure of the seal hunt due to weather conditions or deviations in animal migration patterns could lead to severe hardship. A combination of a poor seal hunt and a poor salmon fishery would be disastrous. The only recourse then was an appeal to the Hudson's Bay Company which might give out a little flour or biscuit on credit or perhaps provide a few days employment cutting wood, shoveling snow, or rendering seal fat.

A particularly vivid, albeit paternalistic description of nineteenth-century life in the Rigolet area in the times leading up to the *Evelena*'s arrival is provided by the American author and sportsman Charles Hallock who visited the area in 1860, publishing an account of his experiences in *Harper's New Monthly Magazine* the following year. Hallock's party was at Tub Harbour, just outside the narrows, when a sixty-tonne schooner came into the cove and dropped anchor: "There were quaint little people on board… dressed in curious smock-frocks of sealskin, trowsers of woolen stuff and neatly-fitting seal-skin boots."[30] The entire crew of the vessel were Inuit. The captain's name was Shugalough (sic). His son Jim Shuglo, who would attend the World's Columbian Exposition, would have been eighteen at the time and was likely among the crew on his father's ship.[31] Hallock learned that Shugalough had built the schooner himself and was working for the Hudson's Bay Company, transporting freight and produce between the posts at Rigolet, North West River, and Sandwich Bay. It is possible that Shugalough was a descendent of Shuglawina, a successful Inuit trader and close associate of the English merchant George Cartwright who had described him in his journals as a chief "whose tent and shallop was both larger and better than those belonging to any of the others."[32] Shuglawina is thought to have perished in the smallpox outbreak that swept through Aiviktok at the end of eighteenth century.

A few days after meeting Shugalough, Hallock visited a nearby fishing camp at Flatwater belonging to Joseph Palliser. His camp consisted of a large sealskin tent or "toupik," two kayaks drawn up on the shore, capelin drying on the rocks, and salmon nets set in the water nearby. The interior of the toupik was lit by a stone lamp suspended in the centre and fed with seal fat.[33] Hallock described Palliser as a clever man, and the head of a household of eight people. He spoke some English and could read and write, having apparently attended school for a time at the Moravian settlement at Okkak on the north coast of

Labrador. He was said to be an expert hunter and fisherman and skilled with both dog-team and kayak.[34] Joseph Palliser was, in fact, a descendent of Mikak, the Inuk woman who had played a central role in helping the Moravians establish their mission in Labrador. She and her son Tutauk had been taken to England by the Governor of Newfoundland, Hugh Palliser, in 1768, in the hopes that the "impressions of the power, splendor and generosity of the British nation" would impress her and her countrymen on their return.[35] Tutauk was later baptised by the Moravians at Nain but subsequently rejected the mission. He moved to Aiviktok where he adopted the Palliser name. There, he became the patriarch of one of the largest surviving Inuit families. Joseph was his grandson. Jonas Palliser, and his brother Peter, both of whom would travel to Chicago with their families, were also descendants.

These profiles of Shugalough and Palliser suggest that even after the demise of their role as middlemen in the trade between northern Inuit and Europeans, Aiviktok Inuit continued to be worldly, enterprising, and fully engaged with Europeans in the economic activities of the region.

After these encounters, Hallock visited the Hudson's Bay Company's post at Rigolet, witnessing the bustle of activity that characterized its operation at the height of the salmon fishery:

> Esquimaux are darting hither and thither in their kayaks; dusky figures are grouped on shore; dogs howl out their doubtful greetings; strange craft are at anchor or drawn up on shore.... Each of the 14 buildings belonging to the post, comprising houses for the officers and servants, store houses for furs and other goods, a sales house, cooper's shop, oil house, fish house, packing house and oven house etc., excited a degree of interest... In the center of the oil house, surrounded by tierces and puncheons, and a villainous smell, Esquimaux were busily cutting flaps of seal blubber into small strips and cubes which they threw into a tank, where they were to lie until they resolved into oil... There are nets hung on pickets to dry; and set nets for salmon sweep out into the cove in semi-circles, like mammoth necklaces of beads.[36]

Hallock appears to have witnessed a particularly prosperous summer for the residents of the region. When the *Evelena* made its appearance at Rigolet some thirty years later, conditions were less favourable and people's livelihoods more precarious. The fishery had been in decline for several years and the summer of 1892 was proving to be part of an emerging pattern.[37] In 1886, Keith McKenzie, Chief Factor for the HBC at Rigolet, claimed that only last-minute Government relief had prevented wide-spread starvation.[38] In 1889, his successor, P.W. Bell, offered his own grim assessment:

> This continued failure of the salmon fishery means in plain English, nakedness and starvation. The inhabitants of this region have apparently lost all heart and courage — no one can blame them under the present depressed state of affairs; their lot for the winter appears sufficiently dismal.[39]

Although the salmon fishery improved in 1890 and 1891, partially alleviating the poverty of the people, the seal hunt was a failure. On 25 June 1891, it was reported that "the miserable cold and wintry weather this spring was seriously against the chances of seal hunting."[40] A similar experience occurred in 1892 when it was reported "the Esquimaux seal hunters came and brought in their spring hunts. They have on the whole, done very poorly."[41]

The precarious fortunes of Inuit hunters, at this time, are recorded in the daily journals of the Hudson's Bay Company. The case of Jim Shuglo was typical. On 8 April 1890, he showed up at Rigolet with only a few feathers to trade. On 15 August, it was reported that he and his brother did well at the salmon. On 21 October, he had a little seal fat to sell. On 4 December, he brought in a white fox. On 6 January 1891, he was begging for food as no seals had been killed for a long time, and on 4 March 1891, he was employed cleaning up around the store and shoveling snow.[42] Jim Shuglo had a wife and four children to feed and like many other residents of the region, he was struggling.

Seals were again scarce in the winter of 1892, and in the spring the salmon fishery would again be a disappointment. A short time after the *Evelena* arrived, an entry in the Hudson's Bay Company journal at Rigolet stated that the salmon "seemed to have disappeared altogether."[43] All signs indicated that Inuit families who had already endured successive years of hunger would be facing another winter of hardship. Under these circumstances, Vincent and Taber's offer of two years of steady employment must have seemed providential, a fortuitous opportunity to escape another season of want.

The *Evelena* paused only briefly at Rigolet before it headed "up the bay" searching for Inuit for the fair.[44] The vessel remained in the region for about twelve days, visiting a number of Inuit fishing camps at places like Back Run, Big Island, Burntwood Cove, Snook's Cove, Palliser's Point, Mason's Point, Double Mer, and most likely, Carawalla, where a number of Inuit families maintained winter homes. Those they met and eventually hired were Jonas and Susan Palliser and their children Lucy, Sam, and John; Jonas' son Tom Palliser and his wife Esther and daughter Susan; Jonas' brother Peter Palliser and his daughter Mary; George and Maggie Deer and their six-month-old son Peter; George's brother Tom Deer; Jim and Salome Shuglo and their children Maggie, Augustina, Liza, and Tom; as well as Peter Mesher.

On 19 July, the vessel headed out the narrows and turned north along the Labrador coast in search of other possible candidates. The Aiviktok families were left to finish the fishery, with instructions to pack up their belongings, collect whatever traditional items they had, such as kayaks, harpoons, winter clothing, and komatiks, and be ready to be picked up when the schooner returned from the north in early September. The Hudson's Bay Company journal reported that they took Peter Palliser with them to act as interpreter. It may well be that his real purpose was to introduce Vincent and Taber to Inuit at Ailik where the Pallisers had close family connections.[45]

CHAPTER 2

The Voyage Of The *Evelena* 1892

PART 2: THE MORAVIAN COAST

As the *Evelena* rounded Cape Harrison and sailed northward from Aiviktok, it encountered increasing numbers of fishing schooners. Thousands of these vessels made annual summer voyages from the island of Newfoundland to fish for cod.[1] They had been visiting the north coast of Labrador in ever greater numbers since the late 1850s and, increasingly, merchant enterprises established seasonal operations on islands south of the Moravian Mission station at Hopedale, most notably at Webeck Harbour, Long Tickle, West Turnavik Island, and Ailik. Inuit families living on the coast also fished cod in the summer, often selling their catch to British and Newfoundland traders as well as the Moravians. Relationships were generally amicable but there were occasions when conflict arose if itinerant schoonermen set gear at fishing berths Inuit considered their own.[2] The annual influx also provided opportunities for Inuit, some of whom were employed by Newfoundlanders: fishing, salting, and packing the season's catch or maintaining stages, wharves, and warehouses.

Ailik was one such place where Inuit and Newfoundlanders worked alongside each other to their mutual benefit. For many years Ailik had been the summer depot of the Hudson's Bay Company post at Kaipokok and had attracted several Inuit families from the region. Kaipokok had operated as an outpost of Rigolet connected by an overland winter travel route. Inuit living in the area were frequently hired by the company to carry mail and supplies between the posts and many travelled to Rigolet to trade their furs. After the

HBC closed the post at Kaipokok in 1878, Ailik remained an important fishing station and was eventually taken over by Newfoundland merchants who maintained summer fishing premises not far from Inuit homes.

The Ailik Inuit, like those from Aiviktok, were among those the Moravians referred to as Southlanders, many of whom worked or traded with southern merchants. In the past, the relationship between these Inuit and the Moravians had been hostile as the missionaries sought to limit the Southlanders' influence on the so-called "mission Inuit." However, by the late nineteenth century, both parties sought closer ties, and by 1892, several Ailik families had become church members with children baptised in the Moravian faith.[3] Ralph Taber, still short of his quota of "Esquimaux," was impressed with Ailik Inuit:

> There are several resident families of Esquimaux here, who speak fairly good English, and any of whom would make acceptable guides.... They are about the first pure Esquimaux to be met with on the coast.[4]

The notion of "pure Esquimaux" was to preoccupy the agents for the "Esquimaux Village" the entire trip and suggests they may have had some misgivings that their recruits from Aiviktok did not quite measure up as ideal exhibit "specimens." Their close association with settlers; their adoption of European culture, manners, and language; and even their physical appearance might call into question any claim that they represented a "race" living in circumstances "untainted by the touch of civilization."[5] They would have similar reservations about "Moravian Inuit," affected as they were by many years under the "civilizing" influence of European missionaries. These considerations made the recruitment of the more remote northern Inuit increasingly important to the Americans.

At Ailik, Taber and Vincent met John Lucy, his brother Joseph, and Simon Manak. John and his wife Katerina lived at Siorniorvik during the winter, a short distance south of Ailik. In the summer, he moved his family to Ailik where he fished and possibly worked for Newfoundland merchants. Although he was a Moravian church member, John Lucy maintained a close relationship with the Hudson's Bay Company and often chose to sell his furs at Rigolet.

HBC Post Journals indicate he was one of the more productive and respected trappers to trade there.[6] Joseph Lucy and his wife Charlotte lived at Ailik year-round as did Simon Manak and his wife Sarah.

Ailik Inuit were industrious and worldly people. Their engagement with Newfoundland fishermen, merchants, Moravian missionaries, and Hudson's Bay Company traders over many years had made them familiar with European attitudes, expectations, and trade practices. The offer of employment by the Americans would have appeared novel but not intimidating. John Lucy, for example, had already travelled outside Labrador.[7] As a result of this experience, the Ailik people likely accepted the prospect of employment in the United States with little apprehension, confident that they could manage whatever challenges lay ahead.

In all, sixteen people from Ailik were recruited for the fair. These were Joseph and Charlotte Lucy (who had no children); John and Katerina Lucy and their five children, Julia Hedwig, Abraha, Simon, Jonas, and Tomasi; and Simon and Sarah Manak and their five children, Maria, Jacobus Marcus, Peterusi, Sarah (Jr.), and Abraha. In addition, another young man joined the group, Abraha Tuktashina, who was likely a relative of Charlotte Lucy, a Tuktashina prior to marriage.[8]

From Ailik, the *Evelena* continued northward into the Inuit heartland, stopping at the southernmost Moravian settlement of Hopedale on 31 July where Taber and Vincent attended church and visited the store.[9] Prior to their departure to Labrador, Vincent had approached Moravian officials in London for help finding Inuit for the fair. The Moravians declined the request because of their previous experience with such ventures.[10] In 1880, Abraham Ulrikab and his family had been recruited from the Moravian community of Hebron and, together with a family from Nachvak, travelled to Europe as part of a Carl Hagenbeck exhibit. They all died of smallpox.[11] The Moravians offered Vincent letters of introduction to their missionaries on the coast but requested that they not recruit Inuit from "their" communities. As a result, the visits to the Moravian settlements at Hopedale, Okkak, Hebron, and Ramah were largely courtesy calls intended to gather information and collect artifacts.

By this time, Vincent and Taber were forming a general opinion of Labrador Inuit and it was not altogether favourable. They believed they were witnessing a race in decline,[12] a defeated people living in a state of semi-servitude. Taber would write:

> War, famine, exposure, intermarriage of blood relations, the introduction of European food and frailties, and with these very likely the germs of pestilence and contagious disease... have all combined to reduce the number of living descendants of these once numerous and powerful aborigines to a few hundred men and women, stunted in stature, blunted in natural intelligence, living in fear of their energetic creditors, the mighty Company or the dominant missionaries.[13]

In a passage that is both admiring and mocking, sympathetic and disparaging, he sums up his view of Inuit character:

> True communists in both theory and practice; unselfishly sharing their last morsel, with a smile; a simple, kindly, dirty, good-natured, child-like race, possessing no hope of betterment; giving no thought to the future; systematically forgetful of the past; living only in the present and making the heaviest burdens of that present light with irrepressible cheerfulness of heart![14]

Had he inquired more carefully, Taber might have learned that "mission Inuit" were far from subservient or fearful and had a history of boldly resisting injustice.

"Mission Inuit"

Although the Moravian mission was principally an evangelical organization, from its beginning it was also a commercial enterprise operating trading stores at all its settlements. The evangelical and commercial arms of the Labrador mission operated somewhat independently. The mission board based in Saxony determined religious doctrine and social practice and was the principal source of missionaries while the financial, commercial, and logistical side of the mission was managed from London by the mission's British agency, the Society for the Furtherance of the Gospel (SFG).

By the late nineteenth century, most Inuit living on the north coast of Labrador were members of Moravian congregations based in six settlements scattered along the coast at Hopedale, Zoar, Nain, Okkak, Hebron, and Ramah.[15] The people tended to live in these communities from Christmas to Easter, at the coldest time of year, when hunting opportunities were limited. The rest of the time, they lived in small camps scattered among the bays and islands, hunting and fishing, only returning to the settlements periodically to sell their produce and acquire provisions from the mission store.

The stores were a central feature of the Moravian communities and were of vital importance to Inuit and missionaries alike. For Inuit, they provided a ready market for their fish, furs, and oil products and a dependable year-round supply of guns, ammunition, fishing gear, tools, utensils, and foodstuffs, such as flour, tea, and biscuits. For the Moravians, the trade initially attracted Inuit to the mission where the Christian gospel was preached, but it also provided the means of paying the expenses of the mission.[16] The trade, however, was not a relationship of equals. The Moravians set the price for Inuit produce as well as for imported goods. Inuit had few alternatives to this system other than to take their business elsewhere, but in nineteenth-century Labrador, there were few options, especially in winter and particularly for those trading in more northerly regions. The terms of trade, as dictated by the Moravians, would naturally be questioned, and if Inuit suspected they were being treated unfairly, suspicion, resentment, and protest would result.

The conflict over prices given for produce and provisions was a central feature of trade relations but the issue that would cause the greatest rift was the matter of credit and debt. If game was abundant and Inuit hunters were doing well, provisions could be paid for and store accounts balanced, but even the most proficient hunters were at the mercy of circumstance. The Moravians' response to credit requests was the same as any other business enterprise. They would issue advances on account and collect against those debts when Inuit next had produce to trade. The balance at the end of the exchange most often left the people in need of new credit, a cycle that was not easily broken and could lead to a perpetual state of indebtedness.

The problem of Inuit debt became a great concern for the SFG in the mid-nineteenth century. Not only were independent traders penetrating traditional Moravian territory and siphoning off valuable Inuit trade, but changing environmental conditions began to impede Inuit harvesting efforts, causing a serious reduction in catches that increased poverty among Inuit and resulted in smaller profits for the SFG.[17] It became more difficult for Inuit to make a living or pay off their debts at the store and the missionaries observed that Inuit were becoming disillusioned and discontented.

This dissatisfaction led increasingly to overt acts of desperation and protest. In Hopedale, in 1856, a man accused of stealing from the store shot at the missionary who had accused him of the theft.[18] Two years later, in the same community, a woman, also accused of stealing, set fire to a woodpile behind the mission residence, nearly burning down the Hopedale mission buildings.[19]

Grievances often simmered below the surface but in the late 1880s, just a few years prior to the World's Columbian Exposition, Inuit dissatisfaction with Moravian trade policy came to a head in several acrimonious confrontations that shook the mission to its core. These incidents were the result of longstanding Inuit complaints about the trade system rooted in the suspicion that the trade was being managed principally for the benefit of the mission. Two of the most significant agitations took place at Zoar (1887–88) and Hebron (1889). These incidents demonstrate a determination among Inuit to stand up for their own interests and to take collective action against perceived injustice. It is a characteristic that would be on full display in Chicago a few years later and undermines any notion that they were a broken or defeated people.

Zoar

Zoar was a recent mission settlement, established at Tappangayok between Hopedale and Nain in 1865, allegedly to serve the spiritual needs of both Inuit and settlers in the region, although some claimed it was "chiefly for the purpose of keeping off southern traders."[20] The Moravians were particularly concerned with the trading operations of Hunt and Henley, which had establishments at Ukkusiksalik (Davis Inlet), north of Hopedale, and at Paul's Island, just south of Nain. These were both acquired by the Hudson's Bay Company in 1869.[21]

Zoar had a short and troubled history. It was a poor place for hunting and fishing and the people who moved there struggled to make a living, resulting in frequent economic hardship, increasing dependence on the stores, and rising debts. The Moravians acknowledged the difficulties created by poor harvests but also questioned Inuit diligence, industry, and honesty. They were particularly critical of the practice of taking produce to other traders instead of paying down debt, but Inuit felt little compulsion to trade exclusively at the mission stores.[22] At Zoar, disputes over prices, credit, and debt eroded the trust between the missionaries and Inuit.

The situation came to a head in 1887–88. That year, not one person among the twenty-six with accounts at Zoar paid their debts, and four men, despite debt owing, chose to leave the community to establish trading relations with the Hudson's Bay Company at Ukkusiksalik.[23] Hunting that fall and winter was a complete failure, which led to an increased demand for credit which the mission store refused to grant. By the new year many people were becoming desperate and at a men's meeting held in January a decision was taken for the people to help themselves to store supplies the next trading day if the storekeeper refused demands for assistance. The missionaries, however, learned of the plan and confronted the men during a church service:

> After this meeting the men stormed into the mission house demanding to know who had betrayed their secret. Happily, they appealed to Br (Theodor) Bourquin (the Mission Superintendent at Nain) and the missionaries were well content that they should fetch him. His visit and the reaction from the outbreak quieted the spirit for the time but there were only too many evidences that the moral tone was unchanged. On Whitmonday, the frequent impudent demands at the store culminated in three shots fired into the window at the

> part where our two missionaries were busy. They were unhurt and at that time unconscious of their danger. The culprit was Caleb and his motive was the expression of revenge for having to leave the store without getting his unreasonable demands.[24]

Bourquin's eventual response to the unrest was to close the store.[25] In his report to the SFG, he made it clear that the latest incident at Zoar was not an isolated occurrence but only the latest manifestation of unrest that had been an ongoing feature of the community for years. He saw no possibility for improvement. The problem, he said, stemmed in part from the poor location of Zoar for hunting and fishing, resulting in a heavy dependence on the mission for relief, but he also claimed the situation was exacerbated by poor leadership in the community and the laziness of the people, which had led to the highest per capita debt of any community on the coast and the mission's greatest single expenditure for poor relief. Bourquin believed that there was no prospect of debts being paid and that the only way to ensure that the existing liabilities did not continue to increase was to close the store.

The closure of the store at Zoar in 1888 led to the gradual departure of the people from the community. The final decision to terminate the mission at Zoar was taken in 1894. The Moravians blamed Inuit for the failure of the community:

> These people have learned no wisdom or thrift in spite of all the love and patience shown them and they have made the last winter a trying time for their devoted missionaries.[26]

Inuit no doubt held a different point of view. The Moravians had withdrawn their support at a time when people were in desperate need. Trading wherever they could get value for what little produce they acquired was not a matter of disloyalty but survival.

Hebron

In Hebron, ongoing tensions between storekeepers and Inuit erupted on 29 September 1889. After church services, one of the Moravian missionaries was approached by an Inuit delegation seeking a meeting to discuss store matters. Despite misgivings, the missionaries agreed to meet in the school room which was attached to the church and the missionaries' residence. Most of the Hebron men attended. One of the missionaries began by asking whether one or all of them had specific concerns and was told: "All of us!"[27] The meeting quickly erupted into a litany of accusations and complaints. The door was barred, and the missionaries were "held captive in our house for four hours" subject to all kinds of "insolence, coarseness and meanness." The discussion ran the gamut of trade issues: the prices offered for produce, the method of weighing trout, the wages paid for labour, and the cost of kerosene. The response of the missionaries gave no satisfaction. "We stood all alone," they later wrote, "not one man stuck with us, and not one word in support or to calm tempers was heard." The missionaries characterized the meeting as an "uprising" and attributed Inuit dissatisfaction to the "untutored and distrustful hearts of people."[28]

At the end of the meeting, Inuit declared that if the missionaries could not help them, then they would no longer help the missionaries. They would withdraw all services such as cutting wood, fetching water, sewing boots, or carrying mail. As well, the work of the women in the mission kitchen, the girls tending the missionaries' children, and the helpers in the store would be suspended. For three days "the disgraceful spirit of rebellion" continued until Inuit sought a peaceful resolution. The missionaries accepted the overture but treated it more as an act of surrender than a desire for reconciliation. They considered the rebellion to be an act of sin, fixed firmly on the "wrongdoing" and "disobedience" of the people, and looked for signs of contrition, a "recognition of trespasses and repentance." At no time in their lengthy report on the incident did the Hebron missionaries suggest that there may have been some merit to Inuit complaints.[29] But, if the missionaries expected repentance and submission to their authority, they were to be disappointed. They suspected that declarations of remorse had a more practical purpose: "We sense that improved heartfelt attitudes have to a lesser extent determined their yielding, than needs, in terms of the store, without which they cannot live."[30] There was residual bitterness on both sides. In the concluding statement of their report to the SFG in London, the Hebron missionaries reported on the prevailing atmosphere in the community after the "uprising." "There is peace," they wrote, "but it is a foul peace."[31]

Vincent and Taber were unaware of the underlying tensions existing between the Moravians and Inuit or of Inuit proclivity to defend their own interests. They had already concluded that they were an oppressed and submissive people. In Chicago they would be forced to revise this presumption.

Continuing North

After leaving Hopedale, the *Evelena* sailed north, anchoring at Daniel's Rattle in Opatik Bay near the Hudson's Bay Company post at Ukkusiksalik on 2 August. The following day, Vincent and Captain McConnell visited the post to explain their purpose. The post was only a short distance from the Moravian community of Zoar but with the mission store now closed, it was the only source of provisions for people in the area. However, the HBC store was poorly supplied, and it was struggling under its own accumulated debts. The manager, John Olsen, wondered how the post or the people could survive another winter under existing conditions: "The future looks anything but bright so far as business is concerned and what the planters and Esquimaux are going to do to keep starvation away from the door is more than I can tell."[32]

Opatik Bay was home to several settler and Inuit families including those of Robert Ford and Âpili Heleneup. Ford had a long association with the Hudson's Bay Company through his family. His father John Ford had managed the company's outpost at Paul's Island near Nain for many years and his brother, George, was then managing the HBC's northern outpost at Nachvak. Âpili was originally from Nain but had moved south to Opatik and had been living with his wife Helene's family. They were members of the Moravian congregation at Zoar. His father-in-law, Itarsoak, who was baptised Jeremiah at

Zoar in 1871, was said to have been the last "heathen Eskimo" to convert to Christianity in the region between Hopedale and Nain.[33] Âpili and Ford were friendly and occasionally hunted together but Olsen had a low opinion of them both.[34]

Vincent and Taber persuaded Robert Ford to accompany the group as its interpreter and translator and further enlisted two Inuit families from the area, those of Âpili and Edward Brown. Brown would not get far; he abandoned the voyage at Rigolet, apparently due to sickness.[35] Those who travelled from Opatik Bay to Chicago were Robert and Susan Ford, and their children William and Mary, and Âpili, his wife Helene, and their pregnant daughter, Esther. Olsen's replacement at Davis Inlet, William Swaffield, took credit for their recruitment and was happy to see them go. They were, as he put it, of "no profit to the company."[36]

The *Evelena* departed Ukkusiksalik on 4 August, arriving at Okkak on 7 August. Here they added to their collection of Inuit artifacts, including such things as carvings, dog-whips, kayaks, and komatiks. Outside Okkak, at a place called Cutthroat, they disassembled an Inuit grave and loaded it onto the schooner for later reassembly in Chicago. Inuit on board raised objections to this but the prospect of adding a significant new attraction to the "Esquimaux" exhibit proved irresistible to the Americans. Vincent was fully aware of Inuit disapproval. He would later write:

> There is now at the Eskimo Village on the world's fair grounds a grave that was taken up from its original place near a harbor known as 'Cutthroat' in Labrador. A photograph of it was made before disturbing it, then care was used in taking it aboard the vessel, for of all deeds unholy in the eyes of an Eskimo that of disturbing the grave takes precedence.[37]

Clearly, Vincent was unmoved by Inuit sentiment. His priority was to create the most engaging exhibit of "primitive" culture possible, and the desecration of Inuit graves served his purpose. His sense of entitlement highlights the ideology underlying the entire enterprise. "Primitive" cultures held value when they served the needs of "civilized" societies. Inuit graves were not the resting place of someone's ancestors or loved ones but, instead, exotic relics whose principal worth lay in educating or entertaining those of more privileged and dominant cultures.

A few days after this episode, the *Evelena* arrived in Hebron, generating considerable interest. When residents of that settlement learned that people were being hired for the fair, several volunteered to go despite the missionaries' objections.[38] Taber and Vincent had no intention of taking anyone from Hebron but one man, Zacharias Naemiup, was insistent and persuaded the Americans to allow him and his family to join the group. The Moravians stated that "he forced himself upon these people, and we could not hold him back," and commented, "he will likely gain from his experience and realize that it would have been better for him to remain where he was."[39] Zacharias left Hebron with his wife Naemi, their four-year-old daughter, Tabea, and Justina, his thirteen-year-old daughter by an earlier marriage. Perhaps as a means of placating the Moravians and compensating for the disruption and possible ill-will, Vincent and Taber paid Zacharias' outstanding debt at the mission store.[40] The missionaries declared they were glad to be rid of him as he was a "trouble-maker."[41] Zacharias likely participated in the rebellion at Hebron a few years earlier. If a troublemaker is someone who won't tolerate injustice, then such he would prove to be. He was the spark that lit the fire in Chicago.

When the *Evelena* left Hebron, it headed farther north towards the more remote regions of Labrador. It was there that Vincent and Taber hoped to contact the long-sought-after "pure Esquimaux": those "who have never before been brought into contact with civilization."[42] On the way, the schooner stopped at Ramah, the Moravians' most northerly settlement, where the exhibit's managers attempted to recruit local Inuit. The presiding missionary recorded the visit in the station diary:

> On 15 August, Mr. Vincent, agent for the world exposition in Chicago, arrived here in a schooner, and with him a few other gentlemen. They looked for archaeological... artifacts as well as curiosities for the exhibition. Its purpose was to exhibit there the life and activities of the Eskimos. For that reason, they would like to have taken with them some Eskimos from our

> station, which we could not permit.... They went to sea from here without any Eskimos and wanted... to go to Nachvak & Aulatsivik, in order to get from there... some Eskimos.[43]

In attempting to recruit Ramah people, Vincent was perhaps hedging his bets. If he was unable to find the ideal candidates, then perhaps those who had only recently become converts to Christianity would be the next best thing. Unable to obtain the cooperation of the missionaries, however, he was forced to look elsewhere. After a short stay, the expedition departed Ramah and headed towards Nachvak fiord where Vincent and Taber hoped to find the prize they were seeking.

CHAPTER 3

The Voyage Of The *Evelena* 1892

PART 3: NACHVAK

Nachvak is a long, deep fiord about 110 kilometres north of Hebron. It is over 40 kilometres long, bordered by the imposing Torngat Mountains. In an article written after the *Evelena*'s voyage but prior to the fair, and most likely for publicity purposes, Vincent evoked the mysterious, magical quality of Nachvak fiord:

> Nachvak, has a weird uncanny... appearance... and everything is so entirely different than anything that may have been experienced in other mountainous countries that there cannot but be wondered what is the cause. It may be that Simigak (sic) exerts his influence over you, for he is among the Esquimaux a wonderful sorcerer. His tent is pitched near the water's edge and at the base of the mountain.... Near his tent is the old whalebone village of Igloosuit and still nearer are the old burial places used by the heathen for hundreds of years. These old graves and ruins make Nachvak a place of desolate oddity and readily satisfies one who wants a change from the ordinary.[1]

It was in Nachvak that the Americans hoped to find their grail: Inuit living beyond the reach of Europeans who met their definition of the "primitive." And yet even here among Inuit who had continually rejected the overtures of the missionaries, Vincent and Taber would find people with a long history of European contact and an established pattern of co-existence.

Nachvak Inuit

Nachvak had been home to Inuit for centuries, well before European records first took note of their presence. Abundant marine and land mammals made the area a reliable location for food and Inuit exploited this ecosystem for generations, moving back and forth between the mouth and head of the fiord according to the season, the migratory patterns of wildlife, and environmental conditions.[2] Inuit tent rings, sod house foundations, food caches, and burial sites can still be found throughout the region.[3]

The earliest European documentation of Inuit activity in Nachvak appears to be that of the Moravian missionary, Jens Haven, who, after establishing the first mission station at Nain in 1771, led a fact-finding expedition along the north coast of Labrador to learn what he could of Inuit population distribution and settlement patterns. Haven spoke a dialect of Inuktitut, the Inuit language, most likely Kalaallisut, which he had learned during his time in Greenland. His numerous conversations with Inuit first revealed the elaborate trade network that had developed all along the Labrador coast after the arrival of Europeans in the south.[4] Haven established that the network had two main terminals, one at Napartok and the other at Nachvak.[5]

When Haven arrived in Nachvak in late August 1773, he found Inuit living in four sod houses about midway up the fiord.[6] At the time of his visit, only women were present at the settlement, the men most likely hunting caribou in the interior. He found the people good natured, "neither too shy nor too familiar," and was impressed by their common-sense approach to trading. Haven estimated the population at Nachvak to have been about eighty people.

The Inuit trade network identified by Haven was eventually disrupted by the Moravians. The year after Haven's journey north, in 1774, the Moravians established their second mission station at Okkak, a short distance south of Napartok. From that time, Okkak became the principal source of European trade goods for northern Inuit, including the Nachvak people until 1830 when the mission established another station north of Okkak at Hebron and the Hudson's Bay Company opened a post called Fort Chimo on Ungava Bay. Once Hebron was established, and especially after the Hudson's Bay Company closed its stores in Ungava in 1843, the mission received many visitors from the north who came to trade. Some came from Saglek, a short distance away, some from Nachvak, and still others from Ungava Bay. The Moravians made every effort to convert these northerners to Christianity, but most expressed little interest in Moravian beliefs, or in abandoning their own lands and way of life, presenting all kinds of "excuses." As one Hebron missionary reported: "one has a long journey to perform, another cannot leave his birthplace; a third cannot act in opposition to his chief."[7]

The Nachvak people in particular were resistant to change, demonstrating a "spirit of opposition and contempt of all that is holy":[8]

> One man... remarked that some of our people were in their conduct little better than himself and his companions... This alas, I was obliged, to some extent to admit, adding however, that those who sought to be saved must walk with the faithful followers of the Lord and not with those who are unworthy to bear his name. Upon this the man cut the conversation short, by saying laughingly, that they had heard enough of such matters, and would like to see some of our European articles.[9]

Although the missionaries found many of these discussions discouraging, northern Inuit often responded more positively when asked whether they would accept teachers going north to live among them. The missionaries understood this to mean that they were not opposed to Moravian teaching as such; they just did not want to leave their homelands. No doubt, Inuit understood that if the Moravians came, they would bring their stores with them which would prove to be a great benefit and convenience. As a result of these discussions, the Moravians began to consider a further expansion northward, a process that would lead to European incursions deep into Nachvak fiord.

The Competition for Northern Inuit Trade

In the 1860s, the Hudson's Bay Company, under the leadership of Donald Smith, embarked on a new and aggressive policy aimed at challenging the commercial hegemony of the Moravian mission on the Labrador coast. Their opening gambit was made in 1865, when the HBC presented the Moravians with an unsolicited proposal, offering to negotiate a buyout of their entire trading operation in Labrador.[10] The proposal came at a time when the Moravians were struggling with trade issues. A significant faction within the church argued that the mission should divest itself of all trade matters to focus exclusively on spiritual affairs. The HBC's offer seemed to present an opportunity to do that. The SFG, however, argued that private traders had no interest in the spiritual and social welfare of Inuit and that acceptance of the offer would deprive the mission of its ability to sustain itself financially. In the end, the SFG's arguments prevailed, and the HBC's proposal was rejected.[11]

The Hudson's Bay Company, however, was determined to have the Moravians' trade, if not by purchase, then by competition. In June 1865, the Board authorized Donald Smith to reopen the post of Fort Chimo at Ungava Bay, and to take whatever actions were necessary to challenge the Moravians for the northern Inuit trade:

> From the information which has recently reached the Board with respect to the operations of the Moravians.... The Board directs me to express their earnest wish that you should take early and effective steps to defeat this opposition and they authorize you to establish a post in any spot in that neighbourhood which may be convenient for the purpose.[12]

The mandate given to Smith was clear, and he would be ruthless in its execution. In 1867, the Moravians sent their trade supervisor Carl Linder to Saglek to set up a new trade outpost there. Saglek, a short distance north of Hebron, was an important fishing area for the Hebron people, as well as the terminus of the overland route for Inuit travelling to and from Nachvak and Ungava.[13] Smith learned of Linder's activities and en route to Ungava had the

HBC vessel *Labrador* offload building materials for its own post in the bay to be called Fort Lampson.[14] Discouraged by this initiative, the Moravians withdrew to consider their options. By establishing Fort Lampson in Saglek and reopening Fort Chimo in Ungava, the HBC essentially cut off Hebron from the trade of northern Inuit. It was up to the Moravians to make the next move.

In February 1868, the Moravian missionary Johann Schneider embarked on a trip to Nachvak in order to explore the prospects of establishing a new mission post at that location. A hundred years after the visit of Jens Haven, Schneider travelled from Okkak and arrived four days later at Naksariktok, a winter campsite near the entrance to Nachvak fiord, where he found between twenty to thirty Inuit living in snow-houses. When asked if they would be willing to receive Christian instruction if a teacher were to come and live among them, most responded positively, however, it was made clear that any final decision would depend on their leader, Tuglavina, who had left for Saglek the previous day. Schneider reported: "They could not ascertain what he would think but if he were willing all the rest would follow."[15] Schneider had already met Tuglavina at Hebron and thought that he would not be an impediment. Schneider would recommend Nachvak as the best site for the mission station, citing abundant fish and game resources as well as numerous sources of fresh water.

In March 1868, Br. Samuel Weiz was commissioned to establish the new mission station at Nachvak and that summer, he and Br. Ernst Beyer travelled there and found a suitable site midway up the fiord at Kitsimagvik where several Inuit, including Tuglavina, were encamped.[16] With Inuit help, they constructed a blockhouse to serve as residence, church, and store.

Donald Smith was in Saglek when news of the Moravians' activities at Nachvak reached him. He wrote immediately to his superiors in London informing them of his plans:

> Mr. Linder is endeavoring to push the trade briskly in the direction of the Company's stations in Ungava Bay. We learn that they are now setting up houses at a place called Nachvak about 60 miles to the north of this bay with the view of intercepting the Esquimaux on their way to this post no doubt, also of drawing away some of those who now resort

> to Fort Chimo. To meet with this move on their part, I have provided building materials and other necessities for establishing another post.[17]

Within weeks, the Hudson's Bay Company steamer arrived in Nachvak and agents of the Company began erecting a trading post next to the newly constructed mission house. Weiz was understandably annoyed. Smith reported that "it is evident our visit gave him no satisfaction."[18] The Moravians were forced to re-evaluate their position and again decided to withdraw.[19] Weiz would recommend moving the mission station to Nullatatok Bay, about a day's travel south of Nachvak, believing it to be a better location as it was thought to be closer to places commonly used by Inuit.[20] It would be three years before the Moravians were able to reorganize themselves and return to the region. In 1871, Samuel Weiz and his wife, Adolphine, accompanied by a store brother, Adolphus Hlavatschek, and two "native helpers"[21] from Hebron, Gottlob and Philip with their families, landed on the north shore of Nullatatok Bay, erected a single dwelling, which combined the functions of residence, church, and school, and founded the Moravians' sixth mission station in Labrador, which was called Ramah.[22] Thus, the two principal European institutions in Labrador established operations in the territory of the Nachvak Inuit.

Change and Adaptation

At this time, Nachvak Inuit consisted of a small number of families related by blood and marriage who generally recognized Tuglavina as their AngajukKâk or leader.[23] Tuglavina was well known to the Moravians as he had visited Hebron and Okkak to trade on numerous occasions. When Weiz and Beyer erected their building at Kitsimagvik, Tuglavina had been camped nearby. The missionaries reported six tents and about thirty-two people at the encampment. Each of the married men had a kayak and Tuglavina had a skin boat as well, which Weiz reported was kept "for the benefit of all." Tuglavina's authority was made clear to Weiz when he spoke to one of the men about the condition of his soul and was told: "You should say this to my chief, not me." Direct discussions with Tuglavina, however, were always inconclusive, although he regularly stated that he would "gladly hear what they had to say."[24]

After the Moravians moved to Nullatatok Bay and established Ramah, Weiz would continue to court Tuglavina but to no avail. Tuglavina rarely visited Ramah and when he did, he remained circumspect and aloof, as the following account indicates:

> On Tuesday in the Passion-week, a company of heathen from Nachvak arrived, intending to leave on the following day for Saglek, where they wished to trade. But being detained here... by the snowy and rainy weather, they had, contrary to their own wishes, a good opportunity for hearing the story... of our Lord's... glorious Resurrection... among them their chief, Tuglavina. They listened to all they heard without contradiction, as something already known to them, but then came the old excuses for not being converted... Eventually they left without leaving upon our minds the conviction that anyone had taken with him a deeper impression.[25]

Tuglavina would continue to resist conversion until his death. Semigak, Tuglavina's brother, would later explain the resistance as fidelity to their father and an attachment to their land: "I will tell you how it is. We promised our father, when he was dying, that we would never leave Nachvak to reside elsewhere."[26]

While the Moravians were intent on converting Inuit, north of Hebron, they were also competing for the trade. Initially, the Hudson's Bay Company had a clear advantage as its trading post was in the heart of the hunting territory of the Nachvak people and could be visited easily by Inuit on trips both up and down the fiord. A visit to the Moravians, on the other hand, required greater effort and mostly occurred during trips to the south or when desired items were unavailable at the HBC post. The HBC referred to Nachvak Inuit as "our Esquimaux" and jealously protected their trading relationship. Clearly, both institutions were trying to impose change on Inuit. The Moravians wanted

Inuit to convert to Christianity and come to live in a religious community at Ramah while the Hudson's Bay Company wanted Inuit to shift their focus from subsistence hunting to trapping and commodity trading, essentially to become indentured labour supplying the Company with fish, fur, and oil.

At the time Europeans arrived in Nachvak, Inuit were already having difficulties securing a livelihood. The Hudson's Bay Company journals for the period 1868–1875 reveal that Tuglavina's people often split into smaller parties attempting to exploit different resources at the same time, some "down below" sealing while others were "up above" trouting.[27] This may have been common practice, but it also suggests that resources were becoming increasingly scarce. The HBC journals constantly refer to people hungry, and sometimes on the verge of starvation, visiting the post even when they had little to trade.[28] The HBC may have contributed to Inuit hardship by employing their own crews to hunt and fish in the area. For example, each year they would set nets in the fiord to intercept the annual migrations of char. The post journals for 1872 report daily catches of hundreds of fish while Inuit at their traditional fishing locations in the upper lakes, using spears and weirs, "seem to do nothing."[29] For the Nachvak people who depended on fish as a vital food resource, especially when all else failed, the depletion of char was an existential threat.

The difficulties of obtaining adequate food resources led, over time, to increasing defections to the Moravian mission at Ramah, threatening the HBC's dominant position in the trade. In the first years after the establishment of the new mission station, there was continual resistance to the Moravians' evangelical efforts and few conversions. This began to change in the early 1880s as Inuit faced greater hardship.[30] It became evident to Inuit that the Moravian community offered greater security and support. The missionaries provided access to medicine, a social safety net in the form of "poor relief," and after the introduction of seal nets in 1874, better prospects of a livelihood. These measures contributed to an increasing number of Nachvak people moving to Ramah between 1881 and 1887.[31]

For the Hudson's Bay Company this meant a decrease in the number of its core clients and an attendant decline of revenues. HBC officials were then forced to re-evaluate their position at Nachvak. On the one hand it was of strategic importance in limiting Moravian trade, but on the other hand it was now operating at a net loss to the company. In 1886, Keith McKenzie, the Chief Factor of the Labrador District, wrote:

> I attach much importance to this post as it prevents the Moravians from establishing themselves in the Bay and encroaching on the trade of the Ungava District... For this reason, I think Nuckvak (sic) should be kept up.[32]

However, the very next year, McKenzie reversed his recommendation:

> At Nuckvak (sic), the trade has been small, and I do not think that there is any probability of it improving, nearly all the Esquimaux have left the Bay and gone either to the missionary station (Ramah) or to George River, it would benefit this District very much if Nuckvak post were abandoned.[33]

In 1889, the Company's Inspecting Officer, Peter McKenzie, reported that the post had been operating at a loss for the past six years. He attributed the situation to the near collapse of the char fishery which he blamed on the overfishing of Newfoundlanders "some years ago" but also on what he perceived as the habits of local Inuit:

> As a rule, the Esquimaux of Nachvak Bay are very poor; they are not good trappers, and they do not care for fishing. As seal hunters they are very good, but somewhat indolent and improvident.[34]

It was a harsh criticism for people who had survived in the region for hundreds of years. McKenzie concluded that, "judging from... the small amount of trade done, I am of the opinion that it is not worthwhile to keep it up much longer."[35]

The Moravians were experiencing their own difficulties. At Ramah, hunting and fishing failures were becoming more common occurrences, possibly due to deteriorating environmental conditions. These failures resulted in increasing poverty among the people based in their community.[36] Between 1886 and 1892, several families decided to leave Ramah and move to Hebron, which reduced the community's population by a third.[37] This movement caused the Moravians to reassess their situation and to consider abandoning Ramah in favour of a new mission station even farther north. This is what eventually happened but not until 1904 when they established their mission at Killinek near Cape Chidley at the northernmost point of the Labrador peninsula.

Searching for the "Primitive"

As the *Evelena* moved slowly up Nachvak fiord, a small encampment came into view where several Inuit families were busy fishing for char. As the vessel approached, Taber and Vincent grew more excited, believing that they had now found the people they had been looking for. Taber wrote:

> From Rama to Cape Chudleigh (sic) on the eastern slope of the height of land, the Esquimaux number barely three-score persons. These have not been visited by the missionaries as yet, and they are probably as primitive and uncivilized as any that exist on our continent today.[38]

He went on to say:

> These Esquimaux have no fixed residence but are... nomadic... shifting from place to place in search of game and dwelling in snow igloos eight or nine months of every year. They are much more healthy and hearty than their southern cousins, with their robust bodies and clear complexions, they bear an air of boldness, pride and confidence, in all of which the others are sadly lacking. Their language is scarcely intelligible to the men from Nain, and our interpreter made very difficult work of the simple questions we desired him to address to them.[39]

After two months on the Labrador coast and numerous conversations with Moravian missionaries, Hudson's Bay Company traders, and local Inuit, Vincent and Taber would have known that many of these claims were misleading or false. Although they lived farther north than other Labrador Inuit, the Nachvak people were neither ignorant of Europeans nor free of their influence. As we have seen, they had been trading with European merchants directly or through middlemen since the time of earliest contact and for decades they had been conducting trading expeditions north to the Hudson's Bay Company posts in Ungava Bay or south to the Moravian communities of Okkak and Hebron on the Labrador coast. In recent years, Europeans had moved into their territory to preach and to trade. By the time the *Evelena* arrived, their independence and self-sufficiency were being challenged and their traditional way of life was changing. But if the Nachvak people did not conform precisely to the stereotype of the "primitive," Vincent and Taber could make them fit the bill. The remoteness and mystique of Nachvak and its people accorded neatly with the fictions that the American entrepreneurs were intent on promoting.

Tuglavina was not present at the Inuit fishing camp when the *Evelena* arrived and was unable to assert his influence. At that time of year, he may have been hunting caribou in the interior. In his absence, the Americans persuaded two families to accompany them south. These included Kangerarsuk, his wife Tuglavina,[40] and an adopted 14-year-old boy, Degouluk, as well as Kupper, his wife Kuttukitok, and their children Mali, Tiguja, and Sikepa. In addition, there were two adolescent siblings, Kamialuit and Pomiuk, who were children of the recently murdered northern chief Kaujasiak and his third wife Aniortama. The teenagers were living with Kupper and Kuttukitok at the time of the *Evelena*'s visit. And so, a total of ten people from Nachvak joined the expedition. The Moravian missionary at Ramah reported on their departure, expressing particular concern for Kamialuit:

> We heard later from Nachvak that from there two heathen families went along to Chicago to have themselves exhibited there. Before their departure, they are supposed to have regretted this step, but too late. Unfortunately, also an

> unbaptized girl who had attended school here for a few years, went along, who just at that time stayed with her relatives.[41]

The return voyage south was uneventful. The *Evelena* stopped at Hebron on 21 August and at Ukkusiksalik on 28 August to pick up families previously engaged. One can only imagine the emotions of those about to set off for a two-year sojourn to the United States. Most would likely have felt a mix of excitement and anticipation, apprehension and fear. Vincent noted the solemnity with which some of them marked the occasion of their leaving:

> At one station the departure of the family of Eskimo... was marked with considerable ceremony. The chief feature of this was the church service held on board the vessel by the missionary helper, who led the party of natives in their prayers and songs. It was a touching sight and one that called forth the thought that home, even in bleak, cold Labrador, is as dear to them as to those whose homes were then thousands of miles away.[42]

The *Evelena* was at Run-By-Guess outside Aiviktok on 4 September.[43] On 5 September, the vessel anchored at Rigolet for two days, gathering the last families on board and taking on supplies for the trip south. On the evening prior to departure, the *Evelena* fired off a celebratory display of fireworks to the delight of those on board and on shore,[44] and early the following morning, with sixty men, women, and children crowded on deck together with dogs, tents, kayaks, komatiks, hunting gear, and numerous barrels of food and artifacts, the schooner departed for the United States.[45] In total there were seventeen men, twelve women, seventeen adolescents, and fourteen children, comprising fourteen families recruited from all over Labrador. Except for those who were related or lived nearby, many would have been strangers to each other.

Later, when a reporter interviewed John Lucy in Boston and asked him why he would choose to leave his home for two years and travel thousands of miles to attend the World's Columbian Exposition in Chicago, he said he had always wanted to travel abroad and that it was an opportunity to do so with his whole family.[46] The motives of the others are less clear. Curiosity and a sense of adventure may have played a role, but for most the deciding factor was likely the economic challenges they were facing at home and the hope that two years of guaranteed employment would provide some respite from months of stress and uncertainty.

In the years leading up to the fair, poor harvests and a tightening of credit had caused widespread hardship throughout Labrador and had led to social unrest in a number of the Moravian communities. It was no different at the Hudson's Bay posts. In 1890, Âpili Heleneup turned up at the post at Davis Inlet in near starving condition, begging for work.[47] The following year, Edward Brown had been so desperate that he had tried to sell his rifle in exchange for provisions.[48] It is a further sign of people's desperation that they found the terms of employment acceptable. For two years' service, the head of each family was to be given 500 Newfoundland shillings (equal to $100 US), and a promise of a hunting outfit on their return. They were to be fed, clothed, and cared for in Chicago and, after two years, provided with a return passage home.[49] Once in Chicago, where a person's labour was not sold so cheaply, the contract would be contested, but in the context of their current prospects in Labrador, it was attractive enough to entice people to venture into the unknown.

It is not known what criteria Vincent and Taber used for selecting those they hired to work in the "Esquimaux Village." If they had expected to find people who aligned with popular notions of Inuit as northern "primitives," clothed in animal fur, living in ice houses, and hunting polar bears and seals, they would have been disappointed. These stereotypes were constantly challenged by the people they met and the way of life they encountered. But time was short and if the expedition was to find enough people by the end of the short Labrador summer, compromises would need to be made. Vincent and Taber may well have feared that the people they were hiring were not exotic enough to meet public expectations. As a result, the recruitment of northern Inuit became increasingly important. This accounts for the special effort they made to acquire "heathen Esquimaux" from the far north who could easily be presented as the "genuine" article.

Whether Vincent and Taber believed their own narratives is also unclear, but the "Esquimaux Village" was never meant to be an authentic ethnographic presentation of Labrador Inuit. It was to be a representation not of Inuit realities but of the imagination: "primitive" people from the "land of the midnight sun." Vincent and Taber were not scientists, after all, but entrepreneurs, and their purpose was to engage the public to maximize potential profits. Fictions would serve their purpose far better than facts.

In Chicago, Inuit were expected to play their part. Inside the "Esquimaux Village" these hunters and fishers would be transformed into side-show curiosities, their clothing would become costumes, their work-a-day tools and utensils, props, and their daily routines, choreographed rituals, designed to meet the preconceptions and imaginings of an inquisitive and intrusive public. Although they may have gained respite from economic uncertainty, little would have prepared them for the new role they had been assigned.

The "Esquimaux Village." Illustration by Charles Warde Traver, *The Illustrated American*, December 1892.

The "Esquimaux Village." Illustration by Thure De Thulstrup, *Harper's Magazine*, March 1893.

The "Esquimaux Village."
Illustration by Charles Warde Traver, *The Illustrated American*, December 1892.

The "Esquimaux Village."
Illustrations by Thure De Thulstrup, *Harper's Magazine*, March 1893.

CHAPTER 4

Chicago and the World's Columbian Exposition

"The people in front of the grandstand could not hear, but it did not matter... They knew they were a part in a memorable scene that was making history. They were in the midst of noble concepts wrought into visible shape. They watched and waited with the patience of those who knew that what was to come would be a study for all time."[1]

Chicago must have been profoundly disorienting for Labrador Inuit when they first arrived to take their place at the World's Columbian Exposition. Their lives in Labrador, although fraught with insecurity, were lived in vast open spaces, in a country where they could travel for days and see no one and where only one or two small trading posts afforded some notion of the outside world. Chicago, on the other hand, embodied all the accelerating developments of the modern world. In less than a hundred years, while the Hudson's Bay Company and the Moravian Mission were slowly establishing themselves in the isolated bays of Labrador, the wild spaces around Chicago had been transformed into a bustling, complex, urban, industrial landscape, home to over a million people. Chicago was emblematic of developments taking place throughout the United States and an appropriate site to stage the massive exhibition that was to celebrate this "American achievement."

The Opening

In the early hours of the morning on 1 May 1893, while "scarfs of mist brooded upon the waters of Lake Michigan,"[2] and the domes and towers of the fairgrounds were still enveloped in fog, a reporter from the *Chicago Tribune* arrived at Jackson Park eager to secure a spot from where he could witness the opening ceremonies of the fair. All of Chicago and much of America had eagerly awaited the arrival of this day. It had taken a monumental effort, but in just two years, Chicago's financiers, architects, engineers, and construction teams had transformed a marshland, a short distance south of the city's centre, into an aristocratic city of ornate classical buildings, pavilions, and exhibition halls. These were elegantly arranged around a network of artificial lagoons, canals, and waterways. The buildings were uniformly painted white, which gave rise to the fairground's popular moniker, the "White City."

The Exposition was conceived as a commemoration of the 400th anniversary of the landing of Christopher Columbus in America, the moment, as some would have it, when the torch of civilization was transferred from the old world to the new.[3] Its stated theme was "civilization's progress," but it was clearly intended to be a declaration of American achievement as demonstrated by the scientific, technological, and industrial products on display in the vast exhibition halls. There for all to see were locomotives, threshers, electric generators, telephones, typewriters, sewing machines, refrigerators, and early prototypes of automobiles and motion pictures. Finally, after years of lobbying, planning, construction, and promotion, the exhibition was ready. As the sun rose higher and the fog began to dissipate, the world was about to get its first glimpse of the World's Columbian Exposition.

At nine o'clock, the gates opened to the public for the first time and "a forest of humanity so dense that its progress was barely perceptible"[4] made its way toward the grandstand in front of the Administration Building in the Court of Honor, the centerpiece of the "White City," where the President of the United States, Grover Cleveland, would preside over the opening ceremonies. At the same time as the gates were opened, the President's procession departed for the fairgrounds from the business district of downtown Chicago. Squadrons of mounted police, Illinois national guard, and troops of the United

States 7th Cavalry escorted twenty-nine horse drawn carriages, carrying the President and Vice-President, members of the federal cabinet, state governors and diplomats, the city's mayor and aldermen, members of the fair's organizing committees, and prominent business and religious leaders.[5] The *Chicago Tribune* reported that thousands of people watched the procession from rooftops, windows, trees, and lampposts, describing "sidewalks choked with people."[6] As the procession approached the fairgrounds, it turned down the Midway Plaisance, a corridor between Washington and Jackson Parks that had been set aside as the Exposition's entertainment and amusement concessions. Here the parade passed the great Ferris wheel, the Ice Railway, Hagenbeck's animal show, and various ethnological villages where people from all over the world were on display. While the President doffed his hat, representatives of the ethnological villages played their traditional music and waved wildly at the passing dignitaries.[7] The parade continued to the "White City" where it was welcomed enthusiastically by the enormous crowd. The *Chicago Tribune* estimated that over four hundred thousand people attended the fair that day.[8]

After prayers, poems, and speeches, President Cleveland took to the podium and heralded the Exposition as a presentation of the "triumphs of a vigorous, self-reliant and independent people."[9] He then stepped forward and pushed a golden key, starting the massive engine in the machinery building a thousand yards away which generated power to all the buildings on the fairgrounds. As a huge stars and stripes unfurled above the President, others followed, and "from the top of every tower and parapet fell flags, ensigns and bunting."[10] At that instant, steam whistles screamed, cannons boomed from naval vessels anchored in the harbour, and the electric fountains shot jets of water hundreds of feet in the air, "the mist falling on the faces of the cheering crowd."[11]

Chicago had fought hard for the honour of hosting the fair and had succeeded largely because of the deep pockets and dogged determination of its investors. A committee of prominent local citizens raised an initial $5 million in stock for the project. When the United States Congress made the award conditional on another $5 million, the additional sum was raised within twenty-four hours.[12] The shareholders of the World's Columbian Exposition were the who's who of Chicago's business elite. No doubt they were motivated by the substantial business opportunities that the fair would offer but the opportunity to host a great international event would also provide Chicago and its leaders with the prestige and recognition they believed they deserved for their contribution to the city's extraordinary growth and prosperity.[13]

The Rise of Chicago

Chicago had its beginnings as a Euro-American settlement with the single homestead of Jean Baptiste Point du Sable in 1779. He had established himself at the mouth of the Chicago River to trade with the Indigenous people of the region, the Potawatomi. This was only a few years after the Moravians established themselves in Labrador. In 1803, the United States army built the garrison of Fort Dearborn on the same site and, after the War of 1812, it became a centre for the American fur trade.[14] A hybrid village of American, French, and Potawatomi developed around the post and prospered until the 1830s when the United States government, in response to Indigenous-settler disturbances in other parts of Illinois, moved to consolidate its control of the remaining Indian territory in the state and, in 1832, forced the Potawatomi to relinquish all claims to the region and move to new lands, west of the Mississippi.[15]

From that time forward, Chicago began to see rapid growth, stimulated by talk of developing the Illinois and Michigan canal which would link the Great Lakes to the Mississippi River, making Chicago, at the head of the canal, the natural funnel for east-west trade.[16] However, it was the railway that would transform Chicago from a small rural town into a bustling metropolitan centre with an extended reach into the rich hinterlands of the American midwest. The railway would change city and country alike, binding the two in a symbiotic relationship, providing farmers with inexpensive access to markets for their grains and livestock and emerging city businesses with new customers for lumber and manufactured products.[17] The first railway was established in Chicago in 1848 and by the 1860s the city was the hub of a large rail network with links to Kansas and Missouri in the south, Iowa and Nebraska in the west, and Minnesota and Wisconsin in the north.[18]

At this time, an increasing number of entrepreneurs were attracted to the area, establishing new businesses and industries, and building stockyards, grain elevators, and sawmills. Access to nearby supplies of coal and iron ore led to the development of steel mills and an array of factories that produced rails, bridge trusses, streetcars, locomotives, and farm machinery.[19] By 1880, Chicago had become, after New York, the second most important manufacturing centre in the United States and home to some of its wealthiest businessmen. Chicago's ascent happened with remarkable speed. In 1830, the city had a population of just seventy people; by 1880, the population was 508,185; and by 1890, it had more than doubled to 1,208,669.[20]

Chicago's rapid expansion created social problems on a scale rarely seen before. The disparities within Chicago's emerging society in the mid-1800s were clearly apparent in the contrasting living conditions of the rich and poor. The elite lived in their custom-designed mansions along the shores of Lake Michigan, or along Michigan and Prairie Avenues, well away from the business district and industrial zones,[21] while most of Chicago's immigrant workers lived in crowded, hastily constructed neighbourhoods near the mills and factories, where living conditions were both unpleasant and unsanitary.[22] By the 1890s, it was estimated that over 49% of Chicago's population lived in houses with at least ten occupants and that over a third had no toilet facilities. Raw sewage was a fact of everyday life and a major concern for Chicago's overburdened health authorities. Outbreaks of smallpox and cholera were common occurrences.[23] In the city's Department of Health Report for 1882, the housing inspector observed: "The whole number of occupants of tenement houses is about equal to the foreign population, not because of their nationality, but because it is the wage workers of all nationalities who are compelled to occupy tenement houses."[24] The root cause of both the housing and health problems was the poor working conditions for most of the city's labour force.

Class Conflict

While Chicago's expanding industrial and manufacturing base demanded workers in ever greater numbers, hours were long, wages were low, and employment was unreliable, subject to unpredictable business cycles and depressions. Industries were mostly unregulated, with management controlling the terms of employment and doing whatever was necessary to keep wages low. Workers fought back, seeking better wages, better working conditions, job security, and shorter hours.

Chicago became a major battleground for capital and labour, with both sides becoming increasingly militant. The number and sizes of unions grew steadily and the number of strikes, protests, and violent confrontations along with them.[25] Chicago unions became the vanguard of the American labour movement and, with the introduction of socialist and anarchist factions, a centre of radicalism. Chicago's capitalists responded with firings, black-listings, lockouts, strike-breakers, court injunctions, spies, and by hiring private security agencies such as the Chicago-based Pinkerton Detective Agency.[26] Between 1887 and 1894, the United States Commissioner of Labour reported over 528 strikes in the city, costing business and labour over $14,000,000.[27]

One particularly notorious event solidified Chicago's reputation as the centre of industrial conflict and tarnished the reputation of its business elite. In 1886, a strike for an eight-hour work week at the McCormick Harvesting Machine Company led to a confrontation between strikers and strike-breakers. Police fired into the crowd, killing two workers. The next day a rally supporting the strike was held at Haymarket Square. Just as labour leaders were finishing their speeches, police arrived, ordering the demonstrators to disperse. Someone threw a bomb, killing one policeman outright and mortally wounding six others. Gunfire was exchanged and, within minutes, four demonstrators were dead and another seventy injured. Anarchists were blamed and seven people were subsequently arrested and brought to trial. With questionable evidence and controversial witnesses, all seven were convicted and four were later executed.[28]

These events solidified Chicago's reputation as a violent and dangerous place, thought to be the inevitable result of unbridled capitalism, radical unionism, uncontrolled immigration, and unplanned urbanization. For many,

Chicago seemed to embody all the negative aspects of modern urban America. The extraordinary effort of Chicago's business leaders to host and stage the fair was in part an attempt to counter these notions. As far as Chicago's business community was concerned, nothing illustrated "civilization's progress" more demonstrably than the speedy transformation of their city from a tiny trading village to a modern industrial metropolis. And if the fair was to celebrate "American achievement," they would ensure that their city and their own deeds would be closely linked to the narrative.

"Civilization's Progress"

By any metric, the "White City" was an impressive achievement. It took two years to complete, cost $28 million, employed forty thousand labourers, and used eighteen thousand tons of steel, seventy-five million board feet of lumber, and over 120,000 incandescent lights. The fourteen main buildings had a total floor space of sixty-three million square feet in which to display over sixty-five thousand exhibits.[29] When it was complete, it stood in stark contrast to the city outside its gates: an idyllic urban landscape complete with clean parks and waterways, electric lights, an elevated rail transport system, modern sanitation facilities, fire hydrants, and clean drinking water.[30]

The creation of the "White City" out of nothing but the swamp of Jackson Park was seen as something of a metaphor for America itself: the proverbial 'City on the Hill' carved from the wilderness. Speaking at the fair's dedication ceremony, the president of the Directory, Harlow Higginbotham, lauded the accomplishment:

> But yesterday these surrounding acres composed a dismal morass — a resting place for wild fowls in their migratory flight. Today they stand transformed by art and science into a beauty and grandeur unrivalled by any other spot on earth. Herein we behold a miniature representation of that marvelous material development, and that unprecedented growth

> of national greatness, which, since the days of Columbus, have characterized the history of this New World.[31]

Michel-Rolph Trouillot has written: "Celebrations straddle the two sides of historicity. They impose silence upon the events that they ignore, and they fill that silence with narratives of power about the event they celebrate."[32] This was certainly true of the celebrations surrounding the World's Columbian Exposition. The interwoven themes of "American achievement" and "civilization's progress" did not allow for any critical examination of Columbus' legacy or acknowledge the collateral damage caused by the development and growth of the United States. Its purpose was the promotion of a heroic national narrative that lauded the achievement of continental expansion while ignoring the processes that had made it possible: slavery and the conquest and destruction of Indigenous nations. This selective narrative was reinforced when organizers denied the applications of African-Americans and Native Americans to create their own exhibits at the fair, thus excluding them from any significant representation in the "White City."[33] "American achievement" was presented as essentially a "white" achievement.[34] In the end, the anniversary of the "discovery of America" was merely the pretext for American businessmen to celebrate themselves as the heralds of progress and prosperity and to reap further commercial rewards in the process. The fair's directors passed responsibility for Indigenous representation to one of the leading ethnologists in the US, Harvard professor Frederic Ward Putnam, who was placed in charge of anthropology and all exhibits pertaining to "the science of man." Putnam's scheme for ethnological exhibits would further limit and marginalize the role of Indigenous Peoples at the fair.

CHAPTER 5

Ethnology and the Fair

"There is nothing barbaric or savage in these nations... what happens is that everyone calls barbaric that which is alien to his customs."
— Michel de Montaigne[1]

It is not known how Vincent and Taber explained to Inuit the concept of an ethnological exhibit or what was to be expected of them. While they were familiar with contracts, and would have understood that in exchange for their labour they would receive wages, food, and accommodation, what that labour was to consist of was likely poorly explained and only vaguely understood. And almost certainly, they would have had no understanding of the ideological and intellectual environment that would shape their experience at the World's Columbian Exposition and largely determine how they would be presented and perceived.

Putnam's Vision

Frederic Ward Putnam, Curator of the Peabody Museum of American Archaeology and Ethnology at Harvard University, was the first to suggest that the World's Columbian Exposition should include a comprehensive "ethnographical exhibition." He had been impressed by the "Village Nègre," an assembly of over four hundred Indigenous people from various French colonies which formed part of L'Exposition Universelle in Paris in 1889.[2] He outlined his own ideas in an article published in the *Chicago Daily Tribune* on 31 May 1890:

> To all who visited the World's Fair in Paris last year, the ethnographical department proved to be one of great attraction.... In this connection cannot Chicago secure and place in the Exposition a perfect ethnographical exhibition of the past and present peoples of America and thus make an important contribution to science, which at the same time will be appropriate, as it will be the first bringing together on a grand scale of representatives of the peoples who were living on the continent when it was discovered by Columbus, and by including as thorough a representation of pre-historic times as possible, the stages of the development of man on the American continent could be spread out as an open book from which all could read(?)[3]

The fair's directors wanted the Exposition to be a great cultural event, a place of learning and enrichment, a forum for the arts and science as well as industry.[4] To achieve this end, and counter critics who suggested that Chicago was a cultural backwater, they undertook a number of artistic and educational programs.[5] A Palace of Fine Arts was built with seventy-four galleries filled with paintings and art treasures from around the world and a World's Congress Auxiliary was established, which held daily presentations and lectures, 5,978 in all, covering a plethora of subjects including ethics, literature, history, economics, labour, and religion.[6] Putnam's vision for a grand ethnological exhibit was endorsed by the Directory and on 5 February 1891, he was hired to head the Department of Ethnology and Archaeology at the fair, to be known as Department M.[7]

Putnam envisioned his exhibit of "the stages of the development of man on the American continent" as twofold: the first part to be a comprehensive display of archaeological and cultural materials representative of all pre-European American cultures; the second part to consist of living exhibits of various Indigenous Peoples occupying traditional housing, wearing traditional clothing, demonstrating crafts, and performing traditional ceremonies.[8] For Putnam, the most significant of the two was the living exhibits. So important were they that without them, he claimed, the entire fair would be deprived of its essential meaning:

> The part of the ethnological exhibit... which will be regarded as an essential display, will be the out-of-doors exhibit of the native peoples of America... for what... is more appropriate, more essential than to show, in their natural conditions of life, the different types of peoples who were here when Columbus was crossing the Atlantic Ocean...? The great object lesson... will not be completed without their being present. Without them, the exposition will have no base. It will show the material prosperity... of our race... but it will... be a monument standing upon nothing... for it will be showing simply America of today.[9]

Putnam was claiming that the story of civilization's progress in America could not be told without reference to pre-European history and cultures. Anthropological exhibits and living cultural displays were needed to provide the baseline against which progress could be measured. The magnitude of the achievement of such things as steam engines, electric lights, and elevators could only be fully appreciated when measured against the "primitive products and inferior technologies" of earlier American societies.

Putnam's philosophical ideas reflected the conventional scientific wisdom of the day. Like most anthropologists of his time, he was an evolutionist who believed that humanity was in the process of evolving towards perfection, both biologically and culturally, and some races were thought to be further along that road than others.[10] This notion led to the then widely accepted construct of a hierarchy of "races" that could be measured on a sliding scale, up to the most "civilized" or down to the most "primitive."[11] The concept was largely accepted by Putnam and many of his contemporaries and influenced the organization of ethnological exhibits at the fair.

The "Stages of Man"

The nineteenth century was for Europe and America a time of remarkable colonial expansion, international war, class struggle, and scientific and technological development. The achievements of the Enlightenment, and particularly the celebration of reason as the principal tool for understanding one's place in the universe, had led to the development of a "science of man" and a belief in the idea of "progress" as the defining characteristic of human history. Archaeological discoveries undermined entrenched biblical explanations for the origin of humanity and replaced the old orthodoxy with the belief that "civilized" states had evolved from ancient "primitive" societies before biblical times.[12] As early as 1748, Montesquieu, the French political philosopher, analyzed human cultural history in *The Spirit of Laws* as passing through stages of "savagery," "barbarism," and "civilization."[13] He defined "savages" as hunter-gatherer societies made up of small clans, while "barbarians" were small nations of herdsmen and shepherds. "Civilized" man was organized into states defined by government and law. Adam Ferguson, the Scottish philosopher and historian, developed Montesquieu's ideas further in his 1767 *Essay on the History of Civil Society*, suggesting the principal characteristic of civilization was the notion of property. The "savage" had no idea of property, while the "barbarian" had some, but nothing protected by law, which Ferguson suggested was the defining achievement of the "civilized" state.[14]

From the fifteenth century, Europeans encountered numerous other peoples and societies during exploratory expeditions and colonial wars in Africa, America, and the Pacific. Few were able to resist Europe's military and technological power. As a result, many Europeans came to believe that Europe was the seat of the most advanced civilization in the world and that Europeans were intellectually and morally superior to those they encountered.[15] The question arose as to why this was, and some European intellectuals began to analyze and compare the characteristics and capacities of different people. It was thought that while some appeared to evolve through the earlier stages of "savagery" and "barbarism," others did not and were destined to live the life of their ancestors. The conclusion was that Europeans were encountering "primitive" societies, anachronisms within the human family, living examples of earlier stages of human culture.[16]

Ideas of socio-cultural evolution received their definitive intellectual expression in the writings of the English philosopher Herbert Spencer in the mid-nineteenth century. Spencer is credited with "biologizing history."[17] He is considered to be the chief proponent of social Darwinism which held that the same laws of natural selection that Charles Darwin had proposed as a determinant among species of plants and animals held to be true for societies as well and that the principal characteristic of human society is the struggle for survival determined by the "survival of the fittest" (a phrase first coined by Spencer). Natural selection ensured that those able to adapt to change in their environment survived, while those who could not died out. Spencer was suggesting that this was also the way humanity improved, evolved, and progressed.

Spencer, wittingly or not, had merged cultural evolutionary theory with racial determinism.[18] His ideas of natural selection and survival of the fittest would have huge consequences. They were used to justify white supremacy, colonial domination, slavery, and the extermination of Indigenous Peoples the world over. If Indigenous people were simply remnants of some earlier stage of man's evolutionary development, then their fate was inevitable. The "primitive," the "savage," and the "barbaric" were destined for destruction. They were thought, in the end, to be anachronisms and impediments to progress.

While Spencer emphasized that human nature was an evolutionary product and that progress consisted of the fit replacing the unfit, his discussion of human hereditary traits also contributed to racial stereotyping. In *Principles of Sociology* published in 1876, Spencer referred to the "nature of social units" and discussed the characteristics of individual members within each human group. He identified the characteristics as both extrinsic and intrinsic, the former being physical and the latter behavioural.[19] The suggestion that behavioural traits are hereditary and common within a given racial group legitimized popular ideas prevalent within nineteenth-century European and American society which asserted rigid racial typologies and stereotypes.[20]

Spencer's work was widely read and became profoundly influential on both sides of the Atlantic. In the United States, his ideas influenced the development of American anthropology and particularly the work of Lewis Henry Morgan. Morgan adopted and popularized the general evolutionary concept outlined by Montesquieu and Ferguson, of humanity progressing through stages of "savagery," "barbarism," and "civilization," and agreed with Spencer that all peoples moved through similar cultural stages but not necessarily at the same time. Morgan stated that the Aryan "race" had advanced beyond the rest "because it produced the highest type of mankind and because it proved its intrinsic superiority by gradually assuming control of the earth."[21] Morgan speculated that there could be other cultures existing in "remote" corners of the world which represented people at earlier phases of the evolutionary process. These cultures could provide insights into earlier eras of human history. Frederic Putnam shared Spencer's and Morgan's view of cultural and racial evolution and these ideas underpinned his notion that ethnological exhibits of pre-Columbian peoples at the fair could serve as a baseline for the measurement of "civilization's progress."

At the time of the World's Columbian Exposition, evolutionary concepts of race were deeply embedded in European and American society and prevailing scientific theories profoundly influenced the perception of non-western societies and cultures. Although Putnam and his colleagues had hoped ethnological exhibits at the fair would be scientific in nature, designed to inform and educate, the scientific constructs used to contextualize the exhibits served to validate prevailing racist perspectives in which observers could see themselves as "civilized" and superior and the observed Indigenous people as "primitive" and inferior.[22]

Ethnological Exhibitions

At the same time as philosophers were defining concepts of evolution and race, a concurrent development was taking place in Europe and America that would profoundly influence the ways that non-European cultures were perceived and understood. This was the development of ethnological exhibits, the public display of non-European people for mass education or amusement. Ethnological exhibitions have a long and varied history. There are innumerable examples of Indigenous people being taken from America to Europe for display, beginning with Columbus, who returned to Spain after his first voyage with several Indigenous Americans whom he presented at the court of Ferdinand and Isabella. Columbus' purpose was most likely to provide proof of his discovery and to solicit from the king continued support for future colonial ventures.[23] It had the desired effect. The Indigenous people's introduction at court created a sensation and they helped validate the existence of a new world. However, the presentation also established the essential nature of the relationship that would characterize such cross-cultural encounters for hundreds of years. It was that of captor and captive, conqueror and conquered, colonizer and colonized. The imbalance of power in the relationship allowed the ideas of the dominant ideology to define the other. The silence and powerlessness of human trophies presented a *tabula rasa* upon which observers could project their own ideas. In a Europe defined by religious orthodoxies and sectarian conflict, they would be defined as "uncivilized" and "savage" because of their ignorance of Christianity, among other things. It was even claimed that they were like animals and had no souls, an argument that rationalized both enslavement and extermination.[24]

Throughout the Age of Discovery, explorers and early colonists repeated Columbus' practice of transporting Indigenous people to Europe, usually through coercion. Inuit were frequently among those targeted. The first appear to have been a 20-year-old woman and her 7-year-old daughter captured by French sailors, probably in Labrador, and brought to Antwerp in 1566. After they arrived in the city, they were exhibited in their sealskin clothing.[25] Martin Frobisher brought Inuit to England following his voyages to Baffin Island in 1576 and 1577. Frobisher perhaps wanted to have something to show for his otherwise fruitless ventures. His pursuit of trophy Inuit was particularly brutal during his second voyage when his men fought a pitched battle with Inuit, killing five or six people, to take prisoners. A man, woman, and child were eventually captured and taken to England. Their brief public display in Bristol included a kayak demonstration on the river Avon. All three subsequently succumbed to European disease.[26] Inuit from Labrador were also transported to Europe by the British Governor of Newfoundland, Sir Hugh Palliser, in 1768, and by the merchant trader George Cartwright in 1773.[27]

In the eighteenth and nineteenth centuries, European colonial expansion created a new interest in foreign people and displays of "human curiosities" from distant lands became common, attracting a more general audience. These exhibits developed somewhat differently in Europe and America. In Europe, they were initially staged as ethnographic presentations for educational purposes, often with the support and endorsement of the scientific community. In America, on the other hand, human exhibits were part of an emerging entertainment industry and people were presented as human "oddities." Both forms of human exhibits became increasingly popular and as their commercial potential became more apparent, the differences between the two traditions became less distinct.[28]

In the United States, ethnological exhibits initially found their home in dime museums, circuses, and sideshows. Dime museums had their origin in the early American museums of the eighteenth century. These museums were mostly privately run, with the owners inviting the public in for viewings for a small fee. The displays would consist of collections of scientific interest such as stuffed birds and animals, books, military paraphernalia, maps, and paintings, occasionally accompanied by lectures. The purpose of these exhibits was to inform and educate a curious public. As the museums proved a popular pastime, entrepreneurs began collecting material with the object of establishing commercial enterprises that could attract increasing numbers of paying customers.

P.T. Barnum, a pioneer of the American dime museum, established his American Museum in New York in 1841. This enterprise, a combination of museum, zoo, lecture hall, and theatre, began to provide more original and daring attractions and shifted the focus away from the educational, creating an entirely new form of mass entertainment. Museums continued to display menageries of stuffed birds and historical artifacts, but they also began to include musical and theatrical performances, magicians, jugglers, and illusionists, as well as vaudeville acts, trained animals, "freak shows," and eventually ethnological exhibits. Indigenous people from Australia, North America, and Africa shared the bill with ventriloquists, sword swallowers, and bearded ladies.

The dime museum was the world of show business, not science. What sold tickets was the exotic, strange, and bizarre. Ethnic displays were in the general category of "human curiosities" and played to racial stereotypes: the "primitive," the "savage," the "wild man," the "cannibal," the "last of a dying race."

By the mid-nineteenth century, dime museums were entertainment staples across the United States, becoming exceedingly popular with America's new industrial working class seeking respite from their lives in factories and slums.[29] The more famous venues in America were Huber's in New York, Austin and Stone's in Boston, Herzog's in Baltimore, and the Kohl-Middleton circuit in Chicago, Cleveland, Cincinnati, and Milwaukee.[30]

When Barnum's American Museum burned down in 1865, he turned his attention to his travelling circuses but did not abandon his interest in ethnological subjects. Barnum had initially conceived of his circus as a travelling dime museum. His first circus, founded in 1872, was called "P.T. Barnum's Great Travelling Museum, Menagerie and World's Fair." From the beginning Barnum had seen the commercial potential of exhibiting exotic people, but had not been able to pull together a major exhibition until 1884 when the Barnum and London Circus staged the first Ethnological Congress with "100 Uncivilized, Superstitious and Savage People."[31] Barnum sent agents to "every part of our little ball of earth"[32] to find his exhibits and succeeded in assembling a collection of "Zulus, Nubians, Burmese, Afghans, Aztecs, and Hindus," among others.[33] The exhibit was hugely successful and financially rewarding. The Ethnological Congress clearly established that the staging of such exhibits could be extremely lucrative.

In Europe, ethnological exhibits also became popular, particularly in the latter half of the nineteenth century. At that time, the entrepreneur Carl Hagenbeck, who specialized in trading and exhibiting wild and exotic animals, turned his attention to importing and exhibiting people from foreign lands. Hagenbeck's early exhibits of Sami (formerly referred to as Laplanders) and Kalaallit (Greenland Inuit), which toured the German cities of Hamburg, Berlin, and Leipzig in the 1870s, created a sensation and proved to be both popular and profitable. In an age of exploration and rapid colonial expansion, public curiosity and interest in exotic people and places had been stimulated by newspaper reports and the popular travel accounts of explorers. Exhibits such as Hagenbeck's enabled mass audiences to encounter foreign peoples and cultures without the expense, inconvenience, and dangers of real travel. Hagenbeck promoted his exhibitions as educational and staged them in respectable venues such as public parks and gardens. He frequently received the support and partnership of museums and the scientific community and used the endorsements to give the exhibits added authority and prestige.[34]

Regardless of these pretensions, the principal purpose of Hagenbeck's enterprise was commercial. It was he who pioneered the concept of the "ethnological village": the creation of a living space that simulated the homeland and natural environment of the people on display to create a facsimile of everyday life. The people were often presented against painted tableaus of their homelands which reinforced the illusion of travel to a foreign place. Against this backdrop, the inhabitants would wear traditional clothing, live in replicas of their native habitations, demonstrate the use of weapons, tools, or musical instruments, and perform ceremonies and dances.[35] Throughout the 1870s and 1880s, Hagenbeck mounted tours of Nubians, Sinhalese, Fuegians, Somalis, and Labrador Inuit.[36] These presentations established an audience for ethnological exhibits throughout the capitals of Europe, including Berlin, Paris, Copenhagen, London, Prague, and Vienna. Hagenbeck's village concept was adopted and amplified at L'Exposition Universelle in Paris in 1889 with the "Village Nègre," a collection of ethnological villages representing people throughout the French colonial empire, including Gabonese, Congolese, Javanese, Senegalese, Arabs, and Melanesians. It was this exhibit that inspired Frederic Putnam to propose an ethnological display for the World's Columbian Exposition.

Putnam's Plan

Putnam's plan for a comprehensive ethnological exhibition was conceived as a non-commercial, purely scientific attraction in keeping with the stated intention of the fair's directory that the Exposition be a great university — a place of learning and enrichment.[37] With a budget of $100,000, Putnam began to plan his indoor-outdoor exhibit. His indoor exhibit was to consist of a comprehensive display of artifacts from the material cultures of Indigenous people throughout North, Central, and South America, including weapons, tools, utensils, clothing, carvings, toys, and religious objects. To this end he solicited contributions from federal and state governments in the US and foreign governments throughout the Americas, as well as private collectors and established museums. He also organized and directed hundreds of field workers, missionaries, and explorers to gather new materials in such far-flung places as Peru, Bolivia, and Chile.[38] The exhibit was somewhat a victim of its own success. The mass of materials that was accumulated required time and space to be properly organized and displayed. It was just five months before the opening of the fair that the Directory decided to construct a special Anthropology Building to house the collection, and the fair would be a third over before its doors would finally open to the public on the Fourth of July. Nevertheless, Putnam was proud of the achievement. In an interview after the fair, he stated that the exhibit had "excited the admiration of scientists from all parts of the world" and that "never before had so much new material been brought together."[39]

Putnam's outdoor exhibit would prove far less successful. He had hoped to create the great "object lesson" by displaying representatives of pre-contact Indigenous cultures living much as they had at the time of the Columbus landing. He envisaged people from all over the Americas in a series of living tableaus with weavers, silversmiths, and potters living in traditional housing and demonstrating ancient crafts.[40] A year prior to the fair's opening he outlined his ambitious plans in a newspaper interview:

> We have offered every possible inducement to native tribes in North, South, and Central America to make their own exhibits at the fair... These representatives will embrace families of Eskimos, Indian tribes of British Columbia and of various parts of the United States, a family of Maya from Yucatán, a family of Mosquito Indians from the Mosquito Coast of Central America, and natives of Guatemala. We will also have from Venezuela, a typical family living in the peculiar houses which they build upon platforms over the water — also several families of Caribs, the lowest of the races that met Columbus on our shores. From Bolivia and Peru are coming families of Amyras (sic) and Quichas (sic). From the district further south, we will get a family of Patagonians and probably, a family of Tierra del Fuegians, lowest of all in the scale of humanity. In all cases these simple people will bring their own habitations with them.[41]

During this planning period, Putnam stated that "schemes for private ends" would not be considered and that those "of a popular amusement character could not be tolerated."[42]

Putnam's plans foundered almost immediately. Principally, he did not have the financial resources to bring to Chicago the number of people he needed for his "object lesson." Nor does it appear that those willing to come were prepared to pay their own expenses or to play the role Putnam had assigned them. Putnam wanted to display Indigenous people as they might have been at the time of Columbus' landing. They were not to represent themselves but rather their ancestors. His field workers had difficulty finding people willing to travel, or in possession of the desired clothing and artifacts, or with the knowledge and skills required to demonstrate traditional trades and practices.[43] As a result, Putnam was forced to adjust his plans. He put his resources into one or two groups and became dependent on government and private enterprise to supply the rest. Private investors, however, expected to make a profit. If anything was to be achieved, Putnam would need to compromise his ideals.

At the same time, the fair's Directory was changing course. Under increasing financial pressure, due to an economic recession and rising construction costs, it reluctantly revised its plan of staging an exclusively refined and cultured exhibition and yielded to the demand for an amusement and entertainment venue to help alleviate costs. So as not to completely undermine the elegant atmosphere of the "White City," they placed the amusement park outside the fairground along a strip of land joining Jackson and Washington Parks, known locally as the Midway. The Directory's President, Harlow Higginbotham, rationalized the decision this way:

> This narrow strip of land gave an opportunity for isolating these special features, thus preventing jarring contrast between the beautiful buildings and the grounds of Jackson Park and the amusing, distracting, ludicrous and noisy attractions of the Midway.[44]

The Midway was proposed as the site of "Ethnology, Archaeology, History, Cartography, Latin American Bureau, Collective and Isolated Exhibits" and was placed under the authority of Putnam. Putnam, however, showed little interest in commercial concessions and played no role in the Midway's development. The Directory initially assigned management of the Midway to Sol Bloom, a theatrical impresario who was managing the Algerian exhibit at the fair and whose orientation toward ethnology had more in common with Barnum than Putnam.[45] Bloom managed the construction of the Midway and helped organize the vendors while the Exposition's Ways and Means Commission negotiated contracts and granted concessions. Neither paid much attention to Putnam's vision of a pan-American Indigenous exhibit. Concessions were granted for an ostrich farm, a hot-air balloon ride, and a Hagenbeck animal show; the original Ferris wheel was built; and numerous "ethnological" villages were constructed representing people from Egypt, Austria, Dahomey, Germany, China, Japan, Samoa, and Turkey. There were two Native American exhibits on the Midway both run privately and independent of Putnam. One was the *Indian Village* consisting of sixty individuals, representing Neshnabek (Potawatomi), Dine (Navajo), Haudenosaunee (Iroquois), Ho-chunk (Winnebago), and Lakota Peoples, who performed dances and songs and demonstrated crafts. The other, an exhibit known as *Sitting Bull's Cabin*, included Oglala Sioux and Crow, some of whom were said to be veterans of the Battle of the Little Bighorn.[46] Putnam's plans to exclude "schemes for private ends" had failed and exhibits of a "popular amusement character" were not only tolerated but actively encouraged.

Putnam's own outdoor "living exhibit" turned out to be a modest affair. He had hoped that his ethnological village would occupy a place of prominence at the fair and attract widespread attention. Instead, it was assigned a place in the extreme southeast corner of the fairgrounds on a piece of land next to South Pond, far from the central attractions of the "White City" and the Midway. Putnam's assistant, Franz Boas, had organized an exhibit of Kwakwaka'wakw (Kwakiutl) from British Columbia. Other exhibits came and went over the duration of the fair. The state of New York sponsored a Haudenosaunee (Iroquois) group; Canada, a contingent of Nehiyawak (Cree) from Saskatchewan; Maine, a group of Panawahpskewi (Penobscots); and the Government of British Guiana sent a delegation of Lokono (Arawak). The state of Colorado had sent a small group of Dine (Navajo) but they soon deserted for the Midway where, it was thought, they could make more money.[47] Putnam's plan for "a perfect ethnographical exhibition of the past and present peoples of America" as a defining feature of the fair and the means by which the public would come to understand the "White City's" message and meaning was a failure. In the end, the ethnological displays at the World's Columbian Exposition had no cohesive theme or organization; they splintered into a jumble of exhibits spread throughout the fairgrounds and the Midway. Most had no relation to either America or Columbus. Any Native American theme was obscured by exhibits from Sudan, Egypt, Algeria, and Java. What occurred was a distortion of Putnam's vision, instead reflecting the influence of other trends affecting the public exhibition of non-European races in the nineteenth century. In Chicago, anthropological exhibits, dime museums, "freak" shows, and circuses all converged in one place, each adding its voice to a confusing cacophony through which ethnological subjects were presented, perceived, and explained. Ethnology became a side-show — a hybrid of perceived science, education, commercial enterprise, and entertainment in varying degrees.

Both Putnam and the fair's organizers had hoped that the World's Columbian Exposition would be a stately and uplifting experience, a place of learning and culture. As it turned out, the attractions of the "White City" would be upstaged by the exhibits of the Midway. The carnival atmosphere to be found there would prove irresistible to much of the public; ethnological exhibits, located there and elsewhere at the fair, quickly degenerated into voyeuristic spectacle.

Whatever Vincent and Taber had said to Labrador Inuit to ready them for their sojourn at the fair, nothing could have prepared them for the realities they would face. The stage had been set, and public response had been largely predetermined.

CHAPTER 6

The "Esquimaux Village"

"The first chance, and probably the last chance, that the American public will ever have of seeing an Esquimau village is afforded them by a visit to the World's Fair at Chicago. On October 19, the little colony of strangers from the frozen North reached their quarters at Jackson Park, and, pitching their seal skin tents, proceeded to make themselves at home. They are the first instalment of Professor Putnam's ethnological exhibit, and comprise twelve families, fifty-nine people in all, selected from widely separated points on the bleak coast of Labrador."[1]

Arrival In America

When the *Evelena* dropped anchor in Boston Harbour on the morning of 14 October 1892, a reporter from the *Boston Globe* came on board to witness the extraordinary event. The schooner had departed Rigolet on 7 September and, after travelling thirty-seven days, finally arrived in the United States. Inuit, many of them dressed in sealskin garments, were perched at prominent points on the vessel, curious to see everything that was happening around them. The deck was packed with sleds, kayaks, skin tents, snowshoes, stoves, lamps, barrels of sealskins, seal oil, blubber, dried codfish, caribou meat, and kennels containing twenty-four "howling Esquimaux dogs." As the reporter observed, it "furnished a strange picture to the innumerable passengers aboard crafts of all kinds that hovered around the vessel and gazed at the strange scene presented." He described Inuit as "children of the north, the primitive people who inhabit the land of the midnight sun."[2]

Ralph Taber told the correspondent that the trip had been successful in securing everything that was needed to create a complete representation of Inuit life. "We have with us," Taber said, "some of the best specimens of the race to be found in their country." He explained that the people had come from various points on the Labrador coast and included "representatives of half civilized tribes at the Hudson's Bay Company posts, converts from Moravian mission stations and heathen aborigines from Cape Chidley and the shores of Ungava."[3] Taber went on to describe in detail the "heathen aborigines" whom he clearly considered his most prized acquisition. He described them as being "typical of the ancient race they represent" and "unsullied by the touch of civilization."[4] Taking his lead from the Taber interview, the *Globe*'s correspondent wrote:

> When the party reached the extreme Northern point of their travels, they were met by the most ignorant class of Esquimaux who stood in terror of anything calculated to disturb the monotony of their dreary lives. Living in houses made of ice, propped up by chance pieces of timber which were washed ashore... they lived absolutely without the slightest semblance of civilization.... They were more primitive in every way than the early Indians of America.[5]

Taber also reported that the party had examined numerous burial sites and had taken one on board, complete with the bones and relics buried inside. The relics included "carvings of dogs and sleds and implements used by natives." Taber stated that it had not been difficult to recruit people for the exhibit, principally on account of there being a very poor salmon and cod fishery that year and because people were facing starvation.[6]

After speaking with Taber, the correspondent wandered among the people on the deck of the *Evelena* and observed that it was easy to distinguish between the "heathen" and their "half-civilized cousins," stating that while they all had similar features, the latter were not as fierce looking, appeared more interested in their surroundings, and could speak English.[7]

The *Evelena* was boarded by US Customs officials in Boston. The Inspector took a list of the names of all on board as well as an inventory of the items that were to be trans-shipped to Chicago.[8] There was some question as to the conditions under which the people were permitted entry to the United States, as they were neither immigrants nor labourers. Delays occurred while US Customs consulted the Treasury Department to determine whether a bond should be required of the men who brought them to ensure that all would return home. The Treasury Department eventually determined that a bond was not necessary if the people were going on exhibition in Chicago.[9] With permission to land, the *Evelena* tied up at Gray's Wharf and everyone was allowed on shore. It was the first time the people had stood on dry land in over a month. The dogs were taken off the vessel and allowed to stretch their legs. The children, reportedly, "ran wild."[10]

The next night, Vincent and Taber took a small group of Inuit, dressed in their sealskins, to the Park Theatre to see a performance of the play *1492*, most likely to garner a little more publicity. The group, consisting of John and Katerina Lucy, Tom and Peter Palliser, Mary Palliser, Kupper, Kamialuit, and Pomiuk, was accompanied by the reporter from the *Boston Globe*. As they drove to the theatre, the people were clearly astonished at all they saw. "Kooper (sic), the young chief, had never seen a horse before his arrival in Boston, nor a house more than one story high. These and the electric cars interested him greatly."[11] According to the reporter, the group found the play interesting but were more taken with the gas and electric lights that could be turned on and off.[12] After the performance, they were introduced to a number of the performers, one of whom was a child dancer named Radloncita (sic), who, according to Taber, presented the young Pomiuk with a ring which, it is said, he would treasure for the rest of his life.[13]

The publicity surrounding the presence of Inuit in Boston brought crowds to the railway station the next day as the group prepared to board their train to Chicago. Arriving at the station by barge, they passed through a double file of curious spectators to get to their coach. Amazed by the "house on wheels" and at first frightened by the steam locomotives, the party had to be reassured before they got on board and settled down. To keep the people comfortable during the trip, "the steam was shut off in the coach and all the ventilators opened."[14]

On the evening of 17 October, the train carrying Inuit and all their belongings arrived at the Polk Street station in Chicago. It was six months before the scheduled opening of the Exposition, but the city was already preoccupied with the upcoming event. It was Dedication Week and a full agenda was planned, including a black-tie reception for the Vice-President of the United States, the entire US Supreme Court, the diplomatic corps, and a who's who of Chicago's political and business elite. The reception would be followed the next day by a massive parade through the streets of Chicago and an official dedication ceremony at the fair site. The arrival of Labrador Inuit occurred just days before these events, and they received widespread interest and press attention. Reporters from the *Daily Inter Ocean*, the *Chicago Tribune*, and the *Chicago News Record* were all on hand when the train pulled into the Chicago station. Inuit stepped onto the platform dressed in their sealskins, and they were described as "fat and jolly,"[15] a "queer and picturesque lot," "short and muscular," and "phlegmatic but intelligent looking."[16] One reporter wrote that they looked like "Indians loaded down with sealskins, except smaller" and that they were "exhausted" and "suffering from the heat greatly."[17]

The press reported that there were two train cars transporting the party: one coach containing Inuit from "the land of the polar bear and the midnight sun," and the other a freight car with "20 Esquimaux dogs, 4 puppies, a number of seal skin kayaks, a komatik, a sealskin tent, several barrels of oil and blubber, a lot of green skins to be made into garments, dried deer and seal meat, and a lot of walrus and fish bones to be manufactured into trinkets."[18] Inside the car, it was said, "the smell of walrus flesh and other delicacies was noticeable, to say nothing of the odor arising from the presence of three score fur-robed people. The excessive heat of the day had been exceedingly uncomfortable for the Esquimaux."[19]

The party led by Taber and Vincent, accompanied by the translator Robert Ford and the *Evelena*'s captain William O'Connell, was met by P.M. Daniels, the president and manager of the newly formed Arctic World American Exposition Company, which had taken over the management of the "Esquimaux Village."[20] In speaking to reporters, the agents for the concession presented their wards as exotic "primitives." They again drew attention to the two "heathen" families from the territory "beyond civilization" and explained that they knew nothing about Christianity, did not speak English, and were polygamous, typically kidnapping young women to be their wives or simply buying them with two or three sealskins.[21] The reporters engaged various Inuit in conversation, even managing to speak to Kangerarsuk, headman of one of the "heathen" families, who was reportedly much impressed with the locomotives at the station. Another who captured the attention of the correspondents was Pomiuk, the young fifteen-year-old "heathen" described as "gay and intelligent" and "the liveliest member of the group," "who loves to dance."[22] He was said to be "the son of a chief who was killed in an attempt to increase his number of wives." Pomiuk was still wearing the ring he received on his night out in Boston.[23]

The "Esquimaux Village" Realized

After their brief appearance at the Polk Street station, and after the passenger and freight cars had been transferred to the Illinois Central tracks, the party reboarded the train and were taken to the fairgrounds where they were expected to live until the close of the Exposition in a year's time. There, for a fee of twenty-five cents, visitors would be able to see the "natives," their "wolfish" dogs, sledges, spears, and canoes, and to watch "the domestic life of this curious people."[24]

The "Esquimaux Village" was in the extreme northeast corner of Jackson Park, on three acres of land that included a grove of trees and a small lagoon. The grounds had been fenced in so that access could be restricted to paying customers. There was a ticket window in the fence and nearby, a turnstile through which visitors could come and go. Initially, the people lived in canvas tents. Management provided materials to construct wood huts, meant to simulate winter homes in Labrador, but the men were expected to build these themselves and it would be mid-December before construction was completed.[25] Even though Jackson Park was still a construction site, and the official opening of the fair was more than six months away, the "Esquimaux Village" was soon doing a brisk business. A reporter from the *St. Louis Post-Dispatch* described an early visit to the site:

> Just at the surface of the water an opening is made in the fence.... Persons using the 57th St. gate are obliged to cross

> the lagoon by a little rustic bridge, and on this the majority of them pause to gaze at the fence hiding this stumpy people from the Arctic regions. One of the Eskimos in full regalia has been trained by his Yankee importers to act as a sort of "capper." He floats upon the hidden hand of the lagoon and ever and anon bends down in his canoe to peer through the aperture towards the bridge outside. When he sees it peopled by visitors, he gives his slender paddle a deft turn or two, shoots towards the hole in the fence and darts through it with a low bridge.... Once in sight of the people on the bridge, he goes through a series of evolutions in his tapering canoe, then wheels about and disappears into the fence hole again. This roly-poly little man is the bait for the show and when he shoots out of sight there's a rush for the ticket window and turnstile.[26]

The "Esquimaux Village" was the first ethnological exhibit open to visitors and throughout the fall and winter prior to the opening of the Exposition it attracted considerable attention. Once construction of the permanent living quarters was complete, visitors to the Village could see twelve huts, one for each family, as well as a number of sealskin tents containing kayaks, paddles, harpoons, whips, nets, sleeping bags, and other tools of the hunt; a dog pen containing the dogs not running wild in the village or hitched to sleds; and the reconstructed gravesite, with skeletal remains and burial relics. The women could be seen curing and tanning skins, crafting sealskin boots and clothing, or making dolls and grass-work for sale while the men carved small likenesses of people and animals in wood and walrus bone. Everywhere children and dogs ran free. When the lagoon froze over, the older boys harnessed their dogs to the sleds and took visitors on rides over the snow and ice around the pond. These rides were particularly popular.[27]

During the fall and early months of winter, the "Esquimaux Village" was well attended, and the concession began earning revenue. Inuit themselves appeared to be content. They were stimulated by their surroundings and apparently as interested in their visitors as their visitors were in them. One journalist wrote: "It seems to be one of the greatest of pleasures to the good-natured little people to entertain their visitors."[28] Another, after speaking to several men, stated that they:

> Evince a candor and good sense with regard to their situation at the exposition and their sojourn in the United States, which do great credit to their powers of observation and judgment. They converse sensibly and give one the impression that they accept the fact that they are part of the fair and hence must tolerate with patience and good humor the sometimes impertinent curiosity of sightseers.[29]

With the onset of winter and the first snowfall, the "Esquimaux Village" took on an irresistible charm. If the village was a stage, winter provided the perfect set dressing. The people, clad in their sealskin clothing, appeared at their most picturesque, aligning perfectly with public expectations. There was even an "igloo" at the edge of the frozen pond which visitors could crawl into.

Sealskin clothing was perhaps the people's most emblematic feature, and the cause of continual public fascination. Almost every writer visiting the village would comment on the native garments.[30] These sealskin clothes, beautifully crafted from the skins of wild mammals, embodied all that was most alluring and exotic about the people who wore them and, more than any other item, identified them in the public mind as "Esquimaux."

As the Chicago winter gave way to spring, the managers of the "Esquimaux Village" sought new ways to attract visitors to the exhibit. The kayaks reappeared on the lagoon, but the dog sled rides which had proved so popular were no longer possible. To overcome this, a small tramway was built with a sled mounted on rollers. Once the dogs were hitched, rides could again be taken around the village.

One of the more popular attractions at the "Esquimaux Village" was called the "Esquimaux whip." What began as a simple demonstration of a hunter's skill with a dog whip evolved into a contest between Inuit men. A visitor would place a coin on edge in the dirt, forty feet away from where the men stood, and each in turn attempted to dislodge the coin from the ground with a flick of the whip. The one who was successful got to keep the coin. It became a popular form of entertainment and a way for Inuit to make a little extra money. Inuit skill with the whip impressed more than one observer:

> The most expert whip among the Esquimau was a little man, not more than 4 feet high, with slanting eyes, and a spiky black beard that made him look very Japanese. A movement of his wrist sent the 40 feet of lash curving back in a straight line like a long snake. Another movement and it came forward, noiselessly shooting through the air just above the surface of the ground until, with a loud report, the tip end of the lash struck the precise spot where the coin was buried, dug it from the ground, and brought it spinning back to the Esquimau artist. Such precision and such force are certainly unknown to any other whips in the world.[31]

Born at the Fair

About two weeks after the arrival of Inuit in Jackson Park, the population of the village increased when two babies were born within days of each other: one to Simon and Sarah Manak, and the other to Kupper and Kuttukitok. Much was made over both babies; the first baptized Columbia Susan because she was the first child born at the fair and the second named Kotuktooka because she was born a heathen and wasn't baptized at all. The births were widely publicized and were promoted by the concession as a new attraction in the village in the same exploitative way that zoos promoted the birth of wild animals in captivity, although one of the Exposition's directors lamented that it was a pity an American child did not have the honour of being the first born at the fairgrounds.[32]

Susan Manak tragically died after only a week of life. Although newspaper items celebrating her birth had described her as 'fat' and healthy, reports of her death stated that she had been frail from the beginning and speculated that perhaps "the climate was too warm for her arctic blood."[33] More likely the damp conditions in the tents that had served as temporary residences for the Labrador people contributed to her death.[34]

The funeral of Susan Manak was vividly described in newspapers the following day and the accounts suggest that the event was deliberately exploited for its commercial potential. Shortly after her death, Susan was taken from her mother and wrapped in deerskin. A tiny coffin was made, and she was placed inside it. This was then put in a small skin tent erected near that of her parents. A few feet from the tent was a box covered in a polar bear skin. As the funeral ceremony began, each family gathered in front of their tents until Lucy and Susan Palliser, both five years old and acting as pallbearers, lifted the tiny coffin and placed it on the bearskin. With the parents at the head of the tiny coffin and the pallbearers at its foot, the families gathered around as an Episcopalian minister conducted a short service, at the end of which they circled the coffin chanting and singing hymns. Susan Manak was then taken to Oakwood Cemetery, a short distance from Jackson Park, where she was buried.[35] The exploitation of Susan Manak's death and the transformation of a solemn ceremony into voyeuristic entertainment echo the insensitivities of the desecration of the northern graves. Commercial interests took precedence over any ethical considerations.

A week after Susan's death, a third child was born, this one to Jonas and Susan Palliser.[36] This child was the first boy to be born at the fair and he was given the name Christopher Columbus. It was reported that his mother celebrated the birth by taking a kayak ride around the pond.[37] This baby too was described as "fair and fat." The fourth and last Inuit child born in Chicago was delivered early in the new year. On 16 January 1893, Esther, the daughter of Âpili and Helene, gave birth to Nancy Helene Columbia Palmer who would in subsequent years become widely known as Nancy Columbia.[38]

"Esquimaux Village," World's Columbian Exposition, 1893.
(Photo: C.D. Arnold, Art Institute of Chicago).

CHAPTER SIX

With Dogteam and Whips, World's Columbian Exposition, 1893.
(Photo: C.D. Arnold, Art Institute of Chicago).

At the Ice House, World's Columbian Exposition, 1893.
(Photo: C.D. Arnold, Chicago History Museum).

Playing on the Pond, World's Columbian Exhibition, 1893.
(Photo: C.D. Arnold, Art Institute of Chicago).

Group Portrait, World's Columbian Exhibition, 1893.
(Photo: C.D. Arnold, Chicago History Museum).

Âpili, Helene, Esther, and Nancy. World's Columbian Exposition, 1893.
(Photo: C.D. Arnold, Chicago History Museum).

Peter, Maggie, and Sarah Deer. World's Columbian Exposition, 1893.
(Photo: C.D. Arnold, Chicago History Museum).

Peter Palliser. World's Columbian Exposition, 1893.
(Photo: The Werner Co., *Portfolio of Photographs of the World's Fair*).

First Impressions

Because the "Esquimaux Village" was the first ethnological exhibit to be established at the World's Columbian Exposition, it immediately attracted attention from the press. Although reporters varied in their perspectives and opinions, they commonly reflected and promoted the preconceptions and stereotypes of Inuit that were current in the public imagination. Little effort was taken to investigate the particulars of Labrador Inuit histories or culture. There was a presumption that Inuit were interesting by virtue of their difference and "otherness" and a general acceptance of their characterization as representatives of "savage" and "primitive" people. They were variously referred to as: "a strange race,"[39] "queer and picturesque,"[40] "a peculiar people,"[41] and "children of the far north,"[42] from "the land of the midnight sun,"[43] "where the days are six months long"[44] or where "there are about ten days of summer and ice and snow the rest of the year."[45] They were described as "oil drinkers,"[46] as "eaters of raw fish and flesh"[47] with "black hair and dark skin,"[48] as "blubber-hunting, blubber fed people of the Arctic region,"[49] and among "the oldest people on the earth, survivors of the stone age and the glacial epoch."[50] The use of familiar and popular tropes drew upon and fed public notions in a kind of feedback loop that perpetuated misconceptions, providing both a language and a set of ideas through which Inuit at the fair were perceived. The notion that the inhabitants of the "Esquimaux Village" were "primitives," remnants of an earlier stage of human evolution, was determined in part by the promotion and publicity efforts of the concession's managers to maximize interest in the exhibit. They tended to highlight the traditional and obscure the modern. The special attention paid to the Nachvak families was part of this strategy. Viewed through this lens, the "Esquimaux Village" fit neatly into Frederic Putnam's original plan for ethnological villages to be "object lessons" by which the public could, through observation of the "primitive," understand "civilization's progress" and their own place in a more advanced and superior culture. One reporter described it this way:

> Away to the north of the grounds a party of Eskimo immigrants have built their huts.... The shadows of these huts,

> when the sun is low in the winter afternoon, are thrown up on the walls of the Art building. Would it be possible for extremes to meet more appositely? The Eskimo is among the races of men nearest to the soil from which all men came. The lines of the Art building express the mature development of the spiritual part of the enlightened man, of the soul in search of ideal beauty. The visitor may comprehend in a glance, the Eskimo and the Art building and in an instant, his mind's eye will show him all that lies between.[51]

It is difficult to assess the attitudes and impressions of the public at large who visited the "Esquimaux Village" in ever increasing numbers in the days leading up to the fair's official opening. These would have run the gamut from the admiring and respectful to the contemptuous and disdainful, reflecting both a genuine fascination with people profoundly different and an acquired prejudice towards people viewed as both ignorant and inferior. Visitors to the exhibit were mostly white Americans, the vast majority of whom probably accepted the misguided view that on the ladder of civilization, they were a few rungs higher than the people they observed in the "Esquimaux Village." The press was generally sympathetic. Although racism is evident in much of the writing about Inuit, it was more ignorant than malicious. However, a more virulent strain occasionally found expression. Julian Ralph, correspondent for *Harper's Chicago and the World's Fair* was particularly offensive:

> Whoever would imagine the face of an Eskimo belle without going to the painful extreme of looking at one, need only picture a Chinaman's visage which has been stepped on and flattened by an elephant's foot. The Eskimo face does not stop being flat — it is dished in the middle. Those polar belles have black horse-hair on their heads, café au lait complexions and very soft fine skins. Their tone of voice is precisely like that of the Edison talking dolls.... Filing a saw produces dulcet strains beside the lullaby of such a woman to her child. It costs $.25 to get into the Eskimo village but is worth $25 to get out.[52]

No doubt, the people inhabiting the "Esquimaux Village" would have seen and heard it all. The tropes, clichés, and stereotypes that framed the understandings and expectations of both the press and the public rarely managed to depict Inuit as anything but caricature. Even before the official opening of the fair, Inuit were becoming disenchanted and restless.

The Spring of Discontent

As the snow and ice melted, the village took on a more desultory appearance. Visitors began to comment on the increasingly sullen nature of the people, and the smell. The Rand McNally Guide to the Fair published the following comment:

> There are men, women, and children in the Village, and their modes of life and the sanitary conditions (or rather the want of them) peculiar to them and their crowded quarters do not "lade the pulsing air with the sweetest perfumes."[53]

This was not an isolated point of view. Early in the new year, casual observation had turned to widespread concern that the deteriorating conditions at the "Esquimaux Village" might harm the reputation of the upcoming Exposition and become a public health risk. In an article published in the *Daily Inter Ocean*, it was observed that the "Esquimaux" were not "the cleanest people in the world" and "delight to daub themselves with seal oil which often becomes rancid and very offensive," the point being that the "primitives" in the "Esquimaux Village" did not have a "civilized" view of hygiene. The situation was not blamed entirely on Inuit, however. The article explained that although the Exposition grounds had developed state of the art sanitary facilities, the site of the "Esquimaux Village" was affected by "every unfavourable feature," including "a stagnant pond that every effort had failed to keep pure." The article also blamed the managers of the Village, claiming that in an effort to recreate living conditions in the "Esquimaux's" native land, they had built houses that were impossible to ventilate and had failed to provide more sanitary quarters for the "Esquimaux" dogs. It went on to raise the possibility of an epidemic if conditions did not improve before the summer. The article concluded with the statement that attendance at the village had been "quite liberal," suggesting, perhaps, that management could afford to do better.[54]

As the physical environment deteriorated, so did Inuit morale. The constant and unchanging routine of receiving curious and intrusive visitors for months at a time must have been tedious. Unlike the representatives of other ethnological villages who would later attend the fair, Labrador Inuit were not seasoned performers. Rather, they were hunters and fishermen who, despite the pressures of subsistence living and merchant debt, led relatively free and independent lives in an open and ever-changing environment. The monotony of their confinement and the repetitive demands and expectations placed upon them would have made them restless, increasingly bored, irritable, and homesick. Food was an issue as well, especially for northern Inuit. The supplies of country food — seal meat, caribou, and fish — which had been brought from Labrador quickly ran out and the adjustment to a southern diet proved difficult and unsatisfying. One visitor to the "Esquimaux Village" was so moved by the apparent condition of the people that she expressed her outrage in a letter to the editors of the *Chicago Tribune*:

> Scarce ever has it been my misfortune to see anything so pitiable as the condition of the Eskimo people at Jackson Park, in the World's Fair Grounds. The motives of the company which brought these poor creatures here, are the most mercenary and should be rebuked by all who respect one common humanity.... (The) helpless people who were brought here as a speculation... are only being demoralized. Some of the children are already becoming brazen, others... are becoming so shrinking as to be a constant rebuke to the staring crowd... As for the women, I have never seen so pitiful a sight. They evidenced their humiliation in a dumb pleading of face and manner that would touch any heart not hardened by greed or vulgarized by curiosity.[55]

Inuit were also beginning to chafe at the rules imposed on them by the concession's management. Principal among these was the restriction of movement. It was one thing to have to remain in the village compound during the day to meet and greet visitors, but management discouraged Inuit from ever leaving the compound. The fence, which was built to keep out non-paying customers, also served to keep Inuit in. There was a clause in the original contract between J.W. Skiles & Co. and the World's Columbian Exposition which stated that the company would be allowed to board and lodge their native employees on the fairgrounds "provided that the said natives shall be confined to the said tract at such times during the night as said Exposition is not open to visitors."[56] The company appeared to be interpreting the contract more broadly and using it to restrict and control people's movements. It may well be that this was an attempt to limit the "contamination" of the village with articles and items that would compromise an "authentic" presentation; the acquisition of American fashion items, particularly skirts and scarves among the women, had already received comment in the press. Restricting contact with the outside world would also help maintain the dependency of Inuit on their employers. Once people began to explore the world outside, their perspective on their own situation began to change. It was most likely through discussion with construction labourers working on the fairgrounds that they learned how cheaply they had sold their labour. This discovery eroded the trust Inuit had placed in their employers and contributed to the discontent. However, it was the efforts of management to impose its authority on all aspects of Inuit life that set in motion the sequence of events that would eventually tear apart the "Esquimaux Village."

The Revolt

Trouble began early in January 1893. According to a newspaper report, one Sunday, Zacharias Naemiup (whom the reporter mysteriously calls Oconomowoe) left the village compound without permission and Robert Ford, the village interpreter and interlocutor between management and Inuit, had the 'delinquent' brought back and upbraided him for leaving. A few days later, the company president and manager P.M. Daniels learned of the incident and, in the presence of Ford, began to reprimand Zacharias for his behaviour. In the middle of the conversation, Zacharias turned on Ford and "proceeded to imitate the automatic vibrator on a big thrashing machine," shaking him violently backward and forward and finally hitting him. Daniels, unable to stop the assault, called in the Exposition police force, the Columbian Guard. By the time they arrived, the village was in "a state of excitement approaching delirium. Dogs were howling, men were shouting, and babies were crying."[57] Zacharias was taken into custody and initially held on the fairgrounds at the headquarters of the Guard. However, Daniels insisted that Zacharias be charged, and he was transferred to the Chicago police at their nearby Woodlawn Station where he spent the night under indictment on several counts of assault. Daniels stated that the arrest and imprisonment was necessary to show the villagers that "they must observe civilized customs or else suffer legal punishment."[58]

The following day, Zacharias was arraigned before Judge V.R. Porter of the Hyde Park Circuit Court. Determined to make an example of him, Daniels demanded that the judge have him locked up for two or three weeks. Porter declined to do so and ordered Zacharias to be released. That night he left the Village, and the next day took a job with a contractor working on the Exposition grounds for $2.25 a day.[59] Under the terms of their contract, Inuit were to be paid $50 a year for their work in the "Esquimaux Village." Working construction, Zacharias stood to make that much in a month. A short time afterwards, a second man, Tom Deer, quit the village, complaining of poor treatment, not enough to eat, and being forced to wear heavy furs on warm days.[60] He too found work with a contractor. A third man, Peter Mesher, also quit. Mesher, who had attended Zacharias' court case, had been impressed with the sympathetic hearing given by Judge Porter and had approached the judge for assistance in finding outside work. Porter had secured him a job with Buffalo Bill's Wild West Show at $1.50 a day.[61] According to later testimony, it was after meeting Mesher that Porter took a deeper interest in the "Esquimaux Village" people and initiated his own investigation of their situation.[62]

The reports of better wages to be found outside the "Esquimaux Village" no doubt fed bitterness and discontent among Inuit but the issue that brought matters to a head was the insistence of the exhibit's managers that Inuit wear their heavy sealskin clothing even in warm weather. From the beginning, Inuit clothing had received admiring comments, and it was clearly one of the most distinguishing features of the people. As temperatures began to rise, however, the heavy skin clothes, normally used as protection in sub-arctic winter conditions, became increasingly uncomfortable to wear.[63] Members of the group began to resist management's directive that these garments be worn throughout the day. The managers of the "Esquimaux Village" believed that visitors expected to see "Esquimaux" dressed in furs, that it was what defined them as authentic denizens of the far north. In effect, they were claiming that only when they donned their sealskins did they become truly "Esquimaux." Without the sealskins, management feared the overall effect and commercial viability of the exhibit would be diminished.

The conflict came to a head on 16 February when Tom and Peter Palliser came out of their huts dressed in blue jeans.[64] Daniels ordered them to put on their sealskin furs and they refused. He then ordered them back into their huts, told them to stay there until they obeyed his orders, and commanded the Columbian Guard to enforce his ruling. The Pallisers continued to defy orders and the forced confinement went on for weeks. It was during this time that Judge Porter visited the village and learned what was taking place. When he asked to visit the prisoners and was refused, Porter contacted the Columbian Guard's commanding officer, Colonel Rice, and informed him that he was likely to find himself entangled in a lawsuit if he continued to enforce the confinement. As a result of Porter's intervention, Rice withdrew the Guard, but Daniels countered by replacing the original security team with private agents. Then, on 18 March, a particularly warm day, Jonas Palliser and John Lucy joined the protest by refusing to wear their sealskins and they too were ordered back into their huts. Porter, who appears to have kept in touch with events at the village through Peter Mesher, thought that the company's action constituted forcible confinement and illegal imprisonment. He and Mesher decided it was time to intervene to see justice done.

On 30 March, Mesher, acting on behalf of James Shuglo, Thomas Palliser, Peter Palliser, and John Lucy, entered the Dade County Circuit Court of Judge McConnell and applied for a writ of habeas corpus against the Arctic World

American Exposition Company and its representatives, including P.M. Daniels, W.D. Vincent, and R.G. Taber.[65] A writ of habeas corpus demands that the custodian of an individual held in custody produce the individual in court so that an inquiry can be made to ensure the detention is lawful. Mesher claimed that the residents of the "Village" were being detained against their will and in his complaint termed the exhibit "a prison within the walls of which his countrymen are being coerced to remain." A reporter from the *Daily Inter Ocean*, who attended the hearing, later visited the village for a first-hand look and spoke to Robert Ford, the interpreter, who explained that the discontent around the obligatory wearing of furs might not be so egregious if the people were compensated fairly:

> Two of the natives have left already. The managers did not want them to leave but they are pretty well-educated and knew that they could not be held. Some of the others want to go but they can't. They are the ignorant ones and can be compelled to do just what the managers want them to. However, there are one or two who are getting ugly, and they may run away any day. The trouble is they are not paid what they think they are worth. As a matter of fact, they receive next to nothing, and they have found out that good wages can be earned outside.[66]

The reporter went on to interview another person who is identified as Jones, most likely Jonas Palliser. He is quoted as saying:

> We are kept in here like so many thieves. We have no rights and are not treated like human beings. If any of us leave the enclosure, our pay is declared forfeited. And some of us are really held as slaves, that is, we cannot really leave if we wanted to. Some sort of agreement was signed before we left the North that we are told makes it impossible for us to quit.[67]

The reporter stated that Inuit were compelled to wear heavy sealskin garments and he observed the people "sweating and lolling around as though it were mid-summer." It was stated that conditions in the "Village" were poor, that the lagoon was "foul and full of debris," and from the dog pen "a stench arises that is enough to sicken the most hardy."[68]

Inuit returned to court on 3 April. Peter Mesher was accompanied by Peter Palliser, Thomas Palliser, Sam Palliser, Jim Shuglo, John Lucy, and Abraha Lucy. Newspaper reports stated that testimony was difficult because of the need for interpretation and that questions were constantly interrupted by the objection of opposing counsel.[69] Mesher testified that Tom Palliser had been confined to his house since 15 February because he would not wear fur clothes all day.[70] He claimed orders were given to withhold food from those who would not wear their furs. Robert Ford, the village interpreter, corroborated Mesher's testimony. Thomas Palliser testified that he was locked up in one of the houses in the "Esquimaux Village" while two guards stood at the door to see that he did not escape. John Lucy also testified that Thomas Palliser had been locked up because he would not wear his sealskins. He said that he wore his furs to avoid the same treatment:

> They did not treat us right. When they coaxed us from Labrador, they told us we would be fed well and only have to wear the skin clothes half the day, but when they got us here, they made us wear them from 9 o'clock in the morning until 6 o'clock in the evening. No man can stand that here.[71]

Finally, Justice Porter testified, explaining that he had got Mesher a job and that afterwards he had visited the "Village" and found Tom Palliser confined to his hut with a guard at the door who refused to let him enter. The company's response to the proceedings was to deny all charges of ill-treatment and to point out that the "Esquimaux" had obligations under their contract with the company and that the company had responsibilities for the "Esquimaux" under conditions set by US Customs which had permitted the group to enter the country in the first place. To clarify the obligations of both parties the contract was read into the court record. For two years' service, the head of each family was promised 500 Newfoundland Shillings (equal to 100 US dollars), and on their return to Labrador they were to be given two hundred pounds of salt, thirty pounds of rice, twenty gallons of molasses, ten pounds of tea, two hundred cartridges, a Winchester rifle, a reloading outfit, twenty pounds of powder, twenty pounds of shot, eighty pounds of lead, one thousand exploding caps, one barrel of pork, one barrel of pilot bread, and other similar articles. At the end of two years, they were to be brought back to Labrador and in the interim fed, clothed, and properly cared for.[72]

When Judge McConnell adjourned the hearing, he informed the plaintiffs that they could wear whatever they pleased and that no one had the right to deprive them of their liberty or to detain them in any way. He expressed the hope that the "Esquimaux" and the company could resolve their differences and ordered a continuance (a suspension) of the case if the "Esquimaux" were allowed full liberty. He also granted the plaintiffs the right to come back to court without a new petition should they be restrained in any way in the future.[73]

It was a clear victory for Inuit and a disaster in the making for the Arctic World's American Exposition Company. The ruling limited the Company's authority and granted Inuit freedom from constraint. They could come and go as they pleased or leave the "Village" altogether. As it turned out, leaving was exactly what many of them intended to do. Mesher and Porter proposed establishing a new "Esquimaux" exhibit where Inuit could share more equitably in the proceeds of the enterprise. Judge Porter, in the meantime, announced his plans to pursue a lawsuit on behalf of Inuit, demanding the Company pay damages.

Exodus

On 5 April, two days after the decisive court ruling, an outbreak of measles was reported in the "Esquimaux Village" with over twenty people infected, including most of the children. In a reckless disregard for public health, the concession remained open for business and hundreds of visitors continued to wander about, interacting with the villagers and poking around the huts "in ignorance of the sufferings of the children who lay on the cots within."[74] It would be weeks before fear of the disease spreading to visiting patrons prompted health authorities to close the village and put its inhabitants under strict quarantine. Teresa Dean, the *Chicago Daily Inter Ocean* correspondent to the fair, visited the village the day after the quarantine was imposed and wrote: "Between you and me... it is a bit like locking up the stable door after the horse is stolen — the disease is just departing. It arrived six weeks ago. The order to close the gates came in the lines of red tape yesterday."[75] Dean reported that the quarantine made the village seem desolate and deserted. As she spoke with Robert Ford and jotted down stories of traditional Inuit spiritual beliefs and practices, she noted that the people who were out and about were not dressed in their sealskin clothes: "They were wearing suits made of white canvas after the style of the skin suits. These were trimmed with narrow red and blue braid and were attractive enough for summer resort suits."[76] Two days before the lifting of the quarantine another baby died, though apparently not from the measles. Peter Deer, the son of George and Maggie Deer, had been the youngest of those to leave Labrador. It was reported that he had never been healthy and, despite medical care, had succumbed to a bad cold.[77]

If the problems surrounding the "Esquimaux Village" had not been bad enough, they were compounded by further negative publicity when a new and devastating article appeared in *The New York Times* on 10 April. Captain William McConnell, skipper of the *Evelena*, gave a scathing interview to a *Times* reporter in which he accused the "Esquimaux Village" managers of cruelty and abuse. He reported that the people had not been permitted to leave the village day or night, and that many had suffered from colds that had developed into consumption. He predicted that a large portion of them would never see their homeland again and that the rest would be abandoned and, most likely, would have to fend for themselves after their contract expired. He reported that it cost the company about fourteen cents per person per day to maintain the "Esquimaux" in the village and suggested the World's Columbian Exposition was complicit in the poor treatment of the people as it received 35 percent of the proceeds from the concession.[78]

Several Inuit within the exhibit had already made up their minds to leave the village. They were just waiting for the quarantine to be lifted before they made their move. Jimmie Shuglo, known to the American press as Joe or Jim Sugarloaf, slipped out one night to buy a trunk. This might have gone unnoticed had he not gotten into a fight and found himself in the newspapers the next day. According to the newspaper report, he was on 55th Street and Lake Avenue walking back to Jackson Park with companions erroneously described as "his four sons"[79] when his way was blocked by eight men from the Algerian Village in the Midway Plaisance. One of the men pushed the newly acquired trunk from his shoulders and Shuglo retaliated by knocking the man down. When he picked up his trunk and attempted to proceed on his way he was attacked again. This time his "sons" joined the fray, and an all-out melee broke out, much to the delight of the spectators who had gathered around. All reports suggested that Shulgo and his companions were getting the best of it when the police arrived and used their clubs to break up the fighting factions before sending both parties on their way. Shuglo returned to the village bruised and battered but not seriously hurt. The trunk, however, caused uneasiness among the exhibit's managers. Daniels was reported to have said that he wouldn't be surprised to wake up some morning and find the village deserted.[80] Such a scheme was now in the works.

On the evening of 18 April, Justice Porter and Âpili Heleneup met with Robert Ford to inform him in advance of the people's decision to abandon the village, most likely to ensure that he understood the court ruling and that the people were within their rights to leave.[81] The quarantine was lifted on 20 April and that same night a number of the families made their move.

At 11 p.m., as two newspaper reporters looked down on the village from the Exposition's elevated railway track, Peter Mesher jumped the fence into the "Esquimaux Village," crept by the dogs, and told his countrymen that friends were waiting for them outside the Exposition gates and that it was time to go. The five families who had chosen to leave that night, those of John Lucy, Jonas Palliser, Peter Palliser, Âpili Heleneup, and Zacharias Naemiup, made for the "Village" gate. They were met there by Joseph Meyer, the company's security guard, who refused to let them pass until Robert Ford intervened and likely reminded him that the court had ruled that they were free to do as they pleased, and that Meyer had no authority to stop them. The families then passed through the gate, and with their bags and trunks, "trotted along through the gloom of the night and the fog-laden atmosphere like so many gnomes away from their village."[82] They made the short walk to the 57th Street fair gate where Justice Porter, accompanied by a policeman, was waiting for them with several carriages. Before allowing them to pass, a member of the Columbian Guard telephoned his superior officer for advice and was told to let the people go but to hold their luggage. This led to strong objections, especially from the women, but after some hesitation, they were persuaded to leave; they boarded the carriages, and headed to a local hotel for the night. A short time later their bags were released.[83] In a subsequent interview with the *Daily Inter Ocean* reporter, Robert Ford declared that he thought the rest would follow:

> They will all go out tomorrow. They have been dissatisfied and misused ever since they were camped and hutted. Everyone feels that he has been duped, that he was misled when induced to leave home and that the promises then made them have been ignored and unfilled. They're all glad to get out and those remaining tonight will join the others tomorrow.[84]

When Daniels woke the next morning, he did not find his village entirely deserted but it had certainly been gutted; five of the families had left and more were about to go. Newspapers were reporting that his company stood to lose $30,000 if the village was forced to close.[85] He had to move quickly. His first job was to stop other Inuit from leaving. By now the biggest issue was money. Inuit knew that they were poorly paid and that the contract was grossly unfair. They knew by the attendance that the "Esquimaux Village" was making good money, while they, in turn, were getting a pittance. It had been demonstrated that they could make better money elsewhere and now the band of deserters was planning to set up their own exhibit and include themselves in the profits. Daniels urgently began negotiating with the families still in the village. It took two days but, in the end, he succeeded. All six of the remaining families agreed to remain with the original concession until the end of the fair. They even consented to wear their sealskin garments throughout the summer. In return, the Company agreed to pay the head of each family $50 in gold and a further $50 a month for the services of each man and his family. The previous commitment of an outfit of guns, ammunition, hunting and fishing supplies, and food staples on the families' return to Labrador was reaffirmed.[86]

Daniels then went on the offensive. The day after the defections, he paid a visit to US Immigration. In a move calculated to undermine the ambitions of his new rivals, he demanded that the dissident Inuit be deported. The Arctic World's American Exposition Company claimed that when Inuit left the village, they broke the terms of their contract and were, as a result, no longer protected by the law and should be forced out of the country. At the same time, Daniels waged war in the media, challenging the widespread stories of ill treatment and claiming that the real reason for people leaving was the inducement of money by outside interests who saw an opportunity to profit themselves. This assertion seemed to gain some credence when a company called the "Esquimaux Exhibition Company" was newly incorporated to exhibit Inuit. Charles F. Duke, Peter Mesher, and Thomas Deer were listed as corporate officers. Justice Porter was the largest shareholder.[87]

On 4 May, the Department of Immigration responded to Daniels' submission. It ruled that Inuit had complied with the law when they entered the country and that what had transpired was a private matter which did not concern the Immigration Department. It stated that the Government had no interest in the matter until the two-year term of the contract was up, when a demand would be made on the company for the peoples' removal. The matter was referred to the United States District Attorney for further investigation.[88] The District Attorney later stated that the Arctic World's American Exposition Company was liable under contract labour law wherever Inuit labourers worked for wages in competition with American workers.[89] Neither the Department of Immigration nor the District Attorney's Office supported deportation. It appeared that Daniels and his partners were on the back foot and would have to accept the presence of two exhibits of "Esquimaux" in competition with each other: one inside the World's Columbian Exposition and one just outside the fairground's gates.

Public Opinion

The rebellion of Inuit within the "Esquimaux Village" occurred just weeks before the official opening of the World's Columbian Exposition on 1 May

1893. Despite the massive publicity surrounding the Exposition's inauguration, the rebellion, court case, and subsequent defections also received widespread coverage in the Chicago press and throughout the United States. Public opinion was generally sympathetic to the plight of the Labrador people, but management also received support. An editorial in the *St. Louis Post-Dispatch* claimed that "the sympathetic soul of Chicago had been touched by the woes of the Esquimaux" and that the way they had been treated was an "outrage on human liberty" but at the same time, it understood management's position calling for the "Esquimaux" to wear sealskin clothes. "One is useless without the other," it stated: "The company does not want to show an Esquimaux dressed like ordinary Chicago citizens." These comments underscore how closely Inuit identity was associated with their clothing in the public mind. The editorial went on to say that the constitution of the United States guarantees the inviolability of contracts and that if the wearing of sealskins was a part of the contract, justice and the law might be in conflict.[90]

The rebellion of Inuit at the World's Columbian Exposition surprised and perplexed many observers and led to a reassessment of the nature of the exhibit and the identity of those within it. An editorial in the *Chicago Evening Journal* suggested that the actions of the "Esquimaux" undermined the very premise of the "Esquimaux" as representatives of the "primitive." It claimed that the way the "Esquimaux" had shown both intelligence and guile in addressing their grievances suggested that the public had been duped:

> These Eskimo, after all, are not very primitive. When it transpires that many... are Episcopalians, it is clear that the World's Fair Arctic Exposition Company (sic) has not procured the people we read about... who inhabit huts of snow, traverse ice flows on their dogsleds in winter and in summer pursue seals and walrus in the dancing kayak. Verily an Eskimo emerges from the glamour of romance when he confesses that he is an Episcopalian.[91]

The *San Francisco Chronicle* took up the same theme, musing that the behaviour of the "Esquimaux" might induce other groups at the Exposition to undertake similar actions. "If the other strangers from strange lands at the World's Fair follow the example of the Eskimo," it said, "there will be little left of native villages that are expected to give glimpses of barbaric life."[92]

Seeking redress in the American courts for injustices perpetrated against them was not the behaviour expected of "primitive" people. Inuit had proved to be neither complacent nor ignorant but instead had demonstrated a capacity for rational action in defence of their own interests based on a strong moral sense of right and wrong. And yet, rather than question the conceptual framework in which Inuit had been placed, the public response, at least in part, was to question their authenticity. The conclusion that many came to was that the "Esquimaux" must be frauds. The problem, of course, was the fiction that was perpetrated in the first place. Inuit were never representatives of the "primitive" and in not conforming to those preconceived imaginings, they simply exposed those notions for the fantasies that they were.

A writ of habeas corpus is a petition against unlawful imprisonment and when Peter Mesher made that claim in Dade County Court, he was concerned with the specific case of the illegal confinement in the "Esquimaux Village" of people who were forced to remain in their huts as punishment for not wearing their sealskin clothes. The ruling was, however, much more. The court, in essence, recognized Inuit as equal under the law, not as "primitives" or aliens occupying some lesser category of the species, but as people with rights like all others. Through the court action, Inuit had essentially undermined the colonialist imaginings to which they had been subjected and freed themselves from the confinement of the ideological framework in which they had been cast. They had established, with the sanction of the court, their fundamental and equal humanity.

The rebellion and the subsequent defection of Inuit families from the "Esquimaux Village" marked a turning point for Inuit experience in the United States. It was both an end and a new beginning. Prior to the revolt, the attitude of Inuit towards the exhibition had evolved from curiosity and interest to dissatisfaction, irritation, and finally rebellion. Afterwards, a new understanding became necessary, and they had to make peace with their circumstances. In Labrador they were hunters and fishermen, but in Chicago they had been turned into performers. Regardless of who they really were, it was in their interest to cater to public expectations and learn to play "Esquimaux." For those in the "Village," this was the basis of the new contract to which they had agreed. And for those who were establishing a new exhibit, it was a necessity for survival and essential for the success of the enterprise they had now undertaken. Perception and reality, fact and fiction, remained at odds but now they would do so with Inuit compliance and participation. It was clear to everyone that the principal purpose of the "Esquimaux" exhibits was to turn a profit so all concerned could make a living.

A Tale of Two Villages

After incorporation, the "Esquimaux Exhibition Company" opened to the public at 5710 Stoney Avenue just outside the Exposition fairgrounds. The whole neighbourhood along Stoney Avenue, stretching for a mile between 56th Street and 64th Street, developed into a minor midway, complete with side-show barkers, merry-go-rounds, fortune tellers, acrobats, fire-eaters, popcorn vendors, and street musicians. All along this stretch were vaudeville theatres and beer saloons, dime museums and "freak shows,"[93] as well as the biggest concession of them all, "Buffalo Bill's Wild West and Congress of Rough Riders of the World," which had leased fourteen acres of land near the main entrance of the fair and constructed an arena capable of housing eighteen thousand spectators, beginning the most profitable season in its history.[94]

There are few records of the "Esquimaux" exhibit at Stoney Avenue and one can only speculate as to the nature of the presentation. It is not clear whether Inuit lived on the site or whether it was simply a performance space. They would have had no pond and no kayaks, komatiks, or skin tents. Publicity photos show the people with few props other than their fur clothing and a single harpoon. Likely, their presentation was more akin to that of a dime museum, where people paid to view them in a salon and listen to an explanatory lecture. This would probably have been delivered by their new manager, Thomas Scott. Scott's *History of the Esquimau Race*, published a short time after the fair, contains short descriptive passages on Inuit traditions and modes of living, and could well have been based on notes developed for lectures.[95] The "Esquimaux Exhibition Company" attempted to compete with the World's Fair exhibit by charging only ten cents for admission instead of the twenty-five cents charged by the "Esquimaux Village."[96] There is no information as to how the concession fared financially or what payments were made to Inuit. It is doubtful, however, that it did particularly well and conceivable that when the people learned of the new contract Daniels negotiated with those in the "Village," some regretted the decision to leave. It is quite possible that those who remained with Daniels were the only ones who truly benefited from the Inuit rebellion.

The "Esquimaux Village" within the Exposition regrouped and carried on, although it was certainly compromised. One review written shortly after the schism and printed in a photographic portfolio would not have encouraged visitors:

> Our picture shows the nearly deserted settlement as it appeared after the revolt... the meager attendance of visitors is representative of the small patronage that rewarded their exhibition. Had the Esquimaux settled on the Midway Plaisance and held together, their remarkable ethnological character would have received earnest public attention.[97]

It was reported that six families remained with the original "Esquimaux Village." Newspaper accounts report that the families who left were those of John and Katerina Lucy, Jonas and Susan Palliser, Thomas and Esther Palliser, Peter Palliser, Âpili and Helene, and Zacharias and Naemi.[98] By elimination this would mean that those who stayed behind were the two families from Nachvak, those of Kangerarsuk and Tuglavina, as well as Kupper and Kuttukitok; the two families from Ailik, Joseph and Charlotte Lucy, and Simon and Sarah Manak; and from Aiviktok, George and Maggie Deer, and Jimmie and Salomie Shuglo. All had been expected to leave but Daniels' intervention with new financial incentives appears to have been decisive in persuading them to remain with the original concession. In addition, the family of the interpreter, Robert Ford, remained with Daniels' group.[99]

After the defections, management attempted to revitalize the "Esquimaux Village" and added at least one new attraction by purchasing two reindeer from the nearby Sami (Lapland) exhibit and offering children cart rides, despite the fact that Labrador Inuit had never domesticated caribou or used them as a mode of transportation. The "Village" eventually recovered from its crisis and subsequent reviews were mostly favourable:

> The little people of the extreme North, in their enforced imitation of semi-tropic customs are not altogether in their proper elements, but they manage to hang on to the ragged edge of existence and give a very faithful representation of their home life in the frigid zone.[100]

The official "Esquimaux Village" could still claim the presence of the only "heathen Esquimaux" in Chicago and two of these, both young boys, proved especially popular among visitors. Pomiuk was described in various press reports as a charming, cheerful, and obliging young man, happy to pose for photographs and to show off his skill with the dog whip.[101] He is referred to as 'Prince' Pomiuk in the press, taking their lead from the village publicists. The story promulgated was only marginally based in fact. Pomiuk's father, Kaujuasiak, was a powerful leader in northern Labrador and had been murdered, but the sobriquet "Prince" was, of course, an invention. Pomiuk was the son of Kaujuasiak's third wife, Aniortama, and had been adopted by Kupper after Kaujuasiak's death. Pomiuk's fair ended badly after an altercation with his stepfather. During the incident, Kupper kicked Pomiuk and broke his thigh.[102] It was a disastrous injury which did not receive proper attention. It failed to heal, became infected, and would eventually lead to a premature death after his return to Labrador. The other young man, Degouluk, was the adopted son of Kangerarsuk and Tuglavina, who was a year younger than Pomiuk. He too was known for his friendly nature and was often assigned to take visitors on sled rides or to demonstrate kayak skills. His fair also ended in tragedy. On 20 August, Degouluk was reported to have been playing in the pond and ventured out too far, falling into a deep hole. Unable to swim, he drowned before anyone could rescue him.[103] The next day, his funeral was held at the

"Esquimaux Village" and appears to have been blatantly exploited for its commercial potential in a manner similar to the funeral of Susan Manak. A reporter from *the Daily Inter Ocean* wrote:

> There was a strange scene which was enacted in the Eskimo Village.... Several hundred persons paid the necessary admission fee in order to witness an Eskimo funeral service. Curiosity was stretched to the highest tension when it was learned that the boy who met an untimely death was an avowed heathen... the curious throngs listen to the howling of the sledge dogs for a while and then press up close to the Chapel windows which were raised and listen to the funeral service.[104]

The ceremony took place in the wooden chapel that had been erected on the exhibit site. The service was simple, consisting of speeches, Moravian hymns, and prayers offered by a Methodist minister. As Degouluk's body departed for Oakwood Cemetery, to join the other two Inuit who were buried there, the reporter covering the event noted that "the rest at once resumed their games for the entertainment of the visitors in the village."[105] The remaining days and weeks of the fair passed largely without incident.[106]

The End of the Fair

On 31 October 1893, the World's Columbian Exposition formally came to an end. The fair, which had opened with parades, pageantry, and cheering crowds, closed without fanfare, overshadowed by the assassination of Chicago's mayor, Carter Harrison, two days earlier. The original plan for a jubilee day of elaborate celebrations was cancelled and instead the Exposition's president Thomas Palmer addressed a small gathering in Festival Hall with a few short comments followed by prayers.[107] With this solemn ceremony, the World's Columbian Exposition passed into history.

Despite its somber end, the Exposition had been an enormous success. Estimates of attendance figures vary, but it is generally agreed that over 27.5 million people visited the fair. As a result, the Exposition paid all its operating expenses, returning $1 million to its 30,000 subscribers. The Exposition also profited from its concessions. Collectively the 450 companies granted concessions provided the Exposition with over $4 million in revenue. The "Esquimaux Village" contributed to this profit. According to Exposition records it paid the Exposition $38,662. Concessions were expected to pay between 25 and 33 percent of their revenue to the fair. This would mean that between 19 October 1892 and 30 October 1893, the "Esquimaux Village" made between $115,986 and $154,648.[108]

Under a photograph of the "Esquimaux Village" published in a portfolio of images of the World's Columbian Exposition shortly after the fair closed, the editor wrote a short descriptive passage containing a wry and insightful observation about the "Esquimaux Village" Inuit:

> In the Fall of 1892, there arrived in Chicago, a colony of Esquimaux, taken from a point as far south in Labrador as Esquimaux could be found and labeled as denizens of the land as far north as could be reached.[109]

There was truth in this statement as well as a pointed suggestion that the public had been deceived. Labrador Inuit were indeed the southernmost dwelling Inuit in the world and those with the longest continuous contact with European society, facts that were sharply at odds with their portrayal as "arctic primitives." However, none of this should have come as a surprise. By the time the World's Columbian Exposition opened its doors, ethnological exhibits were already a hybrid of pseudo-science and show business and neither truth nor honesty necessarily served the agendas of those staging the exhibits. Preconceptions, stereotypes, and falsehoods were all useful marketing tools to generate maximum interest and profit, and for this reason, the ascriptions, imaginings, and misrepresentations of Labrador Inuit were allowed to stand.

Clearly, Labrador Inuit were not responsible for these deceptions. The role they were expected to play was prescribed for them well before they arrived in Chicago, and it was only a result of their resistance to conditions within the "Esquimaux Village" that the public began to learn who they really were and to start to revise previous misconceptions. Thus, while some observers might have felt deceived, others acquired fresh insight and new respect.

The "Esquimaux Whip."
From *Dream City: A Portfolio of Photographic Views of the Columbian Exposition.*

Summer Dress, World's Columbian Exposition.
(Photo: Benjamin West Kilburn, Stephen Loring Collection).

The "Esquimaux" Dogs, World's Columbian Exposition.
(Photo: Benjamin West Kilburn, Stephen Loring Collection).

Reindeer Rides, World's Columbian Exposition.
(Photo: Benjamin West Kilburn, Stephen Loring Collection).

CHAPTER 7

After Chicago

"A crowd gathered around the Esquimaux Village, gazed at the little men and women of the north, and insisted on inspecting the curious snow houses which will be their homes during the fair. The little people themselves were the objects of curiosity. They have donned American clothes and look anything but romantic in them... Before long they will be somewhat more picturesque, but everybody knew them yesterday as they mingled with the throngs on the broad avenues."[1]

Another Deal

As the World's Columbian Exposition was winding down, another American exposition was preparing to open. During the summer of 1893, P.M. Daniels and W.D. Vincent had learned that the California Midwinter International Exposition was to be held in San Francisco. The organizers of that fair were eager to attract exhibits and Daniels applied for another "Esquimaux Village" concession. His troupe of Inuit, however, was getting smaller by the day, as some were eager to return to Labrador. To make up a reasonable contingent for the west coast, Daniels entered into negotiations with Inuit attending both the "Esquimaux Village" and the Stoney Avenue exhibit which had been under the management of Thomas G. Scott.[2] It was agreed that Daniels and Vincent would take one group to the Midwinter Fair in San Francisco while Scott would take another on a tour of dime museums throughout the eastern United States.[3]

The Midwinter Exposition

In the spring of 1893, Michael Henry de Young, founder and publisher of the *San Francisco Chronicle* and California representative to the World's Columbian Exposition, was so impressed with the Chicago fair that he decided a similar event should be held in California to bring San Francisco to the attention of the world. His plan was to open the fair in January 1894, transferring many exhibits and attractions then on display in Chicago directly to San Francisco. Both the governor of California and the mayor of San Francisco thought it would be impossible to organize an exposition in the allotted time, but de Young forged ahead, deploying the considerable influence of his newspaper, raising funds, and gaining the support of a number of San Francisco's leading entrepreneurs. He secured the participation of several western States and California counties as well as the commitment of several exhibits from Chicago, including the "Esquimaux Village."[4]

By August 1893, a board of directors was established and ready to proceed, having chosen Golden Gate Park for the location. In a break with previous fairs, the California Midwinter International Exposition rejected classical architecture for a potpourri of eclectic styles: Moorish, Egyptian, Indian, and Mission, giving the fair an original exotic quality. The Central Court became the principal physical feature of the fair, while the foreign, state, and county buildings, along with the private amusement concessions, surrounded it in a random and festive manner. Unlike Chicago, there was from the outset an acceptance that the success of the fair would depend on its entertainment as well as its educational attractions. The *Official History of the California Midwinter International Exposition* declared that it is a "conceded characteristic of human nature that mankind must be amused as well as educated."[5] As a result, the entertainment exhibits were integrated into the overall concept of the fair from the beginning and not assigned to its geographical and ideological periphery as in Chicago. The Midwinter Exposition, nicknamed "Sunset City," opened on 27 January 1894, and ran for five months, closing on 4 July. The entrance fee was fifty cents, while many buildings, exhibits, and attractions cost an additional twenty-five cents. Most concessions paid a fee and a percentage of gross receipts in lieu of a charge for space.[6] By the time it closed, the Exposition had become a popular and commercial success.

The "Esquimaux Village" in San Francisco

Many of the concessions that appeared at the Midwinter Exposition simply shifted their operations from Chicago to San Francisco in the manner of a travelling circus; among these were the Streets of Cairo, the Samoan Village, the Vienna Prater, the Hawaiian Village, and the "Esquimaux Village." The "Esquimaux Village" was similar to the establishment in Chicago but with a few important differences. There was again a high fence enclosing the village, as well as a pond for kayak demonstrations. Gone, however, were the bark and moss-covered cabins and in their place stood a semicircle of six large white domes, in the fashion of "igloos," said to be "exact reproductions of the houses used by this tribe of Indians in their northern homes."[7] Inserted into these were doors and glass windows for the greater comfort of the families who would live in them for the duration of the California winter and spring. The *Official Guide to the California Midwinter Exposition* claimed that:

> Inside these artificial snow-houses, the Esquimaux household furniture is found in its primitive simplicity. There (are) stone lamps burning seal oil and doing duty as cooking and heating stoves, and the few eating utensils and sleeping furs which are spread on banks of snow.[8]

"Esquimaux Village," California Midwinter Fair, 1894.
(Photo: Isaiah West Taber, Bancroft Library,
University of California, Berkeley).

Kayaks on the Pond, California Midwinter Fair, 1894.
(Photo: Isaiah West Taber, *OpenSF History*).

"Esquimaux Village," California Midwinter Fair, 1894.
(Photo: Isaiah West Taber, Library of Congress).

With Dogteam, California Midwinter Fair, 1894.
(Photo: Isaiah West Taber, *OpenSF History*).

Group Portrait, California Midwinter Fair, 1894.
(Photo: Isaiah West Taber, *OpenSF History*).

This exhibit of the "primitive" was somewhat contradicted by a later newspaper story that reported the inhabitants' rapid adaptation to their new circumstances:

> Those white, glistening houses, built in imitation of the snow huts of their native land are furnished with an eye to comfort and even luxury. There are cook stoves, chairs, beds, tables and other conveniences of civilization in the use of which the Esquimaux have become well versed since coming to live in the home of the white folks.[9]

The village opened for business on 29 January.[10] Newspapers reported that the new exhibit consisted of twenty-nine people, thirty-four dogs, and some reindeer. Inuit attending the fair included the families of Zacharias and Naemi (four), Simon and Sarah Manak (seven), Jonas and Susan Palliser (six, including Christopher, born in Chicago), Tom and Esther Palliser (three), George and Maggie Deer (two, since the death of Peter in Chicago), Joseph and Charlotte Lucy (three, including Abraha Tuktashina) as well as that of Robert and Susan Ford (four). There were later reports that Peter Palliser's daughter, Mary, attended the San Francisco fair, which would mean the Inuit contingent consisted of thirty people.

As in Chicago, the "Esquimaux Village" was advertised as an exhibit of remote "primitive" people from the frozen zones of the far north but also as "a diminishing race" on the verge of extinction. This point was emphasized in publicity literature: "The fact of their decreasing numbers made the Esquimaux a novel as well as educational attraction."[11] The presence of "primitive," "heathen Esquimaux," who have "never come into touch with civilization,"[12] continued to be promoted as a central feature of the exhibit, despite the fact that all the northern "heathen" had returned to Labrador following the Chicago fair. There was reference to the presence of Kamialuits (sic), "the heathen princess" whose father "was a mighty chief among his people."[13] This was a fiction. Kamialuit, the sister of Pomiuk, was, at this time, on her way home.

In addition to the "ice-houses" built in a semi-circle around the pond, the "Esquimaux Village" included the skin tent with its display of hunting gear, a rail track for sled rides, a dog pound, and a reindeer corral. Visitors could see

Inuit in their seal-skin clothes going about their daily chores, watch demonstrations of kayak skills on the pond, go for dog-sled rides on the rail track, or reindeer rides in the back of a cart. And, by placing a coin on the ground, they could witness the men's skill with the famous "Esquimaux dog whip."[14] There is a reference to a stage being constructed at the village for singing and dancing, but there are no newspaper reports of any performances taking place.[15]

In Chicago, the "Esquimaux Village" was isolated on the periphery of the "White City" and outside the entertainment venue, the Midway Plaisance. In San Francisco, it was totally integrated into the mainstream of the fair. It seemed a more comfortable fit and suffered fewer problems. No doubt this was also because Inuit had an acceptable financial arrangement with management and understood and accepted the role they were expected to play. Management made a further concession by agreeing to keep the village closed on Sundays in deference to the wishes of Moravian Inuit. It was the only exhibit at the Midwinter Fair to close on Sundays and over the course of the fair this would have amounted to a considerable financial sacrifice.

Throughout its run at the Midwinter Exposition, the "Esquimaux Village" was both positively reviewed and well attended. The following review, written midway through the fair, was typical:

> Among all the concessions at the Fair there is, beyond a shadow of a doubt, not one that eclipses the Esquimaux Village as a unique, amusing, and instructive exhibit. The strange little brown people in their odd habiliments, with their interesting dogs, their kayaks, and kometiks, attracted 488,046 paid admissions to their village at the Midwinter Fair, and if the large percentage of the Midwinter Fair's visitors that have already seen them here is a criterion, they certainly give promise of being a big paying adventure. The reason for their popularity lays in the fact that on the streets of any large city, at almost any time, any other race of people may be seen, and also in the fact that the public evidently realizes this will be the last opportunity they will ever have to see this rapidly diminishing race of people. The village is unlike most

> propositions of its ilk at the Fair... it has none of the attributes that make up what is usually termed as a side-show, and it is complete down to the smallest detail. It is, as a concession, an intellectual feast and a great source of amusement.[16]

If the figure of 488,046 paid customers is correct, the “Esquimaux Village” in San Francisco had, by the end of March, grossed more than $120,000 with three months left to run.

As in Chicago, much fuss was made of births and babies and similarly, joy was followed by tragedy. On 13 February, George and Maggie Deer, who had lost their son Peter in Chicago, celebrated the birth of a daughter. The occasion was a cause for elation throughout the fairground and the baby quickly became a major attraction for the “Esquimaux Village.”[17] The child was baptized Francesca Deer, a name selected by a vote of San Francisco school children attending the fair on Children’s Day.[18] Francesca, however, lived only forty-four days. Doctors said the cause of death was, in part, malnutrition.[19] On the evening of her death, a wake was held in the village in the child’s honour. It was reported that Zacharias offered up prayers to “Kekuk,” the God of Water, because “the Esquimaux believes that a departed soul has to descend through the waters of the ocean to get safely into heaven.”[20] A short two weeks after Francesca’s death, the 16-month-old child of Jonas and Susan Palliser, Christopher Columbus Palliser, who was born at the Chicago fair, passed away. His mother was reported to have been devastated and wanted nothing but to return home.[21]

Apart from these tragedies, the time spent in San Francisco appears to have been generally quiet and routine. Inuit attended to their audiences at the village during the day but otherwise were free to wander about on their own time. They were often observed strolling about the fair or shopping, dressed casually in their ‘American’ clothes.[22] The young people enjoyed attending dances at the neighbouring Arizona Indian Village.[23]

Although most of the grievances of Chicago had been resolved, there was at least one occasion of labour unrest. It began on 2 April when Inuit refused to work, insisting that the village close its gates to visitors in order that they might celebrate a traditional feast held each year to honour the return of hunters. Despite objections from their employers, they got their way, and the village was closed for the day. As preparations for the feast were being made and before village officials knew what was happening, several men killed one of the exhibition's reindeer. The feast of raw fish and deer meat reportedly went on well into the night.[24] The next day, with relationships strained, Inuit refused to go to work. Joseph Lucy was appointed spokesperson and informed management that unless salaries were raised by $10 per month per man, there would be no exhibition. Their demand was refused, and the villagers were reminded that they were already receiving more money than provided for in their original contract, that all their medical bills were being paid, and that their request to keep the village closed on Sundays had been granted. Furthermore, the strikers were told that if they did not commence work by one o'clock that day, they would be removed from the village and made to fend for themselves. As the deadline approached, the strikers capitulated and the crisis passed.[25]

On 8 June, a group of Alaskan Inuit joined the "Esquimaux Village" at San Francisco. The Alaskans had been in the country for about a year under the charge of Captain Miner Bruce. Bruce had brought them to the United States to raise political and financial support for a project establishing a colony of Siberian reindeer at Port Clarence, to provide Inuit in that region with a more secure source of food. They had met with President Cleveland in Washington and appeared before House and Senate committees from whom they received an appropriation of $7500 for the project. They were in the process of returning home but would take over the "Esquimaux Village" for the final weeks of the fair.[26] On 16 June, the Labrador Inuit gave their last show at the Midwinter Fair and on 24 June departed San Francisco for New York en route to Labrador.

A month after Labrador Inuit left San Francisco, an article appeared in the *San Francisco Morning Call* claiming that a baby belonging to Simon and Sarah Manak was buried illegally under a tree on the grounds of the "Esquimaux Village." The child, it said, was born on the train travelling from Chicago, had been sickly, never received medical attention, and died that December. The source of the story was W.D. Sneathen, said to be a man connected with the concession. He claimed that Manak had spoken to him at the time of the death of Francesca Deer, complaining that he did not see why his daughter had not received a burial like that of Francesca. He apparently referred to it again at the time of departure from San Francisco, saying that he did not like to go and leave the baby there. Burial without a permit was illegal in California. The article blamed P.M. Daniels for breaking the law and accused him of inhumanity in violating accepted practices regarding the treatment of the dead and suggested that he ignored the law to save costs associated with a burial.[27]

Inuit on the Dime Museum Circuit

While Daniels' and Vincent's group spent five months on exhibit in San Francisco, Thomas G. Scott took a smaller contingent of ten Inuit on a tour of dime museums throughout the eastern United States. This group consisted of Âpili and his wife Helene, their daughter Esther, and her daughter Nancy, as well as James and Salome Shuglo, their three daughters, Margaret, Augustina, and Liza, and their son, Tom. Nancy, the last baby to be born in Chicago, was the star attraction of the group and was featured prominently in advertising and publicity.[28]

The dime museum circuit consisted of several commercial museums, theatres, and lecture halls which catered to the public's curiosity for the strange, exotic, salacious, and bizarre. Human oddities were the main attraction, and ethnological exhibits shared the stage with "freak show" and circus acts. The group appeared at museums in Chicago, Boston, and New York, sharing the bill with the likes of Tocci, the two-headed boy; Matthew Lee Price, the elastic skin man; and Mungo Park, the razor walker.[29] Little is known of the exact nature of their performances but most likely Inuit would have appeared on stage in salon rooms dressed in their sealskins, holding harpoons and dog-whips, while the public filed in and out, content to feast their eyes on "real Esquimaux" and in particular to catch a glimpse of the famous "World's Fair baby." As on Stoney Avenue, the "performance" may have been accompanied by a descriptive and explanatory lecture. The dime museum tour continued into the spring of 1894, at which time the Shuglos chose to return to Labrador while Âpili and Helene's family joined the circus.

"The Ethnological Congress of Strange and Savage Races"

Although P.T. Barnum died in 1891, the Barnum and Bailey Circus remained one of the most popular and lucrative entertainment enterprises in the United States during the last decade of the nineteenth century. In 1894, largely in response to the opportunity presented by the presence of so many foreign groups at the World's Columbian Exposition, the Barnum and Bailey circus renewed its featured Ethnological Congress with its assemblage of "savage, cannibal, semi-civilized and barbarous races."[30] The Congress of 1894 consisted of "Esquimaux, Malays, Klings, Javanese, Nubians, Matabeles, Papuans, Samoans, Moors, Singhalese, Hindus, Cossacks, Burmese, Australians, New Zealanders, Numidians and many others."[31] Representing the "Esquimaux" race were Âpili, Helene, Esther, and Nancy.

The Barnum and Bailey Circus was a three-ring affair with performances happening simultaneously in all rings. The Ethnological Congress was presented as a pageant of nations in the opening ceremonies and except for this, was not a part of the main event. Instead, it formed a kind of midway open to the public an hour prior to the circus performance, at a location inside the animal menagerie. Running down the centre of the tent, surrounded by animal cages, was a long "street of nations" where the various people, dressed in their native costumes, "some with little or nothing to speak of upon them," displayed their huts, canoes, weapons, and tools. At either end of the "street" were raised platforms where performances of songs, dances, games, and religious ceremonies took place.[32] The principal attraction of the "Esquimaux" group was the "World's Fair baby," Nancy Columbia:

> At one end of the long enclosure a howling Dervish muttered an unintelligible prayer to Mohammet, while opposite two Turkish girls danced gracefully with curious swaying motions to the weird music of pipe and drums played by natives.... Below these in the dress of their country were... a little party of Esquimaux surrounded by the only American born child of this race who bears the unique name of Columbia Palmer in honor of the World's Fair where she first saw the light of day.[33]

Locating the Ethnological Congress in the animal menagerie was perhaps no accident. It was promoted as an educational opportunity, a chance to see "the family of man" in all its diversity, but these "strange and savage peoples" were clearly meant to illustrate the "primitive" stages of human development. Placing the people of the Congress next to Chico and Johanna, "the only living Gorillas in captivity," made a point that was not lost on either the press or the public. As one reporter observed:

> The Ethnological Congress is even more interesting than the collection of beasts, birds, and reptiles and with Chico and Johanna, there is presented a pretty good study in evolution from brute to man.

Âpili, Helene, Esther, and Nancy toured with the circus for two seasons. The Barnum and Bailey tour of 1894, from the end of March to the end of October, included stops in 138 American cities and towns across the eastern seaboard, the midwest, and the south. The 1895 tour, from the end of March to early November, visited 129 locations in the US and a further thirteen in Canada.[34] During the 1894 tour a delegation from the Ethnological Congress, including Âpili and Helene's family, were guests of President Grover Cleveland at the White House. Esther was reported to have presented Mrs. Cleveland with a photo of Nancy while Âpili demonstrated the "Esquimaux" whip on the White House lawn.[35]

After their stint with the circus, Âpili and Helene were employed for a time by Franz Boas, Putnam's former assistant in Chicago and the newly-appointed curator of the American Museum of Natural History in New York. They were hired to help with the preparation of the museum's growing collection of Inuit artifacts. This work most likely consisted of the manufacture and repair of clothing, tools, and utensils, including kayaks.[36] Âpili and Helene were themselves subjects of interest at the museum. They were photographed and body casts were made of them for study and display.[37] It would not be until the summer of 1896 that Âpili, Helene, and Nancy finally returned to Labrador. Esther would remain behind in New York as she had just given birth to a baby boy.[38]

Getting Home

The original group of Labrador Inuit who arrived in the United States to work at the World's Columbian Exposition splintered into smaller groups after the Chicago fair. Some began their journey home, others travelled to California, and others embarked on the dime museum tour. One family returned to Labrador in the fall of 1893, most would get home in the summer of 1894, and another family returned in the summer of 1896. A few would not return at all, choosing instead to make a new life in the United States.

The first family to leave for Labrador was that of John and Katerina Lucy. The Lucys had been among the group that defected from the "Esquimaux Village" to start up the new exhibit outside the fairground on Stoney Avenue, a venture that seems to have failed to live up to expectations. According to one newspaper report, "their means began to diminish" after they left the "Esquimaux Village."[39] The manager of the Stoney Avenue exhibit, Thomas Scott, claimed that the Lucys left due to illness, and this appears to be true, but they may also have been simply disillusioned and homesick. They left Chicago weeks before the fair ended on 30 October 1893 and well before Daniels proposed a new contract to exhibit at the San Francisco fair. Those who abandoned the "Esquimaux Village" and did not sign a new contract to travel to San Francisco would have received no support for their journey home. After leaving Chicago, the Lucys arrived in Montreal, "in sore straits," where they received help from the Hudson's Bay Company. They were put on board a ship belonging to the Newfoundland merchant company R. Prowse and Sons and arrived in St. John's in late September.[40] They headed north from there, most likely on the *Virginia Lake*, which departed for Labrador two weeks later.[41] On 25 October 1893, the Hudson's Bay Company's Rigolet manager noted the arrival of "a family of Esquimaux from the Chicago exhibits."[42] From there, the Lucys would have continued north to Ailik either by ship or, if it was too late in the season, overland by dogteam which John Lucy had done many times before.

The northern families from Nachvak were the next to leave, departing Chicago in November 1893. These would have been Kupper and Kuttukitok, their children Mali, Tigujak, Sikepa, and Kotuktooka (also called Evelina), as well as Kangergarsuk and Tuglavina, and Kajuatsiak's children, Kamialuit and Pomiuk.

It is difficult to understand the way the Nachvak people were treated at the end of the fair. They had been Vincent and Taber's prized recruits and the star attraction of the "Esquimaux Village" and had remained its core asset after the defections which had so diminished the original exhibit. Daniels and Vincent were obliged under contract to ensure the safe return home of the people in their care, and they should have shown special concern for the Nachvak families as they spoke no English and had the greatest distance to travel. And yet, they were kept on display in Chicago until the final days of the fair and it was well into November before they were put onboard a ship bound for Newfoundland, too late in the season for the families to reach their home. It may well be that Daniels and Vincent had wanted to include the Nachvak families in the San Francisco exhibit and hoped to persuade them to stay, but after a full year in the United States the Nachvak people had had enough. They arrived in Bonne Bay, on the west coast of Newfoundland, on the steamer *Harlaw* on 21 November 1893 with no hope of travelling north until the shipping season re-opened in the spring of 1894. They were simply abandoned and left to fend for themselves.

A correspondent for the *Evening Telegram* reported that "a contingent of the Esquimaux colony en route from the World's Fair" consisting of four adults and six children — "one a cripple on crutches" — caused "much comment and some pity." They appeared "much dejected," having to remain in Bonne Bay until spring. The correspondent observed that they spoke no English and seemed to have no means of support. He feared what might happen to them over the winter and suggested an enquiry be made into the matter.[43] Fortunately, it appears that the people of Bonne Bay rallied around the Inuit families. They spent the winter in a house belonging to the Bonne Bay postmaster[44] and the following summer were able to connect with the Newfoundland coastal boat travelling north to Nain.

Of the families that had remained in America after the World's Columbian Exposition, the Shuglos were the first to head home. For much of the winter and spring of 1894, they were on the dime museum tour with Âpili, Helene, Esther, and Nancy. The Shuglos arrived in Newfoundland on 3 May.[45] A St. John's newspaper noted at the time that the wife of James Thuglow (sic), "an Esquimaux," gave birth to a son at the Poor Asylum on 4 May.[46] They sailed north on the first mailboat of the season arriving home at Rigolet on 11 July 1894.[47]

The families who had gone west left San Francisco in June 1894. They made good time, travelling across the continent to New York by train, and arrived in St. John's via the SS *Sylvia* on 16 July. R.G. Taber, one of the original recruitment agents, was in St. John's at the time, preparing to undertake a mining venture in Labrador,[48] and he appears to have helped ensure that everyone was safely on board the coastal steamer *Grand Lake* when it left for Labrador the following day.

As the group gathered on the St. John's waterfront, they caught the attention of a local newspaper reporter:

> The company of Esquimaux which arrived yesterday by the *Sylvia* from New York took passage this morning in the *Grand Lake* homeward bound. They are from the midwinter fair at California and will find the change from the temperature of India's coral strand to that of Greenland's icy mountains an agreeable and beneficial one. It was rather a novel sight to see the group as they squatted on the fore hatch of the steamer. There were Esquimaux young and Esquimaux old, from the toddling youngster arrayed in the garb of a young American to the white-haired old sire, who might be taken, at a distance, for a Dutchman. Some of these poor creatures were suffering from climactic effects on the constitution; one had contracted dropsy and was hardly able to walk. Before leaving some of the men purchased guns and ammunition where with they propose hunting the walrus and the polar bear. No doubt they yearn for their native place and a good feast of blubber.[49]

It is not clear if these purchases were part of the "outfit" promised Inuit under the original contract. There is no other known reference to suggest that those terms were honoured.

The *Grand Lake* travelled to the south Labrador port of Red Bay where the people transferred to the coastal steamer *Winsor Lake*.[50] Somewhere along the route, the Nachvak families came on board. The *Winsor Lake* arrived at

Rigolet on 25 July and there the families of Jonas and Susan Palliser, Tom and Esther Palliser, and George and Margaret Deer disembarked. The event, which must have caused considerable interest at the time, was barely noted in the HBC Post Journal. A succinct sentence states: "World's fair Esquimaux back."[51] The only observation on record is that of Lydia Campbell, a long-time resident of the region, who, shortly after the families returned, visited the summer encampment of some of the people on 3 August 1894 and reflected on the changes in the people she had seen over the years:

> I have seen 15 or as far as 20 Eskimos seal skin tents in my time, scattered here in little groups not far from each other five or six tents together and such a bustle, women cleaning sealskins and covering kayaks. Their little boats, the men out on the water after a large scove of seals throwing their darts at the large harps with a large bladder at the end of their houliack-harpoon strap... What work to kill them then, it was pretty to see them at that time. I don't know when I saw the last sealskin tent, the few left now is living in wooden houses and I see one kayak this summer, only one now. There was only three or four small families before but the World's Fair people is come now. They are across on the Big Island, we are just going over to see them... Well off we goes, a pretty day, I would like for you to see them... how changed, all can talk English and dress like the people in another country. They has the picture of the World's Fair in different forms.[52]

The remaining Inuit continued north, the coastal boat stopping in Ailik where it dropped off Joseph and Charlotte Lucy and Abraha Tuktashina as well as the family of Simon and Sarah Manak. It then headed farther north to Nain with only the Nachvak and Hebron families left onboard. At Nain they boarded the Moravians' fish collector, the vessel *Gleaner*, and finally arrived at Ramah on 12 August 1894.

For the Nachvak families, it had been nine months since they left Chicago, and their ordeal wasn't over yet. Br. Adolf Stecker, the Moravian missionary, writing in the Ramah station diary, noted the death of Kamialuit, a short time after their arrival:

> With the *Gleaner* came... the Eskimos from Chicago, one family from Hebron, and two from Nachvak... the latter remained here a few days, then the one (family) went to Nachvak while the other remained here in order to convert. With the latter was also an unmarried 20-year-old female heathen as well as her 15-year-old brother. The latter had broken his left leg in America, but, when he embarked for Labrador, it was well enough again, that he could walk on crutches.... The unmarried female heathen... became sick... but no one believed that it would lead to her death. After three days, she sat up by herself, and a few minutes later, she was a corpse.[53]

Another death occurred a short time later. The daughter of Kupper and Kuttukitok, named Kotuktooka (also known as Evelina), who had been born in Chicago on 5 November 1893, died soon after arriving at Ramah.[54] Kupper and Kuttukitok eventually returned to Nachvak with their other children, accompanied by Pomiuk.

Pomiuk's condition slowly deteriorated after his return. Dr. Wilfred Grenfell, who established a medical mission for Newfoundland fishermen on the Labrador coast in 1892, visited Nachvak in the summer of 1895, and was told by the Hudson's Bay Company agent, George Ford, that a boy was dying at a camp nearby. Grenfell found Pomiuk in Kupper's tent and saw that his thigh was broken and diseased. With Kupper's permission, Grenfell removed him from the camp, performed a preliminary operation on him at the HBC post, and took him south where he had set up a makeshift cottage hospital at Burnt Cove near Rigolet.[55] There Pomiuk would undergo further operations, but he never fully recovered. He died from his injuries in September 1897.[56]

After the Nachvak families disembarked at Ramah, the *Gleaner* took its remaining passengers to Hebron. The Hebron missionaries had expressed apprehension about Zacharias' return home. When he left the community, two years prior, the missionaries had been happy to see him go. They had called him a "troublemaker" and feared "his influence for mischief would be increased if he came back with big stories of America and if the large wages, promised him, should make him rich in the estimation of his countrymen."[57] Zacharias had managed to save some money, depositing £30 into his store account on his return,[58] but according to the Moravians, he was a chastened man:

> It seems that Zacharias has had to learn the lessons of adversity instead of being made proud by prosperity. On his way back to Hebron with his family, he landed at Nain, where his former missionary now lives. Almost his first words in entering Br. Kahle's room were these: "I have returned quite a different man. Trouble has taught me to pray, and the only course left to me was to seek the Saviour, of whom you have so constantly taught us."[59]

Several years after Zacharias returned home, August Wirth, another missionary who had known him at Hebron, suggested there were deeper reasons for the regret. In 1899, R.G. Taber began recruiting Inuit for another tour, this one in Europe, but Wirth wrote that Zacharias had no interest in going and claimed that any who went would suffer as he and his family had:

> Morally there will be present much sin and misery, and they will be much damaged… The 11 or 12-year-old daughter of Zacharias was seduced at that time in Chicago by 4 Americans and used sinfully. God have mercy with the weak people and save their souls that they will not perish in sin.[60]

Zacharias' daughter, Justina, was slightly older than Wirth states here but nonetheless the experience must have been devastating and would explain Zacharias' reluctance to expose his family to similar dangers by embarking on another tour.

Two other Inuit returned to Labrador in the summer of 1894 but independent of those returning from San Francisco. Peter Palliser does not appear to have attended the California Midwinter Exposition, although there is evidence that his daughter did. It is not known where he spent the winter of 1893–1894, but by early July both Peter and Mary were in New York in the company of Frederick Cook who was organizing a voyage to supply Robert Peary's expedition in Greenland. The previous summer, Cook had travelled to Labrador and returned with two young Inuit from Rigolet, Clara and Will Manasse. They lived with Cook over the winter and that year became a feature attraction in his fund-raising lectures.[61] Peter and Mary may have participated in the last of these events[62] and together with Clara and Will were offered passage home on Cook's vessel, the *Miranda*, which left New York on 7 July 1894. The ship hit an iceberg off Cape Charles and after a preliminary assessment, it was decided to travel to St. John's for repairs. Its Inuit passengers were left at Cape Charles but only after a collection was taken up to pay for their passage home by mail steamer.[63]

The last group to return to Labrador was the family from Zoar: Âpili, Helene, Esther, and Nancy. They would not return until 1896 after their short stint at the American Museum of Natural History. Despite working in the US at the World's Fair, at dime museums, and at Barnum and Bailey's circus, the family was suffering financially. An article published in *The Chicago Tribune*, at the time of the family's departure for Newfoundland, reported that Âpili once made as much as $110 a week but that he was returning home "with nothing except some articles of clothing, a few utensils, and a hunting outfit that was provided by friends in New York."[64] It was the Secretary of the American Museum of Natural History, John Winser, who made arrangements with Harvey and Co. in St. John's for their passage home.[65] R.G. Taber put together an outfit of hunting equipment and supplies but requested that it remain under wraps to ensure Âpili did not "under any circumstances, part with any portion" of it.[66] The newspaper reported that Esther would remain in New York.[67] Âpili, Helene, and Nancy sailed on the *Silvia* from Johnson, New Jersey on 12 July 1896 and arrived in St. John's on 20 July.[68] They then transferred to the Labrador coastal steamer and returned to their home at Opatik near Ukkusiksalik.

In New York, Esther maintained her association with Franz Boas, being employed, for a time, as housekeeper and translator for a group of Greenland Inuit brought to New York by Robert Peary at Boas' request.[69] In 1899, she was approached by Ralph Taber to help organize a new "Esquimaux Village" exhibit for the 1900 Exposition Universelle in Paris. It is not clear whether she returned to Labrador as part of the recruitment effort, but among the first to be persuaded to join the tour was Esther's family, Âpili, Helene, and Nancy. This was the next step in what would become a twenty year career for Esther and Nancy as professional Inuit performers with stints in Europe (1899–1901), the Pan-American Exhibition in Buffalo (1901), Luna Park, Coney Island (1903–1905), the Louisiana Purchase Exhibition in St. Louis (1904), the Alaska-Yukon Pacific Exposition in Seattle (1909), and innumerable state fairs throughout the United States.[70] Esther's parents Âpili and Helene played a leading part in these exhibits until Âpili's death in New York in 1905, at which time Helene returned to Labrador. Esther and Nancy subsequently took up permanent residence in the United States and would never return. After almost twenty years of touring, they settled in California, setting up an "Esquimaux Village" in Santa Monica, which supplied props, costumes, and dogs to a number of Hollywood films.[71] Two films produced by the Zelig Polyscope Company in 1911, *The Way of the Eskimo* and *Lost in the Arctic*, are considered to be the first films with a credited Inuit cast, predating Robert Flaherty's *Nanook of the North* by eleven years.[72] Nancy starred in both films, and received a writer's credit for *The Way of the Eskimo*, likely the first writing credit for any Indigenous person in film history.[73]

Three other Inuit remained in America after the fair. Peter Mesher, who had initiated the court case in Chicago with the assistance of Judge Porter and who was one of the founding officers of the "Esquimaux Exhibition Company" that set itself up in competition with the "Esquimaux Village," lived in the United States for nearly eighteen years. He would eventually return to Labrador and marry Lucy Palliser who had also attended the World's Columbian Exposition. Tom Deer, who left the "Esquimaux Village" before the rebellion to take a construction job, and who is also listed as a founding officer of the "Esquimaux Exhibition Company," appears to have struck out on his own. He disappears from Labrador records and seems to have remained in the United States. Tomasi Lucy, one of the sons of John and Katerina Lucy, also appears to have lived out his life in the United States and never returned to Labrador. He is absent from all known subsequent records relating to the Lucy family.

CHAPTER 8

Aftermath

"We have cried out to the Lord, day and night... that He would have mercy on us... and that he would end this nasty disease here and now, but his thoughts were different from what we wished. Men and women, from infants to grandparents, have been gathered into heaven by the Lord of life and death."[1]

On 5 July 1895, a year after most Inuit had returned to Labrador from the United States, a story was published in the *Harbour Grace Standard* and reprinted in the *St. John's Daily News* the following week. It reported that an epidemic had occurred in Labrador the previous winter, "the nature of which was not known," killing over two hundred people, eighty in Nain alone. The report went on to say that the disease had been brought to Nain "by the natives who had attended the World's Fair." There were few details in the story, and no evidence to support the claim that the disease originated with Inuit returning to Labrador from the US.[2] Later that summer, the Moravians provided details of the tragedy, but did not speculate as to its cause or assign blame. It would be a few years later, after doctors of the Mission to Deep-Sea Fishermen (MDSF) visited the afflicted communities and repeated the allegation, that it gained new authority and assumed the status of an established fact. Eventually colonial authorities would use the assertion to justify legislation restricting movement of Inuit outside Labrador for any purposes other than hunting, fishing, or guiding.

A "Grave Illness Among Our People"

When the Newfoundland newspaper accounts first arrived in London in July 1895, Moravian authorities reacted with concern.[3] Labrador was ice-bound for six months of the year and they had yet to hear directly from the Labrador missionaries. It would be several more weeks before firsthand reports reached them, confirming their worst fears. The missionaries at Nain (Brs. Martin, Kahle, Lundberg, and Waldmann) stated that shortly after the mission's ship the *Harmony* left their community in the autumn of 1894, illness spread throughout the population, attacking both those in the village and those at the fishing camps outside the community. They were overwhelmed by the devastation wrought by the disease but did their best to alleviate the suffering of the people, comforting the sick and administering medicines while their wives continuously prepared soups to help feed those who were unable to feed themselves. With little knowledge of disease, the missionaries leaned heavily on their faith, believing that God had his purpose whether they understood it or not. The entries of the Nain diaries make grim reading:

> Now began a rather grave illness among our people. Swellings of all kinds appeared, soon they became rose-like, then it was more like mumps. Small, unnoteworthy wounds had soon nasty results, and the suffering and need was extensive.... Almost all persons... had to suffer much pain on their deathbeds... and the illness is not over, quite the contrary, of the sick, there are many still and constantly new cases are to be found.[4]

By October, the sickness had a firm hold on the community with few people escaping its grip. In November, people from the outlying fishing camps began returning to Nain for the winter but the epidemic had already reached many of those places with similar catastrophic results. By Christmas, the extent of the devastation was apparent:

> Because of illness, the (church) gatherings were very poorly attended and on the last day of the old year we had to realise

> that the Lord... had called out no less than... 46 since late August. And still so many are very ill here, that we doubt their recovery.[5]

The new year began much as the old one had ended, with more sickness and death, but by February, the number of deaths was down slightly, and by March the missionaries believed the worst was over. Easter, normally the high point of the Moravian calendar year, was a sad and mournful occasion:

> The passion-time we celebrated as usual. It was to us a great joy that many sick had already recovered and returned to visit God's house. It made a very melancholic impression to see the many pale, sunken faces, the heads robbed of their hair, the tottering weak figures arisen from the illness.[6]

The sickness had run its course. There were several more deaths, but new cases were rare. By the time the epidemic was over, Nain had lost almost a third of its population. Of three hundred inhabitants, eighty-eight persons had died, of which there were sixty adults and twenty-eight children.[7]

Nain was not the only Inuit community affected by the epidemic. The missionary at Okkak, ninety miles north of Nain, reported that the disease also ravaged that community:

> After our ship had left us in the autumn of 1894, our people began to suffer from pains in the body and swellings of the limbs. The worst time was in November when two or three deaths occurred every week.[8]

By the time the sickness had ended at Okkak, twenty people had died.[9]

The Moravians had no idea what they were dealing with. Deadly epidemics of measles, smallpox, influenza, whooping cough, and tuberculosis afflicted Inuit communities year after year but the Moravians were not a medical mission and were ill-equipped to deal with such calamities, having only a rudimentary knowledge of the causes of disease and limited access to medicines. It would be well over a year before they learned that the epidemic had been typhoid fever. As to its origins, the Moravians offered no speculation, although the missionaries at Nain observed that the outbreak began "shortly after the *Harmony* left"[10] and those at Okkak reported the people began to suffer "after our ship left." These testimonials suggest the disease might have come from a passenger or crew member on board the mission ship. But like other theories, it is merely conjecture.

The probability that typhoid fever was brought to Nain by way of the exhibition Inuit seems unlikely. Of all Inuit returning to Labrador in the summer of 1894, only three families, two from Nachvak and one from Hebron, passed through Nain. They arrived on the mail steamer *Winsor Lake* in early August and remained there about ten days before departing for the north on the mission brig *Gleaner*. They were not the only passengers on the mailboat nor was the *Winsor Lake* the only vessel in port at that time. A Newfoundland steam ship, conducting surveys of cod north of Nain, was in the harbour prior to the arrival of the *Winsor Lake*, as was the *Gleaner*. The same day the mailboat arrived, the *Swallow*, a small steamship chartered by R.G. Taber's mining venture, also reached Nain. The Moravians marvelled at the sight: "Three steamships and a sailing ship at the same time in the harbour, an event which Nain, until now, had not experienced."[11] All ships carried passengers and crew.

In addition to these vessels, hundreds of Newfoundland schooners visited the coast during the summer to fish for cod. Dr. Wilfred Grenfell, writing in the *Illustrated London News* in 1894, estimated the Newfoundland fishery involved as many as twenty-five thousand men, women, and children, many of whom, he said, lived in conditions of poverty, disease, and "abject misery." The schooners ranged the full length of the Labrador coast from the Strait of Belle Isle to Cape Chidley. Inuit families, living at their summer camps on the outer islands, frequently engaged in both commercial and social activities with the Newfoundlanders and disease could easily spread during these transactions. The Moravians clearly believed that Newfoundland fishermen were the source of many maladies that afflicted the coastal population. A few years after the typhoid epidemic, W.W. Perrett, the missionary at Makkovik wrote:

> The year 1900–1901 will be remembered for the "grippe" and for a malignant skin affliction which broke out among the inhabitants of these parts. Two years previously there was an epidemic of measles; the year before that, diphtheria put in an appearance; and before that again scarlet fever. All or nearly all of the diseases have been brought to the coast by Newfoundlanders who are there in the hundreds annually to fish and with whom our people are obliged to mix for trading purposes.[12]

Despite these assertions, there is no evidence that Newfoundland fishermen were the cause of the typhoid epidemic. This too would be unsubstantiated speculation.

On 13 August, a few days after the *Gleaner* left Nain for the north with the Hebron and Nachvak families aboard, a "large number" of Inuit came to Nain from their fishing camps outside the community in anticipation of the arrival of the mission's ship, *Harmony*, and to join the annual celebration of the church commemorating the birth of the Moravian community in Saxony.[13] These people are yet another possible source of the sickness.

How then did the exhibition Inuit get the blame? After the Harbour Grace newspaper report, no further attribution occurs in public records until medical personnel working under the direction of Dr. Wilfred Grenfell visit the coast a number of years after the disease overwhelmed the community of Nain.

Diagnosing the Disease

Grenfell began his work in Labrador in 1892, the year Inuit were recruited for the World's Columbian Exposition. He was employed by the Mission to Deep-Sea Fishermen (MDSF), a British charity, which provided a medical mission to British fishermen in the North Sea and was expanding its work to meet the needs of Newfoundland fishermen. With the support of the Governor of

Newfoundland and several St. John's merchants, Grenfell established two cottage hospitals on the coast, one at Battle Harbour in southern Labrador and one at Indian Harbour in Hamilton Inlet. From these bases, the mission began extending its influence along the entire Labrador coast, bringing medical services to the Newfoundland fishing fleet and to many established Labrador settlements. In their first two years, Grenfell and his staff travelled extensively, including visits to Moravian communities where they formed friendly relations with the missionaries. However, in 1894, the year of the typhoid epidemic, the work of the MDSF was severely hindered when Grenfell, who often insisted on piloting his own ships, ran his vessel aground outside Battle Harbour. As a ship was required to tow the damaged vessel to St. John's for repairs, the MDSF lost two of its ships for much of the summer and plans for the season were seriously disrupted, including a trip north.[14]

Grenfell did not get to Nain until the following year, 1895, when he first learned of the epidemic. It was Grenfell who informed the missionaries that the outbreak was typhoid fever.[15] By this time the epidemic had abated in Nain, but Grenfell discovered that other communities were still dealing with outbreaks. Hopedale had experienced several cases the previous winter and Grenfell found people sick at Uviluktuk (Double Island), Hopedale's principal fishing station. North of Nain, he discovered active cases at Okkak, as well as Cutthroat, a fishing camp outside the community "where many of the best men have died."[16] He claimed that two men who had travelled to Nain during the winter had brought the disease north. While at Okkak, Grenfell conducted a post-mortem on a recent victim and claimed convincing proof that typhoid fever was the cause of death.[17]

The same year, Grenfell also visited Ramah and Hebron, the home communities of the northern families who had passed through Nain on their way home. At Ramah, he made his usual rounds and made no mention of typhoid fever. At Hebron he claimed the people were in good health and reported: "They are better off and healthier here than at the other stations; and this year at least, they have cause to be, the epidemic had not reached them."[18] This is particularly interesting in that the families returning from the United States who were blamed for bringing typhoid to Nain do not appear to have brought the sickness to their own communities.[19]

When Grenfell returned to Newfoundland in November 1895, he was interviewed by the *St. John's Daily News* in Harbour Grace. The correspondent describes the importance of Grenfell's work and comments that much time had been given to attending to Inuit whose population was decimated by typhoid fever. In the same sentence the writer repeats the earlier allegation that the disease was "brought home by those who returned from the miserable visit to the Chicago Exhibition."[20] It is not clear if this assertion originated with Grenfell or the reporter. Indeed, at this time the only suggestion that the exhibition Inuit were responsible for introducing the disease to Labrador came from the earlier newspaper report also written from Harbour Grace, quite possibly by the same correspondent. Grenfell, who published a detailed account of his 1895 trip in the MDSF's periodical *Toilers of the Deep*, made no mention of the epidemic's cause. However, things were about to change.

Fixing Blame

At the end of the 1895 season, Grenfell assigned Dr. Frederick Augustine Robinson to over-winter in Labrador. Initially, Robinson took up residence at the Hudson's Bay Company post at Rigolet to oversee a number of patients there and to prepare for a trip north as soon as ice conditions permitted.[21] That trip would become an epic five-month journey by dog-team from Rigolet to Nachvak and back, followed by a similar trip from Rigolet to Blanc Sablon, and from there returning to the hospital at Battle Harbour, a distance of over 1,800 kilometres. During the northern portion of the trip, he stopped at Hopedale, where he found people infected with typhoid. In his account, later published in *Toilers of the Deep*, he repeats the allegation that the disease originated with Inuit who had been in Chicago: "Today, I visited eight Esquimaux sick with typhoid, which they had contracted at the World's Fair."[22] It is a remarkable statement considering no residents of Hopedale attended the fair, and the nearest being the families from Ailik, two of which Robinson visited prior to his arrival in Hopedale, making no mention of illness.[23] It may well be that

Robinson was treating people afflicted with typhoid fever, but he had no basis for claiming that Inuit who had travelled to the United States were responsible.[24] His published report, however, gave new life and credibility to the allegation and the damage was done.[25]

A few years later, and shortly after Queen Victoria bestowed the title "Royal" on the MDSF, it published *The Story of the Labrador Medical Mission*, its official history, which summarized the first six years of work in Labrador. One of the achievements noted was the assistance given by the MDSF to the Moravian communities during the typhoid epidemic:

> An epidemic of most virulent typhoid fever had been raging, among them, imported by Eskimo returning from the World's Fair at Chicago. Out of 350 at the station of Nain, 92 had died. The doctor at once set about disinfecting houses and properties, isolating the sick, insisting on precautionary measures against the relapses which are so common, and had here proved so fatal to those unaware of danger. Sixty-two new and old cases were treated; only two died. The epidemic came to an end; and probably owing to the careful assembling of the Eskimo at each station, explaining to them the contagious nature of the affection (sic), instructing them in precautionary measures, and leaving medicines with the Moravian missionaries, it did not rekindle in the winter when the Eskimo from one station visit those at another.[26]

The accusation that "Eskimo returning from the World's Fair" were the cause of the epidemic was now embedded in the official history of a distinguished medical organization in Great Britain and the transformation of an unsubstantiated rumour into an established fact was complete.

Restricting Exhibits

In the summer of 1896, Grenfell again brought his medical mission to the Moravian communities along the north Labrador coast. At Nain, Okkak, and Hopedale, he found the people to be in good health.[27] The epidemic was over, and the survivors were getting on with their lives. The typhoid epidemic was a fading memory and would remain that way for several years until the Moravians, Grenfell, and the Governor of Newfoundland joined forces to restrict all further attempts at recruiting Inuit for international exhibitions. These efforts had their origins in events that began in 1899, when R.G. Taber returned to Labrador to recruit Inuit for a new exhibition tour. He had enlisted the help of Esther Eneutseak,[28] an original member of the "Esquimaux Village" who had remained in New York after the fair. She recruited her father, Âpili, mother, Helene, and daughter, Nancy, to form the core of the new group.[29] In the fall of 1899, thirty-three Inuit from Labrador arrived in London to begin a European tour that would include appearances at the Olympiad in London and the Exposition Universelle in Paris, as well as at venues in Barcelona, Madrid, Constantine, Algiers, Tunis, and Naples.[30] As on previous occasions, the Moravians tried to discourage Inuit from participating in the exhibit but failed. Their greatest fear was that Inuit would succumb to disease, but they were also afraid that once Inuit left their communities and the supervision of their teachers, they would face moral challenges that would imperil their souls. One incident led directly to Moravian efforts to end Inuit participation in all future international exhibitions.

In early 1901, while Inuit were on exhibit in Madrid, two of the participants decided to marry and a civil ceremony was performed with Esther's father Âpili presiding. A short time later R.G. Taber approached a local Protestant clergyman with a request to bless the marriage to which the minister agreed. In the presence of Taber and his wife, Esther and her husband, an interpreter, and the mother of the bride, the formal blessing was given.[31] Unfortunately, it turned out that the groom was already married and when Moravians in Europe discovered what had occurred, they were shocked and outraged. The blessing, a sacrament of the church, had essentially sanctified a bigamy. All of this reinforced the notion that no good could ever come from

Inuit leaving their communities in Labrador and that action should be taken to end the practice.

A few months later, Moravian authorities in Germany, who had made inquiries into the circumstances of the marriage, wrote to their counterparts in the SFG in London requesting they draft a petition to the Newfoundland Government "to forbid the export of Esquimaux from Labrador for exhibition purposes." The petition was written and submitted to the government of Sir Robert Bond early in 1902 and that summer, representatives of the SFG met with Bond while he was in London for the Colonial Conference. He listened to the Moravians' request but would not commit his government in any way.[32] The following year, Bond informed the Moravians that no legislation would be forthcoming as it was not the place of government to infringe on people's freedoms. Br. H.O. Essex, who attended the meeting, reported to the SFG that "the Premier holds out little hope of anything being done to prevent this practice since after all any man on the coast is free to do as he likes in such matters. The liberty of the individual cannot be interfered with."[33]

The Inuit exhibition tour of Europe ended in April 1901.[34] A number of people returned to Labrador at that time but others extended their tour, travelling to the US to exhibit at the Pan American Exposition held in Buffalo in the spring and summer of 1901, followed by subsequent appearances at venues in Charleston, South Carolina, and Crystal Palace, London.[35] Slowly the people returned to Labrador, some in November 1902, others in September 1903, while still others appear to have been abandoned and had difficulty getting home. In several cases, the Newfoundland government was forced to intervene and pay the people's return fare.[36] The Moravians claimed that no one received the bonus that was promised at the end of their engagement and on their return some "were absolutely desperate and had to be supplied with food."[37] What they learned of the people's experiences only fortified the Moravians' opposition to such ventures. The missionary at Hebron discussing the state of the souls of those who had recently returned from Buffalo wrote: "They led a life even more immoral than that of the heathen.... No wonder they now want to know why the white missionaries are so strict with them in these matters, when white people in America and elsewhere are apparently... so lax in their morals."[38]

While the Bond government refused to take action to restrict the recruitment of Inuit for exhibition purposes, the Moravians found a strong ally, in 1904, when William MacGregor was appointed Governor of Newfoundland. Shortly after his arrival, MacGregor expressed interest in touring the Labrador coast to better understand the colony. During his tenure, he would undertake two tours of Labrador, one in the summer of 1905 and another in the summer of 1908. On both occasions he submitted reports to the government with recommendations to improve conditions in Labrador.

In 1905, MacGregor, accompanied for a portion of the trip by Wilfred Grenfell, visited the Moravian stations at Hebron, Okkak, Nain, and Hopedale and was deeply impressed with the Moravian mission and its commitment to the spiritual and physical well-being of the Inuit population. At Okkak, he visited the Moravians' new hospital and listened attentively to the observations and opinions of its administrator, Dr. Samuel King Hutton. MacGregor was, himself, a trained medical doctor and acutely interested in health issues. He became alarmed at what he learned of the numerous diseases and infections that continually decimated the Inuit population. The latest tragedy had occurred the year before when Okkak experienced an epidemic of influenza which infected over three hundred people and killed forty-three.[39] The continual recurrence of lethal disease in Inuit communities led some to predict the inevitable demise of the Inuit race. MacGregor knew the danger. While chief medical officer of Fiji in 1875, he had witnessed an epidemic of measles that killed an estimated 40,000 people out of a population of 150,000.[40] It is unclear from whom he heard the story of the typhoid epidemic of 1894 and the notion that it had been brought to Labrador by Inuit returning from US expositions. It might have been Grenfell or possibly Hutton, but the story was repeated in the report of his first Labrador tour and was subsequently used to bolster arguments in favour of legislation banning Inuit from travelling outside Labrador:

> There can be no doubt... that the Innuit (sic) are decreasing in number. The causes of decrease are chiefly two: Epidemics of European diseases and the High Death rate among Children. Half a score of years ago the population of Nain was

> 350 people. Of these 80 people died of typhoid fever brought from Chicago, that is, in round numbers, the appalling mortality from such a cause of 23 per cent. The disease was carried to Okkak where 20 persons succumbed to it there. How many more died at other stations I am not able to state but there remains the lamentable fact that thus 100 persons died at two stations of a disease brought from Chicago to which place some of their number had been carried as an exhibition speculation.[41]

MacGregor's solution to avoid a recurrence of this situation was legislation:

> I see no reason for believing that these destructive epidemic diseases could not have been kept out of Labrador... It would at all events, be practical for the Newfoundland legislature to prevent the deportation of the native Innuit for speculative show purpose, or indeed for any reason, without special permission granted by the executive under proper precautions.... As likely as not, the next lot of natives carried to the United States may bring back small-pox or some other disease deadly to the natives.[42]

In another part of MacGregor's 1905 report, he referenced the massive influx of fishermen from Newfoundland each summer but did not consider them as a possible source of disease, accepting instead the prevailing orthodoxy that Inuit were responsible for their own demise.[43] The Moravians thought otherwise:

> Each year brings evidence that Labrador is no longer so isolated as formerly. Our Eskimos come increasingly into contact with Newfoundlanders, Americans and Europeans. Not only do more fishermen come up the coast, but mining operations have begun in earnest... The presence and influence of more white men renders it increasingly difficult for the missionaries to keep the Eskimos to the simplicity of life

> suitable to their country and climate, and healthful for them both physically and spiritually.[44]

Although MacGregor recommended legislation to ban Inuit travel outside Labrador, Robert Bond remained resistant, and the issue was dormant until 1907 when the matter received renewed attention. That year, J.C. Smith, the husband of Esther Eneutseak, attempted to recruit Labrador Inuit for yet another exhibit, this one to be held at Jamestown in Norfolk, Virginia. When MacGregor learned of Smith's plans, he wrote to Edward Morris, the Minister of Justice, requesting he intervene. Morris informed him of what he already knew: there was no legislation to prevent the recruitment of people for exhibition purposes.[45] However, Morris promised action in the next legislative session if MacGregor could furnish him with any precedents for such legislation. MacGregor was aware of a law enacted in British New Guinea and wrote to the Earl of Elgin, the Secretary of State for the Colonies, requesting a copy of the ordnance.[46] Elgin sent MacGregor the British New Guinea "Labour Ordnance of 1900" as well as the "Settlements Ordinance of 1901 restricting the engagement of Asiatics for Exhibition outside the Colony."[47] McGregor passed these on to Edward Morris.

In 1908, MacGregor undertook his second tour of Labrador, visiting the Moravian communities of Nain and Hebron accompanied again by Wilfred Grenfell. Again, he focused on Inuit health issues but by this time the Moravians were struggling to contain an outbreak of syphilis that had spread through the population and was blamed on Inuit who had travelled to Buffalo as part of the Pan-American fair. Venereal disease had been present on the coast for some time and yet MacGregor, Hutton, and Grenfell concluded that the communities could best be protected from disease by restricting Inuit travel outside Labrador.[48] During his second visit, MacGregor spoke directly to the people, appealing to them to resist the temptation to travel and to remain at home. At a gathering of people at Nain he stated his case:

> I have heard that some of you have been dissatisfied and wish to leave your country. Some of you have been to other countries and what is the result? On returning home you

> have brought back a disease which has become widespread among your race. This is a direct result of your having gone away, instead of listening to the advice of the missionaries, and remaining in your own land. I must tell you that the result of this disease is likely to be very bad for the whole of your race.... Therefore, I advise you to remain at home and do your best to earn a livelihood.[49]

On his return to Newfoundland, MacGregor wrote another report suggesting measures to improve conditions in Labrador. He again recommended "a law to protect the Eskimo territory, and to prevent their removal from their own country."[50]

MacGregor's term as Governor expired in 1909 and he left the colony for a new posting in Australia, but his efforts eventually bore fruit. That same year, Robert Bond was defeated and a new administration under the leadership of Edward Morris assumed power. Morris proved to be more open to the lobbying efforts of MacGregor, the Moravians, and Wilfred Grenfell. "An Act to Prevent the Deportation of Esquimaux from Labrador" was finally introduced in the Newfoundland House of Assembly in February 1911.[51] The legislation made it an offence "for any person to enter into an agreement with Esquimaux for the purpose of performing any services outside this colony without first obtaining the permission of the Governor and Council."[52] Although the legislation aimed to restrict the activities of entrepreneurs and promoters who wished to recruit Inuit for future exhibitions, it effectively limited Inuit rights and freedoms to choose for themselves opportunities for employment outside Labrador. The expressed justification for these measures was the health and well-being of the Labrador communities which were believed to be threatened by people leaving their settlements and returning home with infectious diseases. As Donald Morison, the Minister of Justice, explained on second reading of the bill:

> On several occasion, Esquimaux have been persuaded to go away with disastrous results... both as regards their morals and health.... The Esquimaux seem to be particularly liable

> to certain classes of disease, such as smallpox, typhoid, etc. They catch these diseases abroad and when they come back, they spread it among their people and the result is an awful mortality amongst them.[53]

Morison bolstered his arguments with examples where Inuit, after travelling abroad, introduced disease into their communities. Among them was the typhoid epidemic of 1894 which he blamed on those who attended the World's Columbian Exposition:[54]

> In 1893, a colony of Eskimos consisting of 57 men, women and children were taken to the Chicago Exposition.... Of their adventures in Chicago little has been learned but at the end of the exposition the survivors were returned to Newfoundland in an absolutely destitute condition, at the expense of the colony... They brought with them the infection of typhoid fever, to which a very large number of Esquimaux from Hopedale to Hebron fell victims. At Nain out of a population of 350 Eskimo, 90 died during the winter, their dead and frozen bodies awaiting burial at the one time the following spring.

There are numerous inaccuracies in these statements but by this time, the damage was done.

There was no opposition to the bill, rather it was seen by many as a duty to help protect Inuit. Even Robert Bond, who had previously viewed such legislation as an infringement of individual liberties, supported the bill. During the brief debate in the legislature, he also invoked Chicago and recommended extending the bill to include Innu:

> I heartily support the bill. It will be within the memory of honourable members of this House that a few years ago, a number of these Eskimos were taken to the Chicago Exhibition... and were the unwitting instruments of sacrificing the lives of hundreds of their fellow beings. They are nature's

> children innocent of the wiles and pitfalls of our so-called civilization and I think we should be perfectly justified in going a little further and impose a heavier fine than is provided in the bill. I would also suggest that it might be desirable to include in this bill the Mountaineer Indians. A superior race to the Esquimaux, but almost as innocent and probably their innocence may be taken advantage of now that the deportation of Eskimo is forbidden.[55]

Bond's recommendations were included in the final bill and on 14 March 1911, "An Act Respecting the Eskimo and Indians Resident in Labrador" became the law of the land. Remarkably, it remained the law until it was repealed in 1951.[56]

Conclusion

Inuit who had travelled to the United States for exhibitions in Chicago, San Francisco, and elsewhere had made a remarkable two-year odyssey facing adversities, tragedies, and innumerable indignities only to return home and suffer the further injustice of being blamed for the outbreak of an epidemic that took the lives of over a hundred people. No doubt they would have been upset by the accusations had they heard them. However, it is more likely that Inuit were never made aware as the allegations were mostly confined to private correspondence and official reports within colonialist agencies and not accessible to those living in the isolated bays or communities of Labrador.

It is noteworthy that an epidemic of this magnitude received little attention outside Labrador at the time it occurred. It was not discussed in Government circles prior to the attempts to draft legislation limiting future Inuit participation in exhibition tours. No inquiries were held and no support for the people was provided. This is perhaps not surprising. Beyond the fortunes of the Newfoundland cod fishery, the men who governed the colony in St. John's had little interest in the affairs of its northern region and even less in the welfare of Inuit. Like the British Government before them, which had first granted land and trading concessions to the Moravians so that they could contain Inuit in the north and allow the fishery to develop unimpeded, the Newfoundland Government left Inuit affairs in the hands of the Moravians and ignored their own responsibilities.[57] In 1894, the Government clearly had other things on its mind. That year, Newfoundland's leading banks crashed under the weight of their debts, resulting in the collapse of the colony's currency, business insolvencies, unemployment, and the impending bankruptcy of the Government itself. Yet, when it came to Labrador, that year was no different from any other; the people were simply out of sight and out of mind. If Inuit were thought of at all, they were viewed as people from the past with a doubtful future and easily dismissed as a "dying race."[58] The men who governed Newfoundland reflected the same presumptions and prejudices that determined perceptions of Inuit in Chicago. The century's pervasive racial theories would have informed and influenced their own attitudes towards Inuit and Innu in Labrador.[59] They believed in the primacy of the Anglo-Saxon race, and the superiority of their own culture and values. Histories of the colony written at the time inevitably begin their narratives with Indigenous Peoples but these only serve as a prelude to the arrival of the colonists after which there is barely another mention of them unless it is to trumpet the heroic self-sacrifice of European missionaries trying to bring civilization to an ignorant people.[60] Those who cared at all were motivated by a kind of European noblesse oblige, the notion that with entitlement and privilege comes the obligation to help those less fortunate than oneself. This is surely what motivated MacGregor and Grenfell, but it took the form of a paternalism that assumed they were better positioned to understand the needs of Inuit than Inuit themselves. Thus, policies were developed for Indigenous people with little consultation. The process that led to "An Act Respecting the Eskimo and Indians Resident in Labrador" was typical of this approach to public policy and set a pattern that would be repeated for decades, sometimes with tragic results,[61] until Inuit established their own political institutions in the late twentieth and early twenty-first centuries.[62]

What did Inuit think of their experience in the United States? Unfortunately, there is almost no record of any recollections or reflections on their two years away from home. No doubt stories were told to family and friends and a few fragments of these were recalled by descendants and passed on to researchers in later times.[63] But there are very few first-hand comments providing any insight into what Inuit thought of the experience. There is, for example, the brief conversation the traveller and author Dillon Wallace had with Mary Palliser in 1906:

> We reached (Mark Palliser's) home at Karawalla, an Eskimo settlement a few miles west of Rigolet... Here we met some of the Eskimos that had been connected with the Eskimo village at the World's Fair at Chicago, in 1893. Mary, Mark's wife, was one of the number. She told me of having been exhibited as far west as Portland, Oregon, and I asked:
>
> "Mary, aren't you discontented here, after seeing so much of the world? Wouldn't you like to go back?"
>
> "No, sir," she answered. "'Tis fine here, where I has plenty of company. 'Tis too lonesome in the States, sir."
>
> "But you can't get the good things to eat here — the fruits and other things," I insisted.
>
> "I likes the oranges and apples fine, sir — but they has no seal meat or deer's meat in the States."[64]

Another, more bitter recollection, is contained in the comments of the Hebron resident Zacharias which were recorded by Moravian missionaries shortly after his return home. He told Brother Wirth that he found the heat oppressive and became tired of the food. He expressed surprise that he met so few believers and was alarmed by the violence. "Probably not a night went by without someone being killed," he said. Wirth reported that Zacharias brought back some wrong ideas "about the judiciary and many other things" but did not elaborate.[65] To Brother Kahle in Nain, Zacharias expressed gratitude for arriving home safely and said that need had taught him to pray. He is reported to have said: "We are glad to be once more at liberty, and not continually looked at as if we were animals." He vowed never to go again.[66]

Postscript

After returning to Labrador, Inuit who attended the World's Columbian Exposition resumed their former lives as best they could, even as the world around them was changing.

In Nachvak, resource depletion made life in the region increasingly difficult. A short time after returning home, Kupper died.[1] In 1897, Kuttukitok, his widow, together with Sikêpa and Tiguja, moved to the Moravian community at Ramah where they were baptized. Kuttukitok was among several residents who later died there of "a kind of typhoid" in 1901.[2] Kangerarsuk and Tuglavina remained at Ramah for a short time after their return and became candidates for church membership before returning to Nachvak in 1896. Kangerarsuk appears in Moravian records in 1899, when the Ramah missionary, Adolf Stecker, decided to investigate reports of a religious awakening among Inuit in the Ungava district and hired Kangerarsuk as a guide.[3] In 1902–3, Kangerarsuk and Tuglavina spent the winter at Ramah where the missionary wrote: "The diligence of these heathen when working or hunting put to shame many of the baptized Christians." That same year, Kangerarsuk acted as pilot aboard the Moravian ship *Harmony*, assisting the missionaries who were investigating prospects of establishing a new mission post near Cape Chidley.[4]

In 1904, an epidemic of influenza swept through the Nachvak population at Komaktorvik. Although only ten people died, it was a significant portion of the population and included Semigak, at the time the most influential leader of the Nachvak group. Among the victims of the flu was Kangerarsuk's wife Tuglavina.[5] Following his wife's death, Kangerarsuk left Nachvak, returning to Ramah where he remarried in 1905.[6] He was baptized the following year[7] and subsequently moved with his new family to Hebron. He would survive the Spanish Influenza of 1918, which took 135 lives at Hebron, and died on 5 April 1927 at age 72.[8]

Zacharias returned to Hebron in 1894 where he remained until his wife Naemi's death and then in 1904 moved to Hopedale where he remarried in 1906. In 1910, he returned to Hebron. His daughter, Justina, also moved south to Hopedale. She married Jonas Noggasak (sic), had two children, Sara and Zacharias, and died at Hopedale on 12 October 1938.[9]

In 1894, the Moravians abandoned the community at Zoar and while some people remained in the area, many of the Zoar people relocated to either Nain or Hopedale. Robert Ford, the "Esquimaux Village" interpreter, returned to Opatik with his family in 1894. Susan Ford died at Opatik on 28 October 1909. Robert remarried in 1910 and died at Opatik on 10 January 1930. When Âpili, Helene, and Nancy arrived back in Labrador in 1896, they returned to their home at Opatik but attached themselves to the church at Hopedale. It is while they were away that the Moravians encouraged their congregations to choose surnames for the first time.[10] Âpili chose his father's name Jacko. His granddaughter "Nanji Jacko" was entered into the Hopedale Church book as being the "illegitimate child of the unmarried" Esther Jacko and David Edmunds who was "baptised by a clergyman in Chicago."[11] Âpili, Helene, and Nancy would only remain in Labrador for three years. They would leave to form the nucleus of a new "Esquimaux Village" that R.G. Taber assembled for the Exposition Universelle in Paris in 1899. They toured Europe and returned to the United States to exhibit at various fairs and exhibitions until Âpili's death in New York in 1905. At that time Helene returned to her home at Opatik where she died in June 1918.[12] Nancy remained with her mother Esther in the United States, continuing to work as a professional "Esquimaux" performer until the 1920s. Neither Esther nor Nancy would return to Labrador. Nancy died in California on 16 August 1959. Esther died there two years later, on 29 March 1961.[13]

John and Katerina Lucy's family returned to Labrador in the fall of 1893, where they resumed their lives at Sioniorvik, near Ailik. They later migrated south, spending their winters at Tasialuk and summers at "Jigger Island," just north of Cape Harrison. Both John and Katerina are buried at "Jigger Island."[14] John and Katerina's daughter Julia Hedwig became pregnant through a liaison with the captain of the ship that brought the families home in 1894.

Her son, John Thomas Lucy, was raised by her aunt and uncle, Charlotte and Joseph Lucy, at Ailik. Julia would later marry John Broomfield but had no other children.[15] She eventually went blind and died in Tilt Cove in 1949.[16] Her brother Abraha Lucy married Alice Tuktashina and had three daughters, Katherine, Ellen, and Charlotte, and two sons, John and Abraha.[17] He continued to live on the coast fishing and sealing at Dunne's Island in the spring and summer, moving to Makkovik in the fall. He would eventually die of cancer. Simon Lucy would marry Bertha Putalik and have a daughter, Nancy, and a son, John.[18] He moved to Makkovik where he worked for the Andersen family and died when he was struck on the head when a wood pile collapsed on him while he was working.[19] Jonas Lucy would never marry but he too moved to Makkovik where he died tragically when he slipped while rigging the mast of a bully boat, falling onto the deck of the boat and breaking his neck.[20]

Joseph and Charlotte Lucy remained in Ailik after their return and became increasingly active members of the new Moravian church community at Makkovik. In 1903 they were both appointed Native Helpers and Chapel Servants, helping missionaries to instruct Inuit members of the new congregation.[21] They lived in Makkovik for a time but later moved to Tilt Cove for the winters where they lived close to their niece Julia.[22] There is little information on Charlotte's relative Abraha Tuktashina, although photographs establish him in Makkovik on church festival days.[23]

Of the other Ailik family that attended the fair there is little in the documentary records except that Simon Manak died very soon after his return to Labrador,[24] and two years later, on 14 April 1896, his widow, Sarah Kunnunak, married Andreas Amos Simon in Esquimaux Bay.[25] No information has been found about the subsequent lives of their children Maria, Jacobus Marcus, Peterusi, Sarah (Jr.), and Abraha.

While the Moravians maintained a comprehensive record of Inuit life on the north coast, the Inuit of Aiviktok are more difficult to track as fewer records exist. Church records for the region are sporadic and incomplete. The Methodists and the Church of England established a more permanent presence in the region towards the end of the nineteenth century, but their records relate only to their own congregations, and most Inuit identified as Moravian. The HBC agent at Rigolet urged the Moravians to establish themselves in the area[26] and the Moravians undertook a series of visits to the region but were reluctant to commit to a new mission, despite a formal written request from Inuit themselves, signed by, among others, Peter and Tom Palliser.[27] The Moravians were establishing their new mission station at Makkovik and investigating the possibility of establishing another in the far north at Killinek and had neither the human nor financial resources to undertake the mission in Aiviktok. Most Inuit in the region accepted the inevitable and eventually turned to the Methodists and Church of England for their spiritual and social needs.

The records of the Hudson's Bay Company are also of limited use in tracking the lives of local Inuit. The journals for the HBC post at Rigolet document the general conditions of the region but provide few details about specific individuals. In the months and years after their return, the Pallisers, Shuglos, and Deers re-established their lives as fishermen and hunters in the area, but it is clear from the records that economic circumstances had not improved in their absence and they were again struggling to make a living.

This was a time of transition for Inuit in Aiviktok. The number of Inuit families continued to decline. The most common explanation for this was intermarriage with the planter population.[28] It may well be that there were fewer Inuit men to marry but the tradition of Inuit women finding partners outside the Inuit community was, by this time, well established. In the 1911 Canada Census for Rigolet, of sixty-four families recorded in the region, only eight are identified as Inuit.[29] Among them are the Pallisers and the Shuglos, but not the Deers.

Jonas and Susie Palliser lived and worked with their son John until Jonas' death around 1913.[30] Jonas' son John married Sarah Kunnunak while his other son, Sam, married Mary Kunnunak.[31] Both would raise families of their own whose descendants still live in the region. Lucy Palliser would eventually marry Peter Mesher after his return from an eighteen-year sojourn in the United States.[32]

Jonas' brother Peter Palliser also resumed the life of a seal hunter and salmon fisherman and worked odd jobs at the Hudson's Bay Company depot at Rigolet. He died on 15 December 1903 at Kenemish, near the head of the inlet.[33] His daughter Mary married Mark Palliser[34] at the same time as Sam Palliser married Mary Kunnunak on 18 September 1894.[35]

The Shuglos and Deers are more difficult to track. Very few records of Jim and Salomie Shuglo's family exist. On their return to Labrador from the United

States, the Shuglos stopped in St. John's, Newfoundland. A St. John's newspaper announced that the wife of James Thuglow (sic), "an Esquimaux," gave birth to a son at the Poor Asylum in St. John's.[36] This is confirmed in the Birth Registers for the Labrador District.[37] The boy's name is given as John and his date of birth as 15 July 1894. He was to live only five months, dying the following autumn on 14 November 1894.[38] A year later, on 20 December 1895, Jim Shuglo would die of erysipelas. He is buried at Back Bay.[39] No subsequent records have been found for Salomie, their daughters Maggie and Augustina, or their son Tom. The only reference for an Eliza Shuglo appears in the Labrador Marriage Records which records her marriage to Albert Broomfield on 13 December 1918.[40]

George and Maggie Deer had two children after returning to Labrador. They had lost their son Peter in Chicago and their daughter Francesca in San Francisco. On 27 October 1895, a daughter Eliza was born.[41] No further records for Eliza have been found. Another girl, Kitty Esther Deer, was born on 9 October 1900.[42] She would not survive, dying in July 1902.[43] George himself would die at Moliak on 3 May 1901.[44] His widow Maggie remarried Adam Mucko of Carawalla at Lester's Point, a short distance from Rigolet, on 14 October 1901.[45] Only one reference has been found for George and Maggie's daughter, Sarah. A Sarah Deer married Mark Marcouie (Mucko) in Carawalla on 7 March 1912. George's brother Tom Deer is among those who disappear completely from the historical record, most likely because he never returned to Labrador but stayed in the United States.

Of the other two men who remained in the US, Tomasi Lucy and Peter Mesher, only Peter Mesher returned to Labrador. It was Mesher's friendship with Judge Porter in Chicago that led to Porter's investigation of the "Esquimaux Village" and subsequently to the decision to take its owners to court. After a sojourn of eighteen years, Mesher returned home and married Lucy Palliser at Grand Village (Mud Lake) on 11 October 1912. He remained in the area for the rest of his life, trapping, fishing, and working in the lumber camps.[46] Peter and Lucy had seven children but three of them would die young. Harriet died on 7 January 1912 at ten months of age. Charles would die at age seven on 1 May 1920[47] and Samuel at ten on 20 February 1929.[48] Four daughters — Alice, Emily, Nellie, and Eva — would all survive to raise their own families in the region.[49]

APPENDIX 1

Passenger List of the *Evelena*[1]

No.	Name	Age	Sex
1.	R.G. Taber	28	M
2.	Lyle Vincent	20	M
3.	Jewell D. Somberger	22	M
4.	W.M. Reed	21	M
5.	Robert Ford	38	M
6.	Susan Ford	35	F
7.	Wm Ford	3	M
8.	Mary Ford	7	F
9.	Kooper	40	M
10.	Kutukituk Kooper	38	F
11.	Mali Kooper	7	F
12.	Tigujak Kooper	2	F
13.	Pamiuk Kooper	15	M
14.	Kanggegatchook	38	M
15.	Tuklavina Kanggegatchook	45	F
16.	Kamialuit Kanggegatchook	16	F
17.	Sikipa Kanggegatchook	7	F
18.	Degouluk Kanggegatchook	14	M

19.	Zacharias	35	M
20.	Naimi Zacharias	35	F
21.	Justina Zacharias	13	F
22.	Tabia Zacharias	4	F
23.	Abila	38	M
24.	Helina Abila	36	F
25.	Esthermiut Abila	15	F
26.	Joseph Locy	42	M
27.	Charlotte Locy	32	F
28.	Tomasi Locy	14	M
29.	Simon Manok	35	M
30.	Sarah Manok	30	F
31.	Maria Manok	14	F
32.	Jacobus Makus (?) Manok	18	M
33.	Peterusi Manok	8	M
34.	Abraha Manok	2	M
35.	John Locy	50	M
36.	Katatina Locy	48	F
37.	Hetvik Julia Locy	22	F
38.	Abraha Locy	20	M
39.	Simon Locy	18	M
40.	Janasik Losy	16	M
41.	Jonas Peliceer	56	M
42.	Susie Peliceer	32	F
43.	Mary Magdaline Peliceer	18	F
44.	Lucy Peliceer	5	F
45.	Sam Peliceer	20	M
46.	John Peliceer	18	M
47.	Tom Peliceer	25	M

48.	Esther Peliceer	23	F
49.	Susan Peliceer	5	F
50.	George Deer	30	M
51.	Maggie Deer	28	F
52.	Sarah Deer	5	F
53.	Peter Deer	6 mo.	M
54.	Jimmie Sugla	50	M
55.	Salomie Sugla	45	F
56.	Maggie Sugla	18	F
57.	Augustinuk Sugla	16	F
58.	Liza Sugla	6	F
59.	Tom Sugla	1 1/2	M
60.	Peter Peliceer	45	M
61.	Mary Magdaline Peliceer	17	F
62.	Abraha Tooktoosina	17	M
63.	Peter Michaud	22	M
64.	Tommie Deer	25	M
65.	Sarah Manak (Jr.)	16	F

APPENDIX 2

Revised Passenger List of the *Evelena*

Family Groupings with Associated Communities

Zoar

5. Robert Ford
6. Susan Ford
7. Wm Ford
8. Mary Ford

23. Âpili
24. Helene
25. Esther

Nachvak

9. Kupper
10. Kuttukitok
11. Mali
12. Tiguja
17. Sikepa

16. Kamialuit (children of Kajuasiak)
13. Pomiuk

14. Kangerarsuk
15. Tuglavina
18. Degouluk

Hebron

19. Zacharias
20. Naemi
21. Justina
22. Tabea

Ailik

26. Joseph Lucy
27. Charlotte Lucy
62. Abraha Tuktashina

29. Simon Manak
30. Sarah Manak
32. Jacobus Manak
65. Sarah Manak (Jr.)
31. Maria Manak
33. Peterusi Manak
34. Abraha Manak

35. John Lucy (brother of Joseph)
36. Katerina Lucy
37. Julia Hedwig Lucy
38. Abraha Lucy
39. Simon Lucy
40. Janasik Lucy
28. Tomasi Lucy

Aiviktok/Esquimaux Bay

41. Jonas Palliser
42. Susan Palliser
44. Lucy Palliser
45. Sam Palliser
46. John Palliser

47. Tom Palliser (son of Jonas)
48. Esther Palliser
49. Susan Palliser
60. Peter Palliser (brother of Jonas)
61. Mary Magdaline Palliser

50. George Deer
51. Maggie Deer
52. Sarah Deer
53. Peter Deer
64. Tommie Deer (brother of George)

54. Jimmie Shuglo
55. Salomie Shuglo
56. Maggie Shuglo
57. Augustinuk Shuglo
58. Liza Shuglo
59. Tom Shuglo

63. Peter Mesher

APPENDIX 3

The "Esquimaux Village" and the Stoney Avenue Exhibit

April 1893

After 21 April 1893, Labrador Inuit split into two groups, one of which remained in the "Esquimaux Village" while the other left to form a new exhibit on Stoney Avenue outside the fairgrounds. We know from newspaper accounts which families left the "Esquimaux Village."[1] The *Daily Inter Ocean* reported that six families remained with the original "Esquimaux Village" as well as that of the interpreter Robert Ford.[2]

"Esquimaux Village" Exhibit (after April 1893):

Jim and Salomie Shuglo; Maggie, Augustina, Liza, and Tom
Joseph and Charlotte Lucy; Abraha Tuktashina
Simon and Sarah Manak; Maria, Jacobus Marcus, Peterusi, Sarah, and Abraha
George and Maggie Deer; Peter*
Kangerarsuk and Tuglavina; Degouluk**
Kupper and Kuttukitok; Mali, Tiguja, Sikepa, and Kotuktooka/Evelina
Kamialuit and Pomiuk
Robert and Susan Ford; Mary and William

*Peter Deer died April 18, 1893
**Degouluk died August 20, 1893

Stoney Avenue Exhibit:

John and Katerina Lucy; Julia, Abraha, Simon William, and Jonas
Jonas and Susan Palliser; Lucy, Sam, John, and Christopher
Tom and Esther Palliser; Susan
Peter Palliser; Mary
Âpili and Helene; Esther and Nancy
Zacharias and Naemi; Justina and Tabea
Peter Mesher

APPENDIX 4

After the World's Columbian Exposition

After the World's Columbian Exposition, the two groups which had made up the "Esquimaux Village" and the Stoney Avenue exhibit fragmented further. A number of families left for Labrador, including John Lucy's family from Ailik and the Nachvak families. P.M. Daniels and W.D. Vincent organized a new exhibit for the Midwinter Fair in San Francisco and persuaded some Inuit from both exhibits to attend. At the same time, a second group was organized by Thomas Scott to undertake a tour of dime museums in the eastern United States. Most Inuit from these groups returned to Labrador in the summer of 1894. One family, however, remained in the United States to tour with Barnum and Bailey's Ethnological Congress. They returned in 1896.

Midwinter Fair, San Francisco, January to June 1894

Zacharias and Naemi; Justina and Tabea
Simon and Sarah Manak; Maria, Jacobus Marcus, Peterusi, Sarah, and Abraha
Jonas and Susan Palliser; Lucy, Sam, John, and Christopher*
Tom and Esther Palliser; Susan
Joseph and Charlotte Lucy; Abraha Tuktashina
George and Maggie Deer
Robert and Susan Ford
Mary Palliser

*Christopher Palliser died in San Francisco on April 10, 1894[1]

Dime Museum Tour, January to Spring 1894

Âpili and Helene; Esther and Nancy
Jim and Salomie Shuglo; Maggie, Augustina, Liza, and Tom

Barnum and Bailey's Ethnological Congress of Strange and Savage Races, March to October 1894 and March to November 1895

Âpili and Helene; Esther and Nancy

It is possible that both Peter Palliser and his daughter Mary were in San Francisco living with his brother Jonas. Both Mary and her father were later reported to be in New York and would return to Labrador onboard Frederick Cook's ship, the *Miranda*, in 1894.[2] Âpili, Helene, and Nancy returned to Labrador in 1896. Esther remained in New York City.

After the World's Columbian Exposition there is no trace of Peter Mesher and Thomas Deer, both early deserters of the "Esquimaux Village" and shareholders in the Stoney Avenue exhibit, or of John Lucy's youngest son, Tomasi. Deer and Lucy likely remained in the United States for the remainder of their lives, while Peter Mesher would eventually return to Labrador after a stay of 18 years.

APPENDIX 5

Imagining "Esquimaux" at the World's Fair

EXPERTS STRIKING FOR A JOB.

World's Fair Puck. June 26, 1893.

World's Fair Puck. June 12, 1893.

AN EVEN THING.

FIRST ESQUIMAU. — What do you think of the cost of living here?

SECOND ESQUIMAU. — It 's about as broad as it is long. What we spend on whale oil cocktails at home, to keep us warm, we must lay out on ice cream here to keep us cool.

World's Fair Puck. May 22, 1893.

Notes

Notes to the Reader

1 This document was discovered by Jim Zwick and first published in *Inuit Entertainers in the United States: From the Chicago World's Fair through the Birth of Hollywood* (Infinity Publishing Co., 2006).

2 Hans J. Rollmann, "The Adoption of Christian Names and Surnames in the Moravian Communities of Nunatsiavut, Labrador," *Journal of Moravian History* 18, no. 2 (2018): 145–158.

3 *Periodical Accounts Relating to the Moravian Missions* 2, no. 24 (December 1895), 616; revised as the result of personal correspondence with Joan Dicker, Inuktitut language specialist, Nain, Labrador.

Introduction

1 "Christmas at the World's Fair," *Chicago Tribune*, December 25, 1892.

2 "Christmas at the World's Fair."

3 "Christmas at the World's Fair."

4 "Christmas at the World's Fair."

5 *The Youth's Companion World's Fair Extra Number* (Boston: Perry Mason & Co., 1893), 18.

6 *The San Francisco Morning Call,* April 3, 1893.

7 "Locked Up," *St Joseph Weekly Gazette,* January 12, 1893.

8 "Locked Up."

9 "Esquimaux Here," *Boston Daily Globe*, October 14, 1892.

10 Organizers of the Fair refused to allow African Americans or Native Americans to create their own exhibits at the Fair. See Anna R. Paddon and Sally Turner, "African Americans and the World's Columbian Exposition," *Illinois Historical*

Journal 88, no. 1 (1995): 19–36; and Lisa Cushing Davis, "Hegemony and Resistance at the World's Columbian Exposition: Simon Pokagon and the Red Man's Rebuke," *Journal of Illinois State Historical Society* 108 (2015).

11 Jim Zwick, *Inuit Entertainers in the United States: From the Chicago World's Fair through the Birth of Hollywood* (Infinity Publishing Co., 2006).

12 Teresa Dean, "Eskimos, Measles and Evil Spirits," in *White City Chips* (Chicago: Warren Publishing Co., 1895), 6.

Chapter 1

1 "Esquimaux Here," *Boston Daily Globe*, October 14, 1892.

2 *Chicago Daily Tribune*, May 31, 1890.

3 "Eskimos for Chicago," *The Roanoke Times*, July 16, 1892.

4 One of Boas' first professional jobs was organizing Bella Coola artifacts, brought to Germany's Royal Ethnographic Museum in 1885 by Johan Jacobsen who was working at the time for Carl Hagenbeck. It was after this that the people of the Pacific Northwest became the principal focus of Boas' ethnographic research. See Lee D. Baker, *Anthropology and the Racial Politics of Culture* (Duke University Press, 2010), 96.

5 Prior to their departure for Labrador to recruit Inuit for the "Esquimaux Village," a representative of Skiles & Co. solicited assistance from the Moravian Mission, presenting himself as part of the "Ethnological Section of the Columbian Exhibition." Whether this indicated a formal relationship with Putnam or was simply a means to enhance credibility is not known. *British Mission Board Minute Book*, vol. 1, June 13, 1892, Moravian Church Archive and Library, Muswell Hill, London.

6 *Concession Agreement Between World's Columbian Exposition and J.W. Skiles and Company* (World's Columbian Exposition Records, Chicago History Museum).

7 *Concession Agreement Between World's Columbian Exposition and J.W. Skiles and Company.*

8 *Concession Agreement Between World's Columbian Exposition and J.W. Skiles and Company.*

9 Charles Carroll Carpenter was a missionary based in southern Labrador from 1858–1865.

10 William Forbush, *Prince Pomiuk: A Prince of Labrador* (Marshall Brothers, 1903), 48–49.

11 Susan Kaplan, "Economic and Social Change in Labrador Neo-Eskimo Culture," (PhD. Diss, Bryn Mawr College, 1983), 29; and Peter Whitridge, "Environmental Imaginaries and the Inuit Colonization of Labrador," in *Settlement, Subsistance and Change Among the Labrador Inuit* (University of Manitoba Press, 2012), 50.

12 Carol Brice-Bennett, *The Northlanders: A History of the Population, Socio-economic Relations and Cultural Change of Inuit Occupying the Remote Northern Coast of Labrador*, unpublished manuscript (Labrador Inuit Association, 1996), 9.

13 W.H. Whiteley, "The Establishment of the Moravian Mission in Labrador and British Policy 1763-1783," *Canadian Historical Review* 45, no. 1 (1964): 39–40.

14 J.K. Hiller, "The Foundation and the Early Years of the Moravian Mission" (Master's Thesis, Memorial University of Newfoundland, 1967).

15 *History of the Mission of the Church of the United Brethren in Labrador for the past Hundred Years* (London: W. Mallalieu & Co., 1871). Also, *Periodical Accounts Relating to the Moravian Missions*, vol. 12, p. 67; vol. 17, p. 176; vol. 23, pp. 59 and 101.

16 Esquimaux Bay was renamed Hamilton Inlet in 1821 by Captain William Martin, after the Governor of Newfoundland who had sent him to report on the region. The Hudson's Bay Company retained the usage of Esquimaux Bay throughout the nineteenth century.

17 Kaplan, "Economic and Social Change in Labrador Neo-Eskimo Culture", 192.

18 Richard Jordan, "Archaeological Investigations of the Hamilton Inlet Labrador Eskimo: Social and Economic Responses to European Contact," *Arctic Anthropology* 15, no. 2 (1978): 176.

19 Norman Anick, "The Fur Trade in Eastern Canada Until 1870," Parks Canada, Manuscript 207, p. 621.

20 David Zimmerly, *Cain's Land Revisited: Culture Change in Central Labrador, 1775–1972* (ISER Books, 1975), 48–49.

21 Marianne P. Stopp, "Eighteenth Century Labrador Inuit in England," *Arctic* 62, no. 1 (2008): 56–59.

22 George Cartwright, *A Journal of Transactions and Events During a Residence of Nearly 16 Years on the Coast of Labrador*, vol. 1 (1792), 274–276.

23 A.M Lysaght, "Letter from George Cartwright to Joseph Banks, 14 September 1778," in *Joseph Banks in Newfoundland and Labrador, His Diary, Manuscripts and Collections* (University of California Press, 1971), 268–269.

24 "Most people in the region identified as Innu or Inuit (the two main indigenous

groups in the area) or counted themselves part of a mixed-heritage (European-indigenous) group called planters." See Kurt Korneski, "Planters, Eskimos, and Indians: Race and the Organization of Trade under the Hudson's Bay Company in Labrador, 1830–50," *Journal of Social History* 50, no. 2 (2016): 307–335.

25 W.H.A. Davies, "Notes on Esquimaux Bay and Its Surrounding Country," in *Transactions of the Literary and Historical Society of Quebec*, vol.4–1 (1843), 70–94.

26 Armenius Young, *One Hundred Years of Mission Work in the Wilds of Labrador* (Arthur and Stockwell Ltd., 1916), 24.

27 Hans Rollmann, *Demographics and Literacy of the Rigolet-Area Inuit During the Second Half of the Nineteenth Century*, unpublished manuscript.

28 The Labrador tradition of exclusive rights was contested by Newfoundland fishing interests both on the water and in the courts. See Kurt Korneski, "Troubles Down North: Unsettling the Settler in Hamilton Inlet, 1871–1883" in *Conflicted Colony: Critical Episodes in Nineteenth-Century Newfoundland and Labrador* (McGill-Queen's University Press, 2016). In 1887, the HBC possessed berths at the following locations in the Rigolet area: Big Island, Cul de Sac, Carawalla, Burnt Wood Cove, Back Run, Mullin Cove, Turner's Bight, Whittle's Point, Palliser's Point, Summer Cove, Gourdoux Point, Dram Brook, Jewel's Point, and Jewell's Head. See also: Report of Keith McKenzie, Esquimaux Bay District (Rigolet), September 2, 1886, HBC Archives, Microfilm 1M1258, B183/e/1, pp. 1–4.

29 Jimmie "Sugla" was outfitted by the HBC to fish salmon at Carawalla and Portage Cove in 1867; Jonas Palliser was contracted by the HBC to fish salmon at Back Run in 1867; Peter Palliser at Big Island in 1867; and both Jonas and his brother Peter at Back Run in 1870 (unattributed excerpt from Hudson's Bay Co. Records displayed on the wall of Strathcona House, Rigolet, Labrador).

30 Charles Hallock, "Three Months in Labrador," *Harper's New Monthly Magazine*, May 1861, 747.

31 Patty Way, personal conversation regarding the genealogy of the Shuglo family.

32 George Cartwright, *A Journal of Transactions and Events During a Residence of Nearly 16 Years on the Coast of Labrador* (1792), 140.

33 Hallock, 750.

34 Hallock, 750.

35 Marianne P. Stopp, "Eighteenth Century Labrador Inuit in England."

36 Hallock, 754–755.

37 Letter from P.W. Bell to S.H. Parsons, February 25, 1890, HBC Archives, Microfilm 1M1146 183/B/3, vol. 2, p. 205.

38 Letter from Keith McKenzie, Rigolet, HBC to Robert Prowse and Sons, St. John's, July 28, 1886, HBC Archives, Microfilm 1M1146 183/B/3, vol. 2, p. 82.

39 Letter from P.W. Bell, District Manager, Esquimaux Bay District, to William Armit, Secretary of the Hudson's Bay Company, London, August 8, 1889, HBC Archives, A.11/58, p. 387.

40 Rigolet Post Journals, June 25, 1891, P.T. McGrath Fonds, The Rooms Provincial Archive (hereafter RPA).

41 Rigolet Post Journals, June 27, 1892, P.T. McGrath Fonds, RPA.

42 HBC Rigolet Post Journals, HBC Archive, B 183/a/24-30, Reel 1020.

43 HBC Rigolet Post Journals, June 25, 1891 and July 25, 1892, P.T. McGrath Fonds, RPA. Also, *Inspection Report*, Rigolet Post, P. McKenzie (Inspecting Officer), October 9, 1889, HBC Archives Microfilm 1M1258 B.183/e/2, pp. 10–11.

44 HBC Rigolet Post Journals, B183/a/30, July 6, 1892, HBC Microfilm 1M1020.

45 John Lucy's wife, Katerina, was a Palliser by birth. Personal communication, Joyce Allen of Rigolet, May 2019.

Chapter 2

1 Ronald Rompkey, *Labrador Odyssey: The Journal and Photographs of Eliot Curwen* (McGill–Queen's University Press, 1996), 152.

2 *Periodical Accounts*, vol. 33, December 1884, p. 190.

3 Baptismal Certificate, *Hopedale Church Book*, p. 173, entry no. 733, Moravian Mission Microfilm 591. For a detailed examination of the relationship between the Moravians and the "Southlanders," see Carol Brice-Bennett, "Two Opinions: Inuit and Moravian Missionaries in Labrador 1804–1860" (MA Thesis, Memorial University of Newfoundland, 1981), 35–52, 171–177, 310–325, and 441–451.

4 R.G. Taber, "Rugged Labrador," *Outing, an Illustrated Monthly Magazine of Recreation*, February 1896, 388.

5 "Esquimaux Here," *Boston Daily Globe*, October 14, 1892.

6 *HBC Rigolet Journal*, B183/a/30, January 1891, HBC Microfilm 1M102016: "John Lucy and Toustachima (sic) arrived here in the morning bringing 5 foxes, 2 fine silver silvers among them"; March 22, 1891: "John Lucy and Toustachina (sic) arrived here with a load of venison, 4 foxes, 2 white a red and a cross"; December 18, 1891: "Toutoushina (sic) and John Lucy in from the north with a few foxes";

January 30, 1892: "Lucy and Toutuchina (sic) in from the north. They brought quite a bit of fur"; March 7, 1892: "John Lucy arrived with 1 silver fox"; May 1, 1892: "Lucy and Jim Toutoucchina (sic) with venison and fat."

7 "Esquimaux Here, Queer Lot on Their Way to the World's Fair," *Boston Globe*, October 14, 1892.

8 Personal communication, Joyce Allen of Rigolet, May 2019.

9 *Liturgiit Upvala*, the Moravian hymn book of Lyle Vincent, in which is noted the location of the *Evelena* each Sunday from June 12–October 9, 1892, courtesy of Kenn Harper.

10 Minutes of the British Mission Board, vol. 1, June 13, 1892, Moravian Church Archive and Library, Muswell Hill London: "Mr. W.D. Vincent the official representative of the ethnological Section of the Columbian Exhibition has received from us letters of introduction to our missionaries in Labrador, whither he goes to collect curiosities for the exhibition. We gave him no sanction to the wish of his employers to engage Eskimos to go to the Exhibition." See also, Minutes of the Society for the Furtherance of the Gospel Among the Heathen (hereafter SFG), May 6, 1892, Moravian Mission Microfilm 513, Reel 3, paragraph 1004.

11 Hilke Thode-Arora, "Abraham's Diary – A European Ethnic Show from an Inuk Participant's Viewpoint," *Journal for the Society for the Anthropology of Europe* (Fall 2002); Abraham Ulrikab, *The Diary of Abraham Ulrikab*, ed. and trans. Hartmut Lutz (University of Ottawa Press, 2005).

12 Taber's quote is an example of what is now called "The Myth of the Vanishing Indian" which was a popular notion in the nineteenth century, and which was used by promoters of ethnological exhibits to attract spectators with the suggestion that it may be their last opportunity to witness a "dying race." See also Brian Dippie, *The Vanishing American: White Attitudes and U.S. Indian Policy* (University of Kansas Press, 1991).

13 Taber, "Rugged Labrador," November 1896, 95.

14 Taber, "Rugged Labrador," November 1896, 96.

15 The reasons for Inuit conversion receive a thorough discussion in Brice-Bennett, "Two Opinions."

16 SFG, Letter to Newfoundland Government, September 2, 1892, paragraph 1014, Memorial University of Newfoundland (hereafter MUN), Centre for Newfoundland Studies (hereafter CNS), Moravian Mission Microfilm 513, Reel 6.

17 Brice-Bennett, "Two Opinions," 452–465.

18 Letter from Hopedale to the SFG, *Periodical Accounts*, August 10, 1856, vol. 22, p. 103.
19 Letter from Hopedale to the SFG, *Periodical Accounts*, July 12, 1858, vol. 23, p. 50.
20 *Periodical Accounts*, December 1876, vol. 30, p. 93.
21 John C. Kennedy, *Encounters: An Anthropological History of Southeastern Labrador* (McGill-Queen's University Press, 2015), 73.
22 Zoar Diary, *Periodical Accounts*, July 1876, vol. 30, p. 97.
23 Report of Theodor Bourquin to SFG, paragraph 36.
24 Report of Visitation in Labrador by Br. Latrobe in 1888, MUN, CNS, Moravian Mission Microfilm 690, vol. 7, R.15.K.a.11.g, p. 29.
25 Report of Theodor Bourquin to SFG, paragraph 38.
26 *Periodical Accounts*, series 2, December 1890, p. 185.
27 Events relating to the Hebron "uprising" are described in detail in "Letter Concerning the Unrest at Hebron on September 29, 1889," MUN, CNS, Moravian Mission Microfilm, Reel M510, pp. 041163-041181, translation by Larrass Translations, Ottawa, ON.
28 "Letter Concerning the Unrest at Hebron on September 29, 1889."
29 Minutes of the SFG, October 31, 1890, Moravian Mission Microfilm 513, Reel 3, paragraph 915.
30 "Letter Concerning the Unrest at Hebron on September 29, 1889."
31 "Letter Concerning the Unrest at Hebron on September 29, 1889."
32 HBC Post Journal Davis Inlet, August 2, 1892, Transcriptions of HBC Journals, Patrick McGrath Collection, Box 11, File 11, RPA, April 1, 1888, and October 25, 1888.
33 "Extract of the Diary of Zoar, Sept. 1870–Sept. 1871," *Periodical Accounts*, vol. 28, p. 177.
34 HBC Post Journal Davis Inlet, February 6, 1889, Patrick McGrath Collection, Box 11, File 11, RPA: "Robert Ford made his appearance again having evidently exhausted the hospitality of Flowers and the people in Big Bay. Abel is with him, two idlers, who seem to agree well together."
35 Moravian Archives, Bethlehem, Zoar Diary, 55719-55720, courtesy of Hans Rollmann.
36 HBC Post Journal Davis Inlet, August 28, 1892.
37 W.D. Vincent, "Home Life of the Esquimaux," *The Graphic*, March 4, 1893, p. 153.
38 Moravian Archives, Bethlehem, Hebron Diary (1892), 48978-48979, courtesy of Hans Rollmann.
39 Moravian Archives, Bethlehem, Hebron Diary (1892).

40 Minutes of the SFG, 4 November 1892, Moravian Mission Microfilm 513, Reel 3.
41 *Periodical Accounts*, series 2, vol. 2, March 1895, p. 442.
42 "The Labrador Expedition," *Decatur Daily Republican*, October 15, 1892.
43 Moravian Archives, Herrnut, Ramah Diary (August 1892 to August 1893), Microfilm 690, R.15.K.b.6A UAH, unpaginated.

Chaper 3

1 Vincent, "Home Life of the Esquimaux,"153.
2 Kaplan, "Economic and Social Change in Labrador Neo-Eskimo Culture," 282–286; also, "Torngat Mountain National Park, A Cultural Landscape," Parks Canada, pc.gc.ca.
3 Kaplan, 134.
4 Brice-Bennett, *The Northlanders*, 9.
5 Hiller, "The Foundation and the Early Years of the Moravian Mission in Labrador," 31.
6 Kaplan, 284.
7 Extract from Hebron Diary, *Periodical Accounts*, August 22, 1832, vol. 12, p. 255. The term "chief" as used by the Moravians is used to identify the perceived leader of a group of Inuit. It is not entirely clear how they understood the term other than someone who exerted influence over others. Inuit used the term *Angajuk-Kâk* to denote a leader, usually of a small group often with strong family ties.
8 Hebron Diary, *Periodical Accounts*, September 23, 1859, vol. 23, p. 242. For the Moravians, an important part of the conversion process was settlement in Moravian communities for converts to be continually schooled and their progress monitored. Conversion became difficult when Inuit refused to abandon their homelands. See J.K. Hiller, *Foundations*, Chapter VII: "The adoption of Christianity… meant more than a change of heart… It implied the adoption of a new kind of economic and social life which took the form of a settled community."
9 Extract from Private Correspondence of F. Erdman, *Periodical Accounts*, vol. 23, p. 300.
10 Letter to the SFG from Thomas Fraser, HBC, December 13, 1865, Miscellaneous SFG papers, Moravian Church Archives and Library, British Province, London.
11 Minutes of SFG, MUN, CNS, Moravian Microfilm 513, Reel 3, vols. 8–10, unpaginated: SFG minutes April 8, 1861; November 6, 1861; and June 3, 1861.

12 Letter from Thomas Fraser, Secretary HBC, to D.A. Smith, Chief Factor Labrador District, June 9, 1865, HBC Archives A6/39, p. 275.

13 Letter from Hebron to SFG, *Periodical Accounts*, London 1866, vol. 26, p. 10.

14 Donald Smith to William Gregory Smith, HBC Secretary, October 18, 1867, HBC Archives, A 11/58, p. 138.

15 Extracts from the Diary of Okak, *Periodical Accounts*, 1867–1868, vol. 27, p. 65.

16 Hebron Diary, *Periodical Accounts*, August 29, 1868, vol. 27, p. 14.

17 Letter from Donald Smith to HBC Board of Directors, September 3, 1868, HBC Archives, Microfilm 1M1252, A11/58, p. 146.

18 Letter from Donald Smith to William G. Smith, Secretary HBC, October 26, 1868, HBC Archives Microfilm 1M125, A11/58, p. 148.

19 Smith would continue to expand HBC operations in his district. In 1869, the HBC reopened Fort Severight on the George River in Ungava and in the same year bought out Hunt and Company's operations at Ukkusiksalik (Davis Inlet) near Zoar as well as Paul's Island near Nain. See John Kennedy, *Encounters*, 73.

20 *Periodical Accounts*, vol. 27, p. 4.

21 Also referred to as National Helpers. See Hans Rollmann, "'So that in this part you should not lag behind other congregations...': The Introduction of National Helpers in the Moravian Mission among Labrador Inuit," *Journal of Moravian History* 17, no. 2 (2017).

22 Nullatatok Diary, *Periodical Accounts*, August 1871, vol. 28, p. 120.

23 Brice-Bennett, *The Northlanders*, 93.

24 Brice-Bennett, *The Northlanders*, 17,

25 "Extracts from the Diary of Ramah 1878–9," *Periodical Accounts*, vol. 31, p. 249.

26 "Extract from the Diary of Ramah, Sept. 1874–Sept. 1875," *Periodical Accounts*, vol. 29, p. 431.

27 HBC Nachvak Post Journal July 21, 1871; July 23, 1871; April 27 and 28, 1873, HBC Archives Microfilm 1M1012B138/a/2-10

28 HBC Nachvak Post Journal March 8, 1872; April 19, 1873: "Semminica (Semigak) arrived from the woods, I hear that no deer are killed since last anyone was out from there — the Eskimo are therefore starving and nearly all their dogs are dead from want of food." See also: Oct. 9, 1871; Jan. 11 and 28, 1872; Feb. 21, 1872; Jan. 14, 1874; April 19 and 21, 1874.

29 HBC Nachvak Post Journals indicate the following catches of individual char for a part of 1872: July 25– 250, July 29– 300, July 30– 370, July 31– 320, August

1– 280, August 9– 240, August 14– 200, August 16– 400. HBC Archives Microfilm 1M1012B138/a/2-10.

30 Brice-Bennett, *The Northlanders*, 104.

31 Brice-Bennett, *The Northlanders*, 96 and 104.

32 Report of Keith McKenzie, Esquimaux Bay District (Rigolet), September 2, 1886, HBC Microfilm 1M1258, B183/e/1, p. 2.

33 Letter from Keith McKenzie, District Manager, Rigolet, to SK Parson, HBC Montreal, October 15, 1887, HBC Archives Microfilm 1M1146, B183/e/3, p. 134.

34 Report on Nachvak Post, 1889, P. McKenzie, Inspecting Officer, HBC Archives Microfilm 1M1257, B.138/e/1, p. 5.

35 Report on Nachvak Post, 1889, p. 6.

36 Brice-Bennett, *The Northlanders*, 105.

37 Brice-Bennett, *The Northlanders*, 105.

38 Taber, "Rugged Labrador," January 1896, 331.

39 Taber, "Rugged Labrador," January 1896, 331. Here Taber is making his own distinctions between Inuit living north of Ramah and those he has previously encountered and recruited to the south of there.

40 Possibly a relative of the aforementioned Tuglavina.

41 Moravian Archives, Herrnhut, Ramah Diary (1892), unpaginated.

42 Vincent, "Home Life of the Esquimaux," 153.

43 *Liturgiit Upvalo*, belonging to Lyle Vincent.

44 HBC Post Journal Rigolet, September 7, 1892, B183/a/30, HBC Microfilm 1M1020.

45 HBC Post Journal Rigolet, September 8, 1892.

46 "Esquimaux Here," *Boston Daily Globe*, October 14, 1892.

47 HBC Post Journal Davis Inlet, January 12, 1890: "Abel Helina and Tom Tucheon (sic) came here with a team of skeletons. I scarcely saw such a sight in my life. The two Indians and these starving brutes would harmonize well together. The Esquimaux said they were starving, these two especially as they cannot get anything from the Mission. They were willing to work and requested for something to do in order to live."

48 HBC Post Journal Davis Inlet, September 3, 1891.

49 "Exodus of the Eskimos," *Chicago Daily Inter Ocean*, April 21, 1893.

Chapter 4

1 "White City Half in Cloud Land," *Chicago Tribune,* May 2, 1893.

2 "White City Half in Cloud Land."

3 C.M. (Chauncey Mitchell) Depew, *The Columbian Oration: Delivered at the dedication ceremonies of the World's Fair at Chicago, October 21, 1892* (New York: E.C. Lockwood, 1892).

4 "How They Looked from Above," *Chicago Tribune,* May 2, 1893.

5 "How They Went," *Chicago Daily Inter Ocean,* May 2, 1893.

6 "Start Made from Lexington," *Chicago Tribune,* May 2, 1893.

7 "Heralded By Cheers," *Chicago Daily Inter Ocean*, May 2, 1893.

8 "Near Half a Million," *Chicago Tribune,* May 2, 1893.

9 "Formally Opened," *Chicago Daily Inter Ocean,* May 2, 1893.

10 "Formally Opened."

11 "Springs Into Being," *Chicago Tribune,* May 2, 1893.

12 Rodney Reid Badger, *The Great American Fair: The World's Columbian Exposition and American Culture* (Chicago: Nelson-Hall, 1979), 51.

13 Lisa Krissoff Boehm, *Popular Culture and the Enduring Myth of Chicago 1871–1968* (Routledge Press, 2004), 50.

14 William Cronon, *Nature's Metropolis: Chicago and the Great West* (W.W. Norton and Co., 1991), 26.

15 Cronon, *Nature's Metropolis*, 29.

16 Bessie Louise Pierce, *A History of Chicago, Volume I: The Beginning of a City, 1673–1848* (University of Chicago Press, 2006), 46.

17 Cronon, *Nature's Metropolis*, 92.

18 "Emergence as a Tranportation Hub," *History of Chicago*, Wikipedia, accessed April 30, 2025, https://en.wikipedia.org/wiki/History_of_Chicago#Emergence_as_a_transportation_hub.

19 Bessie Louise Pierce, *A History of Chicago, Volume III: The Rise of the Modern City, 1871–1893* (University of Chicago Press, 1957), 155.

20 Board of Trade of Chicago, *Annual Report for the Year Ending December 31, 1890* (JME Jones Stationary and Printing Co., 1891), 138.

21 Pierce, *A History of Chicago, Volume III*, 58.

22 Cronon, *Nature's Metropolis*, 347.

23 Pierce, *A History of Chicago, Volume III*, 55.

24 Chicago Department of Health Report 1881 and 1882, p. 47, quoted in Pierce, *A History of Chicago, Volume III*, 56.

25 Pierce, *A History of Chicago, Volume III*, 245.

26 David Moberg, "Antiunionism," Encyclopedia of Chicago, accessed April 30, 2025, http://www.encyclopedia.chicagohistory.org./pages/55.html.

27 U.S. Commissioner of Labour, *Tenth Annual Report, 1894*, I, 22, quoted in Pierce, *A History of Chicago, Volume III*, 298.

28 Pierce, *A History of Chicago, Volume III*, 276–289.

29 Julie K. Rose, "The World's Columbian Exposition: Idea, Experience, and Aftermath" (MA thesis, University of Virginia, 1996), 8–9.

30 Judith A. Adams, "The American Dream Actualized: The Glistening White City and the Lurking Shadows of the World's Columbian Exposition," in *The World's Columbian Exposition: A Centennial Bibliographic Guide*, ed. David J. Betuca (Greenwood, 1996), xxiii.

31 *Dedicatory and Opening Ceremonies of the World's Columbian Exposition* (Chicago: Stone, Kastler and Painter, 1893), 157.

32 Michel-Rolph Trouillot, *Silencing the Past: Power and the Production of History* (Beacon Press, 1995), 118.

33 Lisa Cushing Davis, "Hegemony and Resistance at the World's Columbian Exposition: Simon Pokagan and the Red Man's Rebuke," *Journal of the Illinois State Historical Society* 108 (2015); also Barbara J. Ballard, "A People Without a Nation," *Chicago History Magazine* (1999), and Elliott M. Rudwick and August Meier, "Black Man in the White City: Negroes and the Columbian Exposition, 1893," *Phylon* 26, no. 4, Clark Atlanta University (1965).

34 William De Wiit, James Gilbert, and Robert W. Rydell, *Grand Illusions: Chicago's World's Fair of 1893* (Chicago Historical Society, 1993), 145.

Chapter 5

1 Michel de Montaigne, quoted in Jan Carew, "Columbus and the Origins of Racism in the Americas," *Race and Class* 29, no. 4 (1988): 4.

2 Lauren Cross, Lauren Seitz, and Shannon Walter, "The First of its Kind: A Cultural History of the Village Nègre," *Digital Literature Review* 3 (2016): 21–31.

3 *Chicago Daily Tribune*, May 31, 1890.

4 Chaim M. Rosenberg, *America at the Fair: Chicago's 1893 World's Columbian Exposition* (Arcadia Publishing, 2008), 245.

5 Boehm, *Popular Culture and the Enduring Myth of Chicago*, 33.

6 Rosenberg, *America at the Fair*, 249–252.

7 Anthropology was in its infancy when Frederic Putnam began his career in the mid-nineteenth century, and he had no formal training in this field. He started his career as a naturalist with a focus on ornithology and it was only later in his career that he turned his attention to archaeology with a specific interest in Indigenous burial sites. As director of the Peabody Museum of Archaeology and Ethnology, Putnam supervised numerous archaeological digs and helped train a new generation of archaeologists. See Charles C. Abbott, "Sketch of Frederic Ward Putnam," *Popular Science Monthly* 29 (1886).

8 Curtis M. Hinsley, "Anthropology as Education and Entertainment: Fredric Ward Putnum at the World's Fair," in *Coming of Age in Chicago: The 1893 World's Fair and the Coalescence of American Anthropology*, ed. Curtis M. Hinsley and David R. Wilcox (University of Nebraska Press, 2016).

9 Frederick Ward Putnam Papers, *Speech to the Committee of Liberal Arts, Chicago*, 21 September 1891 (Harvard University Archives), quoted in Hinsley, "Anthropology as Education and Entertainment," 16.

10 George W. Stocking Jr., *Race, Culture and Evolution: Essays in the History of Anthropology* (University of Chicago Press, 1968; 1982), 112: "Turn of the century social scientists were evolutionists almost to a man, and their ideas on race cannot be considered apart from their evolutionism."

11 Stocking Jr., *Race, Culture and Evolution*, 114.

12 Marvin Harris, *The Rise of Anthropological Theory: A History of Theories of Culture* (Altamira Press, 2001), 145–149.

13 Baron de Montesquieu, *The Spirit of Laws*, trans. Thomas Nugent [1752] (1748; Batoche Books, 2001), 176.

14 Quoted in Harris, *The Rise of Anthropological Theory*, 30.

15 Although Europe was not a monolithic culture and these ideas of superiority did not develop in precisely the same manner at the same time in all countries, it was a viewpoint shared by the ruling classes among all the major colonial powers.

16 Harris, *The Rise of Anthropological Theory*, 145.

17 Harris, *The Rise of Anthropological Theory*, 12.

18 Harris, *The Rise of Anthropological Theory*, 12.

19 Herbert Spencer, *Principles of Sociology*, vol.1 (London: W.J. Johnson, 1876), 61, 108.

20 It should be said here that Spencer himself never asserted this, only arguing that common environmental and social factors led to common intellectual and

emotional responses. See Jay Rumney, *Herbert Spencer's Sociology* (Atherton Press, 1966), 214–221.

21 Lewis Henry Morgan, *Ancient Society: Or Researches in the Lines of Human Progress from Savagery Through Barbarism to Civilization* (New York: Holt, 1877), 6.

22 Harris, *The Rise of Anthropological Theory*, 130: "No major figure in the social sciences between 1860 and 1890 escaped the influence of evolutionary racism."

23 Christian F. Feest, ed., *Indians and Europe: An Interdisciplinary Collection of Essays* (University of Nebraska, 1989).

24 Carew, "Columbus and the Origins of Racism in the Americas," 41–42.

25 William C. Sturtevant and David Beers Quinn, "This New Prey: Eskimos in Europe in 1567, 1576 and 1577," in *Indians and Europe: An Interdisciplinary Collection of Essays* (University of Nebraska, 1989), 61.

26 Sturtevant and Quinn, "This New Prey," 69 and 80.

27 Stopp, "Eighteenth Century Labrador Inuit in England," 45–64.

28 Eric Ames, *Carl Hagenbeck's Empire of Entertainments* (University of Washington Press, 2008), 70–71.

29 Ames, *Carl Hagenbeck's Empire of Entertainments*, 4.

30 Andrea Stulman Dennett, *Weird and Wonderful: The Dime Museum in America* (New York University Press, 1997), 41.

31 *Boston Daily Globe*, June 11, 1884.

32 P.T. Barnum, *Struggles and Triumphs: The Life of P.T. Barnum, Written by Himself* (New York: 1855), 228.

33 *Chicago Tribune*, June 4, 1883.

34 Ames, *Carl Hagenbeck's Empire of Entertainments*, 64.

35 Ames, *Carl Hagenbeck's Empire of Entertainments*, 74.

36 See Chapter 2, p. 25; also Thode-Arora, "Abraham's Diary," 2.

37 Rosenberg, *America at the Fair*, 245.

38 Hinsley, "Anthropology as Education and Entertainment," 17 and 22.

39 *Chicago Daily Inter Ocean*, November 1, 1893.

40 Hinsley, "Anthropology as Education and Entertainment," 25.

41 *Springfield Daily Republican*, August 20, 1892, quoted in Ralph W. Dexter, "Putnam's Problems Popularizing Anthropology," *American Scientist* 54, no. 3 (1966).

42 Hinsley, "Anthropology as Education and Entertainment," 17.

43 Melissa Reinhart, "To Hell with the Wigs!," *The American Indian Quarterly* 36, no. 4 (2012): 408.

44 *Dedicatory and Opening Ceremonies of the World's Columbian Exposition*, 85.

45 Hinsley, "Anthropology as Education and Entertainment," 66.
46 Reinhart, "To Hell with the Wigs!," 413.
47 Hinsley, "Anthropology as Education and Entertainment," 38.

Chapter 6

1 "Esquimau Village at the World's Fair," *The Illustrated American*, December 24, 1892.
2 "Esquimaux Here," *Boston Daily Globe*, October 14, 1892.
3 "Esquimaux Here."
4 "Esquimaux Here."
5 "Esquimaux Here."
6 "Esquimaux Here."
7 "Esquimaux Here."
8 See Appendix 1.
9 "Far Away Labrador," *Daily Inter Ocean*, October 15, 1892.
10 "Esquimaux Off to Chicago," *Boston Sunday Globe*, October 16, 1892.
11 "At the Theatre," *Boston Sunday Globe*, October 16, 1892.
12 "At the Theatre," *Boston Sunday Globe*, October 16, 1892, and "Esquimaux in Chicago," *Baltimore Sun,* October 22, 1892.
13 Ralph Graham Taber, *Northern Lights and Shadows* (London: Greening and Company, 1900), 193.
14 "Esquimaux Off to Chicago," *Boston Sunday Globe*, October 16, 1892.
15 "Esquimaux Off to Chicago."
16 "Twelve Families Arrive," *Chicago Tribune*, October 18, 1892.
17 "Jolly Esquimaux," *Daily Inter Ocean*, October 18, 1892.
18 "Twelve Families Arrive," *Chicago Tribune*, October 18, 1892.
19 "Chicago's Esquimau," *Chicago Times* and *Buffalo Morning Express*, October 20, 1892.
20 "New Incorporations," *Chicago Daily Tribune*, November 7, 1892.
21 "New Incorporations."
22 "Twelve Esquimau Families Arrive," *Chicago Tribune,* October 18, 1892.
23 "Jolly Esquimaux," *Daily Inter Ocean*, October 18, 1892.
24 Rand McNally & Co., *A Week at the Fair, Illustrating the Exhibits and Wonders*

at the World's Columbian Exposition (Chicago: Rand McNally & Co. Publishers, 1893).

25 "The Esquimaux Village at Chicago," *St. Louis Post-Dispatch,* December 18, 1892.

26 "The Esquimaux Village at Chicago."

27 H.H. Bancroft, *The Book of the Fair: An Historical and Descriptive Presentation of the World's Science, Art and Industry as Viewed Through the Columbian Exposition in 1893* (Chicago and San Francisco: The Bancroft Co., 1895), 879.

28 "Esquimau Village at the World's Fair," *The Illustrated American,* December 24, 1892.

29 *The Youth's Companion World's Fair Extra Number*, 18.

30 "Esquimau Village at the World's Fair," *The Illustrated American*, December 24, 1892, 653.

31 "The Wonderful Esquimaux Whip," *The Star*, Reynoldsville, PA, June 21, 1893.

32 "In a Strange Land," *Chicago Tribune*, November 1, 1892; also "Another Baby," *The New York Times*, November 5, 1892.

33 "Lived But A Week," *Chicago Tribune*, November 8, 1892.

34 "Esquimaux Don't Like Rain," *Chicago Tribune*, October 19, 1892.

35 "Shrouded in Deerskin," *Democrat and Chronicle*, Rochester, NY, November 11, 1892. The burials of Inuit who died in Chicago are registered in the records of the Oakwood Cemetery, but the graves are currently unmarked.

36 Jonas and Susan Palliser's son Tom, married to Esther, had a daughter also named Susan Palliser.

37 "Boy Born in the Esquimau Village," *Chicago Daily Tribune*, November 13, 1892.

38 The name Palmer is attributed to Potter Palmer, president of the Exposition's Board of Lady Managers who apparently stood as godmother at Nancy's christening; see Zwick, *Inuit Entertainers in the United States*, 16. For a sketch of Nancy's subsequent career as a performer and actress, see Zwick, *Inuit Entertainers in the United States*, 80–82.

39 Rossiter Johnson, *History of the World's Columbian Exposition* (New York: D. Appleton and Company, 1897–98).

40 "Twelve Families Arrive," *Chicago Tribune*, October 18, 1892.

41 *Midway Types* (Chicago: The American Engraving Company, 1894).

42 "Locked Up," *St. Joseph Weekly Gazette,* January 12, 1893.

43 *The San Francisco Morning Call*, April 3, 1893.

44 "Jolly Esquimaux," *Daily Inter Ocean*, October 18, 1892.

45 "Twelve Families Arrive," *Chicago Tribune*, October 18, 1892.

46 "Oil Drinkers Secured," *Daily Inter Ocean*, September 23, 1892.
47 "Eaters of Raw Fish," *The Sun,* October 15, 1892.
48 "Esquimaux in Chicago," *Baltimore Sun*, October 22, 1892.
49 *The San Francisco Morning Call,* April 3, 1893.
50 *The Youth's Companion World's Fair Extra Number*, 18.
51 "Measure of Progress," *The World's Fair Update, Once a Week: An Illustrated Weekly,* March 18, 1893.
52 Julian Ralph, "In the Eskimo Village at Chicago," *Evening Star*, Washington, DC, May 27, 1893.
53 Rand McNally & Co., *A Week at the Fair.*
54 "Esquimaux in Summer," *Daily Inter Ocean*, January 27, 1893.
55 Anna N. Kendall, "The Eskimo Village," *Chicago Tribune,* April 1, 1893.
56 *Concession Agreement between the World's Columbian Exposition Co. and J.W. Skiles and Co.,* March 9, 1892, Records of the World's Columbian Exposition, Chicago Historical Society, Chicago, Ill.
57 "Locked Up," *St. Joseph Weekly Gazette*, January 12, 1893.
58 "Locked Up."
59 "May Abate Itself," *Daily Inter Ocean*, April 1, 1893.
60 "Too Warm for Furs," *Atlanta Constitution*, March 31, 1893.
61 "Exodus of Eskimos," *Daily Inter Ocean,* April 21, 1893.
62 "Too Warm for Furs," *Atlanta Constitution*, March 31, 1893.
63 The mean temperature in Chicago in February 1893 was 28° F, in March, 33° F, and in April, 44° F. Although these temperatures may seem cool, heavy Inuit sealskin clothing was designed for temperatures much lower than this.
64 "Too Warm for Furs," *Atlanta Constitution*, March 31, 1893.
65 The names of the plaintiffs as listed in the *Daily Inter Ocean* report of March 31, 1893, are James Sugarloaf, Thomas Jones, Peter Pallacier, and John Log. In the *Chicago Daily Tribune* of March 31, 1893, they are named as James Sugarloaf, Thomas Jones, Henry and Peter Pallacier, and John Log.
66 "An Esquimaux Revolt," *Daily Inter Ocean,* March 31, 1893.
67 "An Esquimaux Revolt."
68 "An Esquimaux Revolt."
69 "Court Proceedings," *Chicago Mail*, April 3, 1893.
70 "Exodus of Eskimos," *Daily Inter Ocean,* April 21, 1893 reports that "the James Sugarloaf" family was shut up from February 15 to March 25, although this was most likely Thomas Palliser.

71 "Esquimaux Win Habeas Corpus Cases," *Chicago Tribune*, April 4, 1893.

72 "Exodus of the Eskimos," *Daily Inter Ocean*, April 21, 1893 mentions additional items such as one hundred fishhooks and to each woman thirty yards of calico and four blankets.

73 "Court Proceedings," *Chicago Mail*, April 3, 1892, and "Courts of Record," *Daily Inter Ocean*, April 4, 1893.

74 "Measles and Chills," *San Francisco Chronicle*, April 13, 1893.

75 "Christopher Columbus Has the Measles," *Daily Inter Ocean*, April 14, 1893.

76 "Measles and Chills," *San Francisco Chronicle*, April 13, 1893.

77 "Another Esquimau Baby Dies," *Chicago Tribune*, April 19, 1893.

78 "The Esquimaux Village, A Story that the Strangers from Labrador Are Badly Treated," *The New York Times*, April 10, 1893.

79 James Shuglo had four children with him in Chicago, but only one boy, and he was too young to have participated in the fighting.

80 "War of the Races," *Chicago Tribune*, April 15, 1893.

81 A reporter from *The Daily Inter Ocean* appears to have been present at every critical juncture of this story, suggesting advance knowledge of events, probably through the agency of Judge Porter.

82 "Exodus of Eskimos," *Daily Inter Ocean*, April 21, 1893.

83 "Exodus of Eskimos."

84 "Exodus of Eskimos."

85 "Too Much Civilization," *The Dalles Daily Chronicle* (The Dalles Oregon), April 22, 1893.

86 "Two Eskimo Villages," *Daily Inter Ocean*, April 23, 1893.

87 "New Incorporations," *Chicago Tribune*, April 26, 1893.

88 "A Loophole Found," *St. Louis Post-Dispatch*, May 4, 1893.

89 "Esquimaux Competition," *Once A Week: An Illustrated Weekly Newspaper*, May 6, 1893.

90 "Midway Plaisance," *St. Louis Post-Dispatch*, May 7, 1893.

91 "Exodus of the Esquimaux," *Chicago Evening Journal*, April 21, 1893.

92 "Editorial," *San Francisco Chronicle*, April 22, 1893; also "Too Much Civilization," *The Dalles Daily Chronicle* (The Dalles Oregon), April 22, 1893.

93 "Outside the Gates," *Daily Inter Ocean*, May 8, 1893.

94 L.G. Moses, *Wild West Shows and the Images of American Indians 1883–1933* (University of New Mexico Press, 1996), 140.

95 Thomas Scott, *History of the Esquimau Race* (Erie, PA: Dispatch Print, 1893).

96 "Carte de Visite for Esquimaux Exhibit," Chicago, Personal Collection.

97 *The Dream City: A Portfolio of Photographic Views of the World's Columbian Exposition* (St. Louis, Missouri: N.D. Thompson Publishing, 1893–1894).

98 "Exodus of the Eskimos," *Daily Inter Ocean*, April 21, 1893.

99 "Two Eskimo Villages," *Daily Inter Ocean*, April 23, 1893.

100 "Strange Structures," *The Iola Register*, September 1, 1893; also, "People at the World's Fair," *The Cultivator and Country Gentlemen*, September 28, 1893.

101 "The Midway Plaisance," *The Princeton Union*, September 14, 1893.

102 Forbush, *Pomiuk: A Prince of Labrador*, 56.

103 "Esquimau Boy Drowns in the Pond," *Chicago Daily Tribune,* August 21, 1893.

104 "Weird Funeral Rite," *Daily Inter Ocean*, August 22, 1893.

105 "Weird Funeral Rite."

106 Largely without incident, except for the efforts of employees of the Colonies Hotel, situated close to the "Esquimaux Village," to break into the compound to kill the noisy "Esquimaux dogs" which continually disturbed their guests. The invaders were intercepted and arrested before their mission achieved success ("Attempt to Kill Esquimau Dogs," *Chicago Tribune*, September 1, 1893). The other event of note was the international boat races held on the main lagoon of the fairgrounds and won, after numerous heats, by Kupper in his kayak ("Boat Races," *Daily Inter Ocean*, September 21, 1893).

107 "Now a Reminiscence," *Daily Inter Ocean*, October 31, 1893.

108 "Profits On The Side," *Chicago Tribune*, July 15, 1894.

109 J.W. Buel, *The Magic City: A Massive Portfolio of Original Photographic Views of the Great World's Fair and Its Treasures of Art Including a Graphic Representation of the Famous Midway Plaisance* (Philadelphia: H.S. Smith and C.R. Graham, for Historical Publishing Co. Weekly, from January 15, 1894, through May 14, 1894).

Chapter 7

1 "Scenes at the Fair," *San Francisco Chronicle,* January 1, 1894.

2 Scott refers to himself as manager of the "Esquimaux Village" and states that he had been "connected with the Esquimaux Village in Chicago during the six months the World's Fair has been open." Scott, *History of the Esquimau Race*, 3.

3 Scott, *History of the Esquimau Race*, 3.

4 Victoria Dailey, "California's First International Exposition: The Midwinter Fair of 1894," *Quarterly, The Book Club of California* 75, no. 1 (Winter 2010).

5 Raymond Clary Papers, *The Official History of the California Midwinter International Exposition*, Chapter XVII, The Concession (unpaginated manuscript). Compiled from the Official Records of the Exposition and published by Authority of the Executive Committee (San Francisco: Press of H.S. Crocker Co., 1894), courtesy of Christopher Pollack and the Golden Gate Park Commission.

6 Raymond Clary Papers, *The Official History of the California Midwinter International Exposition*, Chapter XVII, The Concession (unpaginated manuscript).

7 *The Official Guide of the California Midwinter Exposition* (San Francisco: G. Spaulding & Co., 1894), 124.

8 *The Official Guide of the California Midwinter Exposition*, 124.

9 "Night in Palm City," *San Francisco Chronicle*, February 11, 1894.

10 "Seeing the Palm City," *San Francisco Chronicle,* January 28, 1894.

11 *California Midwinter Exposition Illustrated*, January 20, 1894.

12 *California Midwinter Exposition Illustrated.*

13 Kamialuit is referred to by name in several newspaper articles. On March 5, 1894, nearly identical stories published in two different newspapers tell of a young woman suffering heartbreak over a failed romance. In one, she is referred to as "Kamealowik, the Esquimau princess" and in the other as Mary Palliser. *San Francisco Morning Call*, March 5, 1894, and *San Francisco Chronicle*, March 5, 1894.

14 "Scenes on the Midway," *San Francisco Chronicle*, January 31, 1894.

15 "To Travel Free," *San Francisco Chronicle*, March 14, 1894.

16 "The Esquimaux Village," *San Francisco Chronicle,* March 24, 1894.

17 "A Brown Midget Arrives at Sunset City," *San Francisco Morning Call*, February 14, 1894.

18 "To Travel Free," *San Francisco Chronicle*, March 14, 1894.

19 "Notes of the Fair," *San Francisco Chronicle*, March 29, 1894.

20 "A Woeful Feast," *San Francisco Call*, March 30, 1894.

21 "Death of Another Baby," *San Francisco Call*, April 11, 1894.

22 "News of the Fair," *San Francisco Chronicle*, February 28, 1894.

23 "Night in Palm City," *San Francisco Chronicle*, February 11, 1894.

24 "Notes of the Fair," *San Francisco Chronicle*, April 28, 1894.

25 "Strike in the Esquimaux Village," *San Francisco Morning Call*, April 29, 1894.

26 "A Little Girl Lost," *San Francisco Chronicle*, June 27, 1894.

27 "A Baby's Grave," *San Francisco Call*, July 27, 1894.

28 Jim Zwick, *Inuit Entertainers in the United States*, 34.

29 *Daily Inter Ocean,* October 8, 1893; also, *The Evening World*, December 19, 1893.

30 "Remarkable Sights, Strange People, Two Gorillas, Trained Animals," *Buffalo Enquirer*, June 14, 1894.

31 "Remarkable Sights, Strange People, Two Gorillas, Trained Animals."

32 "Premium for Promptness," *The Ohio Democrat*, May 22, 1894.

33 "The White Tents," *Wilkes-Barres Times Leader*, May 24, 1894.

34 *The Barnum and Bailey Official Route Book, Season of 1894* (Harvey L. Watkins, 1894), Milner Library, https://digital.library.illinoisstate.edu/digital/collection/p15990coll5/id/2049/; *The Barnum and Bailey Official Route Book, Season of 1895* (George E. Hardy, 1895), Milner Library, https://digital.library.illinoisstate.edu/digital/collection/p15990coll5/id/1914.

35 "Heathen at the White House," *The Washington Post*, May 8, 1894.

36 "Apile, The Globe Trotting Eskimo," *The New York Times*, January 8, 1905.

37 "Apile, The Globe Trotting Eskimo." See also Harlan Smith Photographs, American Museum of Natural History, File No. 42910-42920.

38 "Go Back to Labrador," *The Chicago Tribune*, July 26, 1896.

39 "An Eskimo Family from the world's fair," *Evening Telegram*, September 30, 1893.

40 "An Eskimo Family from the world's fair."

41 "Marine Notes," *Evening Telegram*, October 14, 1893.

42 HBC Records, MG 20-B 183, microfilm reel HBC 1m102, p. 37.

43 *Evening Telegram*, November 22, 1893.

44 William Forbush, *Pomiuk: A Prince of Labrador*, 57.

45 "SS Portia," *Evening Herald*, July 13, 1894.

46 "A Baby Esquimaux," *Evening Telegram,* May 4, 1894.

47 HBC Rigolet Post Journal, July 25, 1894, HBC Archives, B.183/a/31, Reel 1m102, p. 62.

48 A St. John's newspaper reported: "The S.S. Winsor Lake was yesterday morning at Messrs. Harvey and Co.'s premises taking in the implements for the Labrador Mining Co. (Messrs. Taber, Regad, Lloyd and others). These gentlemen intend mining on a large scale in the vicinity of Nain. The *Winsor Lake* took a boiler, 2 cases of boiler coverings, 2 cases of boiler fittings, 12 bdls. Iron piping, 1 coil of wire rope, 2 lots of derrick fittings, 1 flat car, 45 iron rails and about 2,000 feet of lumber. The little steamer 'Swallow' was also packed tight with implements, every available space being occupied. It is to be hoped that this company will meet with the success its enterprise deserves." "Labrador Mining Co.," *Evening Herald*, July 3, 1894.

49 "Homeward Bound," *Evening Herald*, July 17, 1894.

50 "Labrador Mail Season 1894," *Daily News*, July 2, 1894.

51 HBC Rigolet Post Journal, July 25, 1894, HBC Archives, B.183/a/31 reel HBC 1M102, p. 63.

52 Lydia Campbell, "Sketches of Labrador Life," *St. John's Evening Herald*, February 6, 1895.

53 Moravian Archives, Herrnut, Ramah Mission Diary (1894), Microfilm 690, R.15.K.b. 6A UAH, unpaginated, translation courtesy Hans Rollmann. In the statistical part of the diary, there is the following note: "Moved here.... Kangerarsuk, Tuglavina & Sikepâ from Chicago..." which suggests that the family that remained in Ramah was that of Kangerarsuk-Tuglavina.

54 Ramah Mission Diary, 1897.

55 Wilfred Grenfell, "How We Found Pomiuk," *Toilers of the Deep,* 113.

56 *Periodical Accounts*, vol. 3, December 1896, pp. 175–6.

57 *Periodical Accounts*, series 2, vol. 2, March 1895, p. 442.

58 Minutes of the SFG, February 6, 1895, MUN, CNS, Moravian Microfilm 513, paragraph 1158.

59 *Periodical Accounts*, series 2, vol. 2, March 1895, p. 442.

60 Letter of August Wirth circa. 1900, courtesy of Hans Rollmann.

61 "Dr Cook at Home," *The Brooklyn Citizen*, September 23, 1894.

62 Henry Collin Walsh, *The Last Cruise of the Miranda* (New York-London: The Transatlantic Publishing Company, 1896), 15.

63 "Loss of the Miranda," *Boston Globe*, September 9, 1894.

64 "Go Back to Labrador," *The Chicago Tribune*, July 26, 1896. It is reported in this article that the family "travelled with Barnum at a salary... of $110 a week," but made no profit as Âpili was both generous by nature and "easy fruit" for hucksters. See also: Letter from John H. Winser, Secretary of the AMNH to Messr. Bowring and Archibald, July 7, 1896, and Letter from R.G. Taber to Franz Boas, June 3, 1896, American Museum of Natural History (Library Box 16, Folder 5).

65 John Winser, Secretary AMNH to William Lash, July 7, 1896, American Museum of Natural History, Outgoing Correspondence.

66 John Winser, Secretary AMNH to William Lash.

67 John Winser, Secretary AMNH to William Lash.

68 "The *Silvia* Arrives," *Evening Telegram*, July 20, 1896.

69 Kenn Harper, *Give Me My Father's Body: The Life of Minik, the New York Eskimo* (Steerforth Press, 2000).

70 Zwick, *Inuit Entertainers in the United States*, 163–170.
71 Zwick, *Inuit Entertainers in the United States*, 136.
72 Zwick, *Inuit Entertainers in the United States*, 113–120.
73 Kenn Harper and Russell Potter, "Early Arctic Films of Nancy Columbia and Esther Eneutseak," *Nimrod* 10, no. 4 (2010).

Chapter 8

1 Records of the Moravian Mission in Labrador (MUN), Microfilm 511, Reel 6 pp.006871, Letter from the Labrador Mission Conference at Nain Labrador to the Conference of Elders at Berthelsdorf Germany, 12 July 1895.
2 "Labrador Notes," *Harbour Grace Standard*, July 5, 1895.
3 *Periodical Accounts*, vol. 2, no. 23, September 1895, p. 542.
4 Moravian Archives, Herrnhut, Diarien von Nain, vol. 20, R.15.Kb.4g, July 1894–July 1895, pp. 7–8.
5 Moravian Archives, Herrnhut, Diarien von Nain, July 1894–July 1895, p. 13.
6 Moravian Archives, Herrnhut, Diarien von Nain, July 1894–July 1895, p. 25.
7 Moravian Archives, Herrnhut, Diarien von Nain, July 1894–July 1895, pp. 30, 31.
8 *Periodical Accounts*, vol. 3, no. 25, March 1896, p. 40.
9 *Periodical Accounts*, vol. 2, no.24, December 1895, p. 617.
10 *Periodical Accounts*, vol. 2, no. 25, March 1896, p. 38.
11 Moravian Archives, Herrnhut, Diarien von Nain, vol. 20, R.15.Kb.4g, July 1895–July 1896, p. 3.
12 *Periodical Accounts*, vol. 4, no. 48, December 1901, p. 590.
13 *Periodical Accounts*, vol. 4, no. 48, December 1901, p. 4.
14 Ron Rompkey, *Grenfell of Labrador* (University of Toronto Press, 1992), 80.
15 Moravian Archives, Herrnhut, Diarien von Nain, July 1895–July 1896, p. 3.
16 *Toilers of the Deep*, November 1895, 308.
17 *Toilers of the Deep*, November 1895, 309.
18 *Toilers of the Deep*, December 1895, 335.
19 The death of Kamialuit at Ramah (see p. 136) is unexplained but her ailment did not infect the others travelling with her or spread to the community at Ramah.
20 Harbour Grace Notes, *Daily News*, November 29, 1895.
21 *Toilers of the Deep*, vol. XI, January 1896, 22.

22 *Toilers of the Deep*, September 1896, 247.

23 *Toilers of the Deep*, September 1896, 246.

24 Despite there being serious outbreaks of typhoid fever in Chicago in the years leading up to the World's Columbian Exposition, according to modern scholarship there was not a single case in 1893 that is traceable to the fair itself. See Bronwyn Rae, "Water, Typhoid Rates and the Columbian Exposition in Chicago," *Northwestern Public Health Review* 2, no. 2 (2015).

25 A more positive outcome of Robinson's visit to the north coast was his recommendation that the Moravians appoint their own doctor and develop their own medical facilities in Labrador. This recommendation was forwarded to the SFG in London and would eventually lead to the establishment of the Moravian hospital at Okkak in 1903. See MUN, CNS, Moravian Mission Records Microfilm 513 Reel 3, Minutes of SFG, October 7, 1896, paragraph 122.

26 *The Story of the Labrador Medical Mission*, Royal National Mission to the Deep-Sea Fishermen, The Rooms, Wilfred Grenfell Fonds, MG327, Reel 115.

27 *Toilers of the Deep*, vol. XII, July 1897, 191–192 and 215.

28 Esther had been twice married in the US but adopted the stage name Eneutseak, meaning "good people."

29 Jim Zwick, *Inuit Entertainers in the United States*, 53.

30 *Periodical Accounts*, vol. 34, December 1899, p.180; also, Zwick, *Inuit Entertainers*, 56.

31 MUN, CNS, Moravian Microfilm M 511 Reel 12, pp. 15574–15576.

32 MUN, CNS, Moravian Microfilm 513 Reel 4, SFG Minutes, January 9, 1903, paragraph 37.

33 MUN, CNS, Moravian Microfilm 513 Reel 4, SFG Minutes, January 12, 1904, paragraph 8.

34 *Periodical Accounts*, vol. 4, no. 46, June 1901, p. 35.

35 Zwick, *Inuit Entertainers in the United States*, 65.

36 Zwick, *Inuit Entertainers in the United States*, 65; also MUN, CNS, Moravian Microfilm SFG Minutes, January 9, 1903.

37 *Periodical Accounts*, series 2, vol. 5, no. 52, December 1902, p.165 and vol. 5, no. 56, December 1903, pp. 372 and 373.

38 *Periodical Accounts*, vol. 5, no. 56, p. 373.

39 "Serious Epidemic at Okak: Dr. Hutton's Report," *Periodical Accounts* V, no. 60, (December 1904), 622.

40 R.B. Joyce, *Sir William MacGregor* (Oxford University Press, 1971), 307.

41 Reports of His Excellency, Sir E.M. MacGregor, G.C., M.G., C.B., M.D., &C, Governor of Newfoundland, Of Official Visits to Labrador, 1905 and 1908. CNS. HF 3229. N4. N42, 1910, pp. 99–100.

42 Reports of His Excellency, Sir E.M. MacGregor, 102.

43 Reports of His Excellency, Sir E.M. MacGregor, 125: "The summer population of Labrador may be set down, in round numbers at from 20,000 to 25,000; the winter population at 4,000. Of these, some 1300 are native Innuit or settlers about Moravian missions."

44 *Periodical Accounts* VI, no. 63 (September 1905), 148.

45 RPA, GN 2.6, Box 29, Letter Edward Patrick Morris to Sir William MacGregor, 4 May 1907.

46 RPA, GN 2.6, Box 29, Letter to The Earl of Elgin from Sir William MacGregor, 9 May 1907.

47 RPA, GN 2.6, Box 29, Letter to Sir William MacGregor from The Earl of Elgin, 29 May 1907.

48 Anne Budgell, *We All Expected to Die* (ISER Books, 2018), 67 and 95.

49 *Periodical Accounts* VI, no. 76 (December 1908), 193–194.

50 Report of an Official Visit to Labrador By the Governor of Newfoundland, 1908, p. 188.

51 Proceedings of the House of Assembly and Legislative Council During the Third Session of the Twenty Second General Assembly of Newfoundland 1911, February 16, 1911, 105.

52 Proceedings of the House of Assembly and Legislative Council During the Third Session of the Twenty Second General Assembly, February 24, 1911, 204.

53 Proceedings of the House of Assembly and Legislative Council During the Third Session of the Twenty Second General Assembly, February 24, 1911, 205.

54 In 1910, the first comprehensive history of Labrador was published in which the allegation is again presented as fact. William G. Gosling, *Labrador: Its Discovery, Exploration, and Development* (Alston Rivers Ltd., 1910), 312.

55 Proceedings of the House of Assembly and Legislative Council During the Third Session of the Twenty Second General Assembly, February 24, 1911, 206.

56 Statute (Repeal) Act, Statutes of Newfoundland and Labrador, 1951 C.80, 295.

57 Prior to the summer of 1895, no minister of the Newfoundland Government had ever visited the Labrador coast in an official capacity, and prior to 1905, no Governor of the colony had visited the region.

58 Budgell, *We All Expected to Die*, 153–161.

59 Anthony Pagden, *People and Empires: Europeans and the Rest of the World, from Antiquity to the Present* (Weidenfeld & Nicholson, 2001), 135–159.

60 D.W. Prowse, *A History of Newfoundland from the English, Colonial and Foreign Records* (London: MacMillan & Co., 1895) and Gosling, *Labrador: Its Discovery, Exploration, and Development*.

61 The forced resettlement of the Inuit communities of Hebron and Nutak in the 1950s is one example. See Carol Brice-Bennett, *Dispossessed: The Eviction of Inuit from Hebron, Labrador* (Presses de l'Universite du Quebec, 2007).

62 The Labrador Inuit Association was formed in 1973 to promote Inuit interests in Labrador and to prepare a land claim. Upon reaching a land claim settlement with the Government of Canada and the Provincial Government of Newfoundland, the Nunatsiavut Government was created on December 1, 2005, to manage Inuit affairs in the region.

63 Susie Pottle, "Recollections," *Them Days Magazine* 7, no. 4, June 1982 and 8, no. 3, March 1983.

64 Dillon Wallace, *The Long Labrador Trail* (Fleming H. Revell Co., 1907), 279–280.

65 Missionary at Hebron, to Brother Connor, August 22, 1894.

66 *Periodical Accounts* 2, no. 21 (March 1895), 442.

Postscript

1 Ramah Diary for 1896/97, R.15.K.b.6a, UAH.

2 "Special Report from Ramah," *Periodical Accounts*, series 2, vol. 4 (1900), 583. Kuttukitok had wanted to move to Ramah immediately after Kupper's death, but was prevented by Paksaut, one of Tuglavina's half-brothers, who was said to be "feared by almost everyone." See *Periodical Accounts*, series 2, vol. 3 (December 1897), 371 and Ramah Diary for 1897, R.15.K.b.6a, UAH.

3 "Account of Br. Stecker's Tour to Kangiva and Ungava," *Periodical Accounts*, series 2, vol. 4 (1899), 327.

4 *Periodical Accounts* 5 (December 1903), 358.

5 Hudson's Bay Company Nachvak Post Journals, September 26, 1904, RPA: P.T McGrath Fonds.

6 Rama Church Book, MUN, CNS Moravian Microfilm 591, 168.

7 Rama Church Book, MUN, CNS Moravian Microfilm 591, 87.

8 Hebron Church Book, MUN, CNS Moravian Microfilm 592, no. 911, 456.

9 Hopedale Church Book, MUN, CNS Moravian Mission Microfilm 591, pp. 125, 126, and 442.

10 Hans Rollmann, *"I was baptized this winter... and received a new name." The Adoption of Christian Names and Surnames in the Moravian Communities of Nunatsiavut/Labrador*, unpublished manuscript, courtesy of the author, 7.

11 Hopedale Church Book, MUN, CNS Moravian Microfilm 591, no. 1040A, 119.

12 Hopedale Church Book, MUN, CNS Moravian Microfilm 591, Death Records, no. 1197.

13 Zwick, *Inuit Entertainers in the United States*, 136.

14 Personal Communication, Joyce Allen, Rigolet (Julia's great-granddaughter).

15 Personal Communication, Joyce Allen.

16 Personal Communication, Joyce Allen,

17 Personal Communication, Muriel Andersen, Happy Valley/Goose Bay (Abraham's granddaughter) and Makkovik Church Book, MUN CNS, Moravian Mission Microfilm 591, Birth Records nos. 27, 40, 62, 72, 97, 108.

18 Susie Pottle, "Reflections," *Them Days* 8, no. 3 (March 1983): 35; also Makkovik Church Book, Birth Records nos. 54 and 64.

19 Pottle, "Reflections," *Them Days* 8, no. 3, 35.

20 Pottle, "Reflections," *Them Days* 8, no. 3, 35.

21 "Extract from the Station Diary for Makkovik, July 1, 1904–July 1, 1905," *Periodical Accounts*, series 2, vol. 6, 213.

22 Personal communication, Joyce Allen, Rigolet.

23 *Them Days* 11, no. 1 (September 1985): 41.

24 Hopedale Church Book, MUN CNS, Moravian Mission Microfilm 591, Death Records, no. 915.

25 Hopedale Church Book, MUN CNS, Moravian Mission Microfilm 591, Marriage Records, no. 253.

26 "These Eskimos belong neither to the Church of England or the Methodists; they look upon themselves as members of your church, and I will do all in my power to help you if you will only come to Aivektok (sic) Bay." "Attempts to Establish a Moravian Mission at Rigolet," *Them Days* 22, no. 1 (Fall 1996): 16.

27 "Attempts to Establish a Moravian Mission at Rigolet," 20.

28 Armenius Young, *One Hundred Years of Mission Work in the Wilds of Labrador* (Arthur and Stockwell Ltd., 1916), 24.

29 Fifth Census of Canada, 1911, Unorganized Regions, Rigolet, Labrador, Canada.

30 "Grandfather's Stories," *Them Days* 24, no. 1 (Fall 1998): 21.

31 Marriage Records, Northwest River, United Church Archives, St. John's.

32 See below, p. 163.

33 Records of Burials, Northwest River, United Church Archives, St. John's.

34 Wallace, *The Long Labrador Trail*, 279–280.

35 Parish Records, Methodist and United Church for Northwest River, Box 1 (R2-D-2), RPA.

36 "A Baby Esquimaux," *Evening Telegram*, April 5, 1894.

37 Registration Records, Labrador District, Birth Register, 1892–1895, Registration Number 626714, http://ngb.chebucto.org/Vstats/post-1891-birth-1892-1895-620001-634463-lab.shtml.

38 Register of Deaths, District of Labrador, 1892–1897, 167, http://ngb.chebucto.org/Vstats/death-reg-bk-2-1892-1897-lab.shtml.

39 Register of Deaths, District of Labrador, 1892–1897, 168.

40 Registration Records Labrador District, Marriages 1917–1920, 503, http://ngb.chebucto.org/Vstats/post-1891-vol-8-mar-1917-1920-lab.shtml.

41 Hopedale Church Book, Births, 1004.

42 Parish Records, Methodist and United Church for Northwest River, Box 1 (R2-D-2), Baptismal Records 1884–1950, RPA.

43 Parish Records, Methodist and United Church for Northwest River, Box 1 (R2-D-2), Baptismal Records 1884–1950.

44 Methodist Records for Northwest River, Labrador, United Church Archives, Happy Valley/Goose Bay, Labrador.

45 Post 1891, Registration Records, Labrador District, Labrador Marriages 1901–1905, 495, http://ngb.chebucto.org/Vstats/post-1891-vol-4-mar-1901-1905-lab.shtml.

46 Registration Records Labrador District, Labrador Marriages 1909–1912, 485, http://ngb.chebucto.org/Vstats/post-1891-vol-6-mar-1909-1912-lab.shtml.

47 Register of Deaths, Labrador District 1919–1922, 496, http://ngb.chebucto.org/Vstats/death-reg-bk-8-1919-1922-lab.shtml.

48 Register of Deaths, Labrador District 1925–1930, 536, http://ngb.chebucto.org/Vstats/death-reg-bk-10-1925-1930-lab.shtml.

49 Personal communication, Henry John Palliser, Rigolet.

Appendix 1

1 Zwick, *Inuit Entertainers in the United States*, 152. Zwick states that the passenger list was made up by crew members and spellings were often inaccurate. Also of note, Moravian Inuit and Northlanders did not have surnames at this time. In these cases the crew member designated the name of the patriarch of the family as the surname and assigned it to others in the family. These designations were sometimes inaccurate.

Appendix 3

1 "Exodus of the Eskimos," *Daily Inter Ocean*, April 21, 1893.

2 "Two Eskimo Villages," *Daily Inter Ocean*, April 23, 1893.

Appendix 4

1 "Death of Another Baby," *San Francisco Morning Call*, April 11, 1894. The other baby, Francesca Deer, was born and died at the Midwinter Fair.

2 Walsh, *The Last Cruise of the Miranda*, 36.

Bibliography

Primary/Archival Sources

Hudson's Bay Company Archive/Archives of Manitoba. Post Journals. Numbers B183 (Rigolet), B52 (Davis Inlet), and B138 (Nachvak).

Hutchison, George Andrew, ed. *Toilers of the Deep: A Record of Mission Work Amongst Them*. London: Royal National Mission to Deep Sea Fishermen, 1841–1913.

Patrick Thomas McGrath Fonds (MG 8), The Rooms Provincial Archive.

Periodical Accounts Relating to the Mission of the Church of the United Brethren established among the Heathen. London: Brethren's Society for the Furtherance of the Gospel; Series 1, 1790–1889. Centre for Newfoundland Studies, Memorial University of Newfoundland.

Periodical Accounts Relating to the Foreign Missions of the Church of the United Brethren. London: Brethren's Society for the Furtherance of the Gospel among the Heathen; Series 2, 1890–1955. Centre for Newfoundland Studies, Memorial University of Newfoundland.

Society for the Furtherance of the Gospel. Letters, Minute Books, and Accounts. CNS Microfilm 513.

Wilfred Thomason Grenfell Fonds (MG 327), The Rooms Provincial Archive.

Books and Articles

Abbott, Charles C. "Sketch of Frederic Ward Putnam." *Popular Science Monthly* 29 (September 1886).

Adams, Bluford. *E Pluribus Barnum: The Great Showman and the Making of U.S. Popular Culture*. University of Minnesota Press, 1997.

Adams, Judith A. "The American Dream Actualized, the Glistening White City and the Lurking Shadows of the World's Columbian Exposition." In *The*

World's Columbian Exposition: A Centennial Bibliographic Guide (1996), xix–xxix.

Ames, Eric. *Carl Hagenbeck's Empire of Entertainments*. University of Washington Press, 2008.

Anderson, Virginia DeJohn. *Creatures of Empire: How Animals Transformed Early America*. Oxford University Press, 2004.

Anick, Norman. *The Fur Trade in Eastern Canada Until 1870*. Parks Canada, Department of Indian and Northern Affairs, Manuscript Report 207, volumes 1 and 2, 1976.

Appelbaum, Stanley. *Spectacle in the White City: The Chicago 1893 World's Fair*. Dover Publications, 1979.

A Week at the Fair, Illustrating the Exhibits and Wonders of the World's Columbian Exposition. Chicago: Rand McNally and Co. Publishers, 1893.

Badger, Rodney Reid. *The Great American Fair: The World's Columbian Exposition and American Culture*. Nelson-Hall, 1979.

Baikie, Margaret. *Labrador Memories, Reflections at Mulligan*. Them Days Publications, 1976.

Ballard, Barbara J. *A People Without a Nation*. Chicago History Magazine, 1999.

Bancroft, H.H. *The Book of the Fair: An Historical and Descriptive Presentation of the World's Science, Art and Industry as Viewed Through the Columbian Exposition in 1893*, volumes 1 and 2. The Bancroft Co., 1895.

Banks, Rosemarie. "Representing History: Performing the Columbian Exposition." *Theater Journal* 54, no. 4 (December 2002): 589–606.

The Barnum and Bailey Official Route Book, Season of 1894. Harvey L. Watkins, 1894. Milner Library, https://digital.library.illinoisstate.edu/digital/collection/p15990coll5/id/2049/.

The Barnum and Bailey Official Route Book, Season of 1895. George E. Hardy, 1895. Milner Library, https://digital.library.illinoisstate.edu/digital/collection/p15990coll5/id/1914.

Beck, David R.M. and Rosalyn R. Lapier. *City Indian: Native American Activism in Chicago, 1893–1934*. University of Nebraska Press, 2015.

Blake, Thomas. *The Diary of Thomas Blake*. Them Days Incorporated, 2000.

Board of Trade of Chicago. *Annual Report for the Year Ending December 31, 1890*. JME Jones Stationery and Printing Co., 1891.

Board of Control of the World's Columbian Exposition. *Memorial Volume of the World's Columbian Exposition.*

Boehm, Lisa Krissoff. *Popular Culture and the Enduring Myth of Chicago, 1871–1968*. Routledge, 2004.

Brice-Bennett, Carol. *Dispossessed: The Eviction of Inuit from Hebron, Labrador.* Presses de l'Universite du Quebec, 2007.

Brice-Bennett, Carol. "Missionaries as Traders: Moravians and Labrador Inuit 1771–1860." In *Merchant Credit and Labour Strategies in Historical Perspective*, edited by Rosemary E. Ommer. Acadiensis Press, 1990.

Brice-Bennett, Carol. *The Northlanders: A History of the Population and Socio-Economic Relations and Cultural Change of Inuit Occupying the Remote Northern Coast of Labrador,* unpublished manuscript written for the Labrador Inuit Association, 1996.

Brice-Bennett, Carol. *Our Footprints are Everywhere: Inuit Land Use and Occupancy in Labrador*. Labrador Inuit Association, 1977.

Brice-Bennett, Carol. "Two Opinions: Inuit and Moravian Missionaries in Labrador 1804–1860." MA thesis, Memorial University of Newfoundland, 1981.

Brown, Rev. P.W. *Where the Fishers Go*. Cochrane Publishing Co., 1909.

Budgell, Anne. *We All Expected to Die.* ISER Books, 2018.

Buel, J.W. *The Magic City: A Massive Portfolio of Original Photographic Views of the Great World's Fair and Its Treasures of Art, Including a Vivid Representation of the Famous Midway Plaisance*. St. Louis, Historical Publishing, 1894.

Bullock, Alan and Stephen Trombley, editors. *The New Fontana Dictionary of Modern Thought*, 3rd Edition (1999).

Campbell, J.G. *Illustrated History of the World's Fair*, volumes 1 and 2. Sessler and Dungan, 1894.

Campbell, Lydia. "Sketches of Labrador Life," *Evening Telegram*, December 1896.

Carew, Jan. "Columbus and the Origins of Racism in the Americas," *Race and Class* XXIX, no. 4 (1988).

Cartwright, George. *A Journal of Transactions and Events, during a residence of nearly sixteen years on the coast of Labrador*. Cambridge University Press, 2012.

Conkey, W.B. *Official Catalogue of the World's Columbian Exposition*. Department of Publicity and Promotion, Chicago 1893. The Lakeside Press, 1894.

Cronon, William. *Nature's Metropolis: Chicago and the Great West.* W.W. Norton and Co., 1991.

Cross, Lauren, Lauren Seitz, and Shannon Walter. "The First of its Kind: A Cultural History of the Village Nègre." *Digital Literature Review* 3 (2016): 21–31.

Dailey, Victoria. "California's First International Exposition: The Midwinter Fair of 1894." *Quarterly News-Letter, The Book Club of California* 75, no. 1 (2010): 3–8.

Davies, W.H.A., "Notes on Esquimaux Bay and the Surrounding Countries." *Literary and Historical Society of Quebec* 4, Part 1 (1842): 70–94.

Davis, Lisa Cushing. "Hegemony and Resistance at the World's Columbian Exposition: Simon Pokagon and the Red Man's Rebuke." *Journal of Illinois State Historical Society* 108, no. 1 (2015): 32–53.

Dean, Teresa. *White City Chips*. Chicago: Warren Publishing Co., 1895.

De Boilieu, Lambert. *Recollections of Labrador Life*. London: Saunders, Otley & Co., 1861.

Dedicatory and Opening Ceremonies of the World's Columbian Exposition. Chicago: Stone, Kastler & Painter, 1893.

Dennett, Andrea Stulman. *Weird and Wonderful: The Dime Museum in America*. New York University Press, 1997.

Dexter, Ralph W. "Putnam's Problems at the Fair." *American Scientist* 54, no. 3 (1966): 315–331.

Dippie, Brian. *The Vanishing American: White Attitudes and U.S. Indian Policy*. University of Kansas Press, 1991.

The Dream City: A Portfolio of Photographic Views of the World's Columbian Exposition. St. Louis: N.D. Thompson Publishing Co., 1893.

Feest, Christian F. *Indians and Europe: An Interdisciplinary Collection of Essays*. University of Nebraska, 1989.

Fleming, Herbert E. "The Literary Interests of Chicago." *American Journal of Sociology* 11, no. 3 (November 1905): 784–790.

Forbush, William Byron. *Pomiuk: A Prince of Labrador.* Marshall Brothers, 1903.

Gordon, Tom. *Called Upstairs: Moravian Inuit Music in Labrador*. McGill-Queen's University Press, 2023.

Gosling, W.G. *Labrador: Its Discovery, Exploration, and Development*. Alston Rivers Ltd., 1910.

Grenfell, Wilfred T. "How We Found Prince Pomiuk." *Toilers of the Deep,* 111–113.

Hale, Wm H. "Strange People at the World's Fair." *The Cultivator & Country Gentleman,* September 28, 1893: 760–761.

Hales, Peter Bacon. Introduction to *Spectacle in the White City: The Chicago 1893 World's Fair*. Dover Publications, 1979.

Halligan, J. *Halligan's Illustrated World's Fair: A Pictorial and Literary History of the World's Columbian Exposition*. Chicago: The Lakeside Press, 1894.

Hallock, Charles. "Three Months in Labrador," *Harper's New Monthly Magazine,* May 1861, 577–599 and 743–765.

Harper, Kenn. *Give Me My Father's Body: The Life of Minik, the New York Eskimo*. Steerforth Press, 2000.

Harper, Kenn and Russell Potter. "Early Arctic Films of Nancy Columbia and Esther Eneutseak." *Nimrod* 10, no. 4 (2010).

Harris, Marvin. *The Rise of Anthropological History: A History of Culture.* Altamira Press, 2001.

Harris, Neil. "Memory and the White City." In *Grand Illusions: Chicago World's Fair of 1893*, Neil Harris, William de Wit, James Gilbert, and Robert W. Rydell. Chicago Historical Society, 1993.

Hawthorne, Julian. *Humors of the Fair*. Chicago: E.A. Weeks & Co., 1893.

Hickson, Thomas. "Excerpts from Journals." *Wesleyan-Methodist Magazine*, vol. 4 of the 3rd Series, 1825, 58–62, 136–138 and 206–207.

Hiller, J.K. "Early Patrons of the Labrador Eskimos: The Moravian Mission in Labrador, 1764–1805." In *Patrons and Brokers in the Eastern Arctic*, edited by Robert Paine. Institute of Social and Economic Research, Memorial University of Newfoundland, 1971.

Hiller, J.K. "Eighteenth Century Labrador: the European Perspective." In *Moravian Beginnings in Labrador: Papers from a Symposium held in Makkovik and Hopedale*, edited by Hans Rollmann. Newfoundland and Labrador Studies, Occasional Publication no. 2, Memorial University of Newfoundland, 2009.

Hiller, J.K. "The Foundations and the Early Years of the Moravian Mission in Labrador, 1752–1805." MA Thesis, Memorial University of Newfoundland, 1967.

Hiller, J.K. "Jens Haven and the Moravian Mission in Labrador." *Newfoundland Historical Society* (October 1968).

Hiller, J.K. "The Moravians in Labrador 1771–1805." *The Polar Record* 15, no. 99 (1971): 839–854.

Hinsley, Curtis M. "The World as Marketplace: Commodification of the Exotic at the World's Columbian Exposition, Chicago, 1893." In *Exhibiting Cultures: The Politics and Poetics of Museum Display*, edited by Ivan Karp and Stephen D. Levine. Smithsonian Institution Press, 1992.

Hinsley, Curtis M. and David R. Wilcox. *Coming of Age in Chicago: The 1893 World's Fair and the Coalescence of American Anthropology*. University of Nebraska Press, 2016.

Holley, Marietta. *Samantha at the World's Fair New York*. New York: Funk & Wagnalls, 1893.

Jenks, Tudor. *The Century World's Fair Book for Boys and Girls; Being the Adventures of Harry and Philip with their Tutor Mr. Douglass, at the World's Columbian Exposition.* New York: Century Co., 1893.

Johnson, Rossiter. *A History of the World's Columbian Exposition held in Chicago in 1893*, vols. 1–4. New York: D. Appleton & Co., 1897.

Joyce, R.B. *Sir William MacGregor*. Oxford University Press, 1971.

Kaplan, Susan A. "Economic and Social Change in Labrador Neo-Eskimo Culture." PhD Thesis, Bryn Mawr College, 1983.

Kennedy, John C. *Encounters: An Anthropological History of Southeastern Labrador.* McGill-Queen's University Press, 2015.

Kennedy, John C. (editor). *History and Renewal of Labrador's Inuit-Metis.* ISER Books, 2014.

Kleivan, Helge. *The Eskimos of Northeast Labrador: A History of Eskimo-White Relations 1771–1955.* Norsk Polarinstitutt, 1966.

Korneski, Kurt. "Planters, Eskimos, and Indians: Race and the Organization of Trade under the Hudson's Bay Company in Labrador, 1830–50." *Journal of Social History* 50, no. 2 (2016): 307–335.

Korneski, Kurt. "Trouble Down North: Unsettling Settlers in Hamilton Inlet, 1871–1883." In *Conflicted Colony: Critical Episodes in Nineteenth-Century Newfoundland and Labrador*. McGill-Queen's University Press, 2016.

MacGregor, E.M. *Reports of His Excellency. Sir E.M. MacGregor G.C. M.G. C.B., M.D., Governor of Newfoundland, Of Official Visits to Labrador, 1905 and 1908.* Centre for Newfoundland Studies, Memorial University of Newfoundland.

"The Magic City, A Portfolio of Original Photographic Views of the Great World's Fair and Its Treasures of Art." *Historical Fine Arts Series* 1, no. 6, H.S. Smith, C.R. Grau (19 February 1894).

Midway Types, A Book of Illustrated Lessons About the People of the Midway Plaisance, World's Fair 1893. Chicago: The American Engraving Co., 1894.

Montesquieu, Baron de. *The Spirit of Laws*. 1748. Translated by Thomas Nugent, 1752. Batoche Books, 2001.

Morgan, Lewis Henry. *Ancient Society: Researches in the Lines of Human Progress from Savagery, through Barbarism to Civilization*. New York: Holt, 1877.

Moses, L.G. *Wild West Shows and the Images of American Indians, 1883–1933*. University of New Mexico Press, 1996.

Mumford, Lewis. *Sticks and Stones: A Study of American Architecture and Civilization.* Boni and Liveright, 1924.

Naylor, Robert Anderton. *Across the Atlantic*. The Roxburghe Press, 1893.

Official Guide to the World's Columbian Exposition, compiled by John J. Flynn. Chicago: The Columbian Guide Co., 1893.

Official Views of the World's Columbian Exposition, Department of Photography. Chicago: Chicago Photo Gravure, 1893.

Paddon, Anna R., and Sally Turner. "African Americans and the World's Columbian Exposition." *Illinois Historical Journal* 88, no. 1 (1995): 19–36.

Pagden, Anthony. *The Burdens of Empire: 1539 to the Present*. Cambridge University Press, 2015.

Pagden, Anthony. *People and Empires: Europeans and the Rest of the World from Antiquity to the Present.* Weidenfeld & Nicholson, 2001.

Pauls, Elizabeth Prine. "Cultural Evolution." *Encyclopedia Britannica*, 2008.

Photographs of the World's Fair: The Columbian Portfolio. Chicago: The Jones Publishing Co., 1893.

Pierce, Bessie Louise. *A History of Chicago, Volume l, The Beginning of a City, 1673–1848*. University of Chicago, 1937.

Pierce, Bessie Louise. *A History of Chicago, Volume III, The Rise of the Modern City, 1871–1893*. University of Chicago Press, 1957.

Pierce, J.W. *Photographic History of the World's Fair and Sketch of the City of Chicago*. Baltimore: R.H. Woodward and Co., 1893.

Portfolio of Photographs of the World's Fair. Chicago: The Werner Co., 1893.

Prowse, D.W. *A History of Newfoundland from the English, Colonial and Foreign Records*. London: MacMillan & Co., 1895.

Raibmon, Paige. *Authentic Indians: Episodes of Encounter from the Late-Nineteenth Century Northwest Coast*. Duke University Press, 2005.

Ralph, Julian. *Harper's Chicago and the World's Fair*. New York: Harper and Bros., 1893.

Reinhart, Melissa. "To Hell With the Wigs: Native American Representation and Resistance at the World's Columbian Exposition." *The American Indian Quarterly* 36, no. 4 (Fall 2012): 403–442.

Rollmann, Hans. "The Adoption of Christian Names and Surnames in the Moravian Communities of Nunatsiavut, Labrador." *Journal of Moravian History* 18, no. 2 (2018): 145–158.

Rollmann, Hans. *Demographics and Literacy of the Rigolet-Area Inuit During the Second Half of the Nineteenth Century*. Unpublished manuscript.

Rollmann, Hans. "Hopedale: Gateway to the South and Moravian Settlement." *Newfoundland and Labrador Studies* 28, no. 2 (2013): 153–192.

Rollmann, Hans. "*I was baptized this winter... and received a new name." The Adoption of Christian Names and Surnames in the Moravian Communities of Nunatsiavut/ Labrador*. Unpublished manuscript.

Rollmann, Hans. "Moravians in Central Labrador: The Indigenous Mission of Jacobus and Salome at Snook's Cove." *Journal of Moravian History* 10, no. 9 (2010): 6–40.

Rollmann, Hans. "'So fond of the pleasure to shoot': The Sale of Firearms to Inuit on Labrador's North Coast in the late 18th Century." *Newfoundland and Labrador Studies* 26, no. 1 (2011): 5–24.

Rollmann, Hans. "'So that in this part you should lag behind other missionary congregations...': The Introduction of National Helpers in the Moravian Mission among the Labrador Inuit." *Journal of Moravian History* 17, no. 2 (2017): 138–159.

Rompkey, Ronald. *Grenfell of Labrador*. University of Toronto Press, 1992.

Rompkey, Ronald (editor). *Labrador Odyssey: The Journals and Photographs of Eliot Curwen on the Second Voyage of Wilfred Grenfell, 1893*. McGill-Queen's University Press, 1996.

Rose, Julie K. "The World's Columbian Exposition: Idea, Experience, and Aftermath." MA thesis, University of Virginia, 1996.

Rosenberg, Chaim M. *America at the Fair: Chicago's 1893 World's Columbian Exposition*. Arcadia Publishing, 2008.

Rudwick, Elliott M. and August Meier. "Black Man in the White City: Negroes and the Columbian Exposition, 1893." *Phylon* 26, no. 4 (1965).

Rumney, Jay. *Herbert Spencer's Sociology*. Atherton Press, 1966.

Rydell, Robert W. *All the World's A Fair*. University of Chicago Press, 1984.

Rydell, Robert W. "The World's Columbian Exposition of 1893: Racist Underpinnings of a Utopian Artefact." *Journal of American Culture* 1, no. 2 (Summer 1978).

Schneirov, Richard, Shelton Stromquist, and Nick Salvatore. Introduction to *The Pullman Strike and the Crisis of the 1890s*. Cornell University, 1999.

Scott, Gertrude. *Village Performance: Villages at the Chicago World's Columbian Exposition, 1893*. Unpublished Doctoral Dissertation, New York University, 1991.

Scott, Thomas G. *History of the Esquimau Race*. Erie, PA: Dispatch Print, 1893.

Shaw, Marion. *World's Fair Notes: A Woman Journalist Views Chicago's 1893 Columbian Exposition*. Pogo Press, 1992 (Compilation of Original Articles).

Skrupskelis, Ignas K. and Elizabeth M. Berkeley. *William and Henry James: Selected Letters*. University of Virginia Press, 1997.

Slotkin, Richard. *The Fatal Environment: The Myth of the Frontier in the Age of Industrialization 1800–1890*. Atheneum, 1985.

Snider, D.J. *World's Fair Studies*. Chicago: Sigma Publishing, 1895.

Spencer, Herbert. *Principles of Sociology*. London: W.J. Johnson, 1876.

Stocking Jr., George W. *Race, Culture and Evolution*. University of Chicago Press, 1982.

Stopp, Marianne P. "Eighteenth Century Labrador Inuit in England." *Arctic* 62, no. 1 (2008): 45–64.

Stopp, Marianne P. "'I Old Lydia Campbell': A Labrador Woman of National Historical Significance." In *History and Renewal of Labrador's Inuit-Metis*. ISER Books, 2014.

Stopp, Marianne P. Introduction to *George Cartwright's The Labrador Companion.* McGill-Queen's University Press, 2016.

Stopp, Marianne P. *The New Labrador Papers of Captain George Cartwright*. McGill-Queen's University Press, 2008.

Stopp, Marianne P. "Reconsidering Inuit Presence in Southern Labrador." *Etudes/Inuit/Studies* 26, no. 2 (2002): 71–106.

Sturtevant, William C. and David Beers Quinn. "This New Prey: Eskimos in Europe in 1567, 1576 and 1577." In *Indians and Europe: An Interdisciplinary Collection of Essays*. University of Nebraska, 1989.

Swift, L.S. *The Yankee of the Yards, The Biography of Gustavus Franklin Swift*. A.W. Shaw Co., 1927.

Sullivan, Louis H. *The Autobiography of an Idea*. Press of the American Institute of Architects, 1924.

Taber, Ralph Graham. *Northern Lights and Shadows*. London: Greening and Co. Ltd., 1900.

Taber, Ralph Graham. "Rugged Labrador." *Outing: An Illustrated Magazine of Recreation*, vol. 27, October 1895; November 1895; December 1895; January 1896; February 1896.

Taylor, J. Garth. "Labrador Eskimo Settlements of the Early Contact Period." *National Museums of Canada, Publications in Ethnology*, no. 9 (1974).

Trachtenberg, Alan. *The Incorporation of America, Culture and Society in the Gilded Age*. Hill and Wang, 1982.

Trouillot, Michel-Rolph. "Good Day Columbus: Silences, Power and Public History (1492–1892)." *Popular Culture* 3, no. 1 (1990): 1–24.

Trouillot, Michel-Rolph. *Silencing the Past: Power and the Production of History*. Beacon Press, 1995.

Truman, B.C. *The History of the World's Fair, Being a Complete Description of the World's Columbian Exposition from its Inception*. Chicago: Mammoth Books, 1893.

Turner, Frederick J. *The Significance of Frontier in American History*. Annual Report of the American Historical Association for the year 1893.

The Vanishing City: A Photographic Encyclopedia of the World's Columbian Exposition. Chicago: Laird and Lee, 1893.

Vincent, William David. "Home Life of the Esquimaux." *The Graphic*, March 4, 1893.

Wallace, Dillon. *The Long Labrador Trail*. F.H. Revell, 1907.

Walsh, Henry Collin. *The Last Cruise of the Miranda*. New York-London: The Transatlantic Publishing Company, 1896.

Way, Patricia. "The Story of William Phippard." In *History and Renewal of Labrador's Inuit-Metis*, edited by John C. Kennedy. ISER Books, 2014.

White, Richard. *The Rise of Industrial America 1877–1900*. The Gilder Lehraman Institute of American History, gilderlehraman.org.

Whitely, George. "The Story of Pomiuk." *The Newfoundland Quarterly* 58, no. 2 (June 1959).

Whitley, W.H. "The Establishment of the Moravian Mission in Labrador and British Policy 1763–83." *Canadian Historical Review* 45 (1964).

Wilson, William. *Newfoundland and Its Missionaries*. Cambridge, Mass.: Daikan and Metcalfe, 1868.

Young, Arminius. *One Hundred Years of Mission Work in the Wilds of Labrador*. Arthur and Stockwell Ltd., 1916.

Zimmerly, David. "Cain's Land Revisited: Culture Change in Central Labrador, 1775–1972." *Newfoundland Social and Economic Studies*, no. 16, 1975.

Zumwalt, Rosemary Lévy. *Franz Boas: The Emergence of the Anthropologist*. University of Nebraska Press, 2019.

Zumwalt, Rosemary Lévy. *Franz Boas: Shaping Anthropology and Fostering Social Justice*. University of Nebraska Press, 2022.

Zwick, Jim. *Inuit Entertainers in the United States: From the Chicago World's Fair through the Birth of Hollywood*. Infinity Publishing Co., 2006.

Index

Photographs are indicated with page numbers in *italics*.

Ailik, 21, 23–25, 111, 132, 135, 147, 160–161, 169, 173

Aiviktok, 8, 11, 15–19, 21, 23–24, 48, 111, 161–162, 169; *see* Baie St. Louis, Baye Esquimaux, Baye Kessessakiou, Hamilton Inlet

Algiers, 149

Âpili, xv, 32–33, 49, 85, *91*, 105, 111, 129, 130–131, 133, 138–139, 149, 160, 168, 172, 174

Back Run, 21

Baffin Island, 12, 69

Baie St. Louis, 15; *see* Aiviktok, Baye Esquimaux, Baye Kessessakiou, Hamilton Inlet

Baltimore, 71

Barcelona, 149

Barnum and Bailey Circus, 71, 130, 138

Barnum and Bailey Ethnological Congress, 71, 130, 173, 174

Barnum, P.T., 70, 71, 75, 130

Baye Esquimaux, 15; *see* Aiviktok, Baie St. Louis, Baye Kessessakiou, Hamilton Inlet

Baye Kessessakiou, 15; *see* Aiviktok, Baie St. Louis, Baye Esquimaux, Hamilton Inlet

Bell, P.W., 20

Big Island, 21, 135

Boas, Franz, 12, 75, 131, 138

Bond, Robert, 150–151, 153–156

Bonne Bay, 133

Boston, 48, 71, 77, 78, 79, 81, 129

Boston Globe, The, 77–79

Bourquin, Theodor (Br.), 29–30

Burnt(wood) Cove, 21, 136

Cape Charles, 14, 16, 138

Cape Chidley, 11, 46, 78, 144, 159

Carawalla, 17, 21, 163

Cartwright, George, 16, 18, 69

Caubvick, 16

Chicago, 1–4, 13, 19, 28, 32–34, 47–50, 55–61, 64, 71, 74, 76, 77, 79–80, 83, 85, *86*, *87*, *88*, *89*, *90*, *91*, *92*, 99, 108–109, 112, 113–115, 120–121, 125–129, 131, 132–133, 135–139, 147–148, 152, 155, 156–158, 160, 163

Chicago Daily Inter Ocean, The, 80, 96, 101, 104, 106, 113, 171

Chicago News Record, The, 80

Chicago Tribune, The, 1, 56–57, 64, 80, 97, 138
Cincinnati, 71
Cleveland, 71
Cleveland, Grover, 56–57, 128, 131
Columbus, Christopher, 12, 56, 62, 64–65, 68–69, 73–74, 76, 85, 127.
Constantine, 149
Cook, Frederick, 138, 174
Cutthroat, 33, 146
Daniel's Rattle, 32
Daniels, P.M., 80, 99–101, 105–107, 111, 119, 129, 132–133, 173
Davis Inlet, 9, 29, 33, 49; *see* Ukkusiksalik
de Young, Michael Henry, 120
Deer, Eliza, 163
Deer, Francesca, 127–128, 163
Deer, George, 21, 104, 111, 126–127, 135, 163, 167, 170, 171, 173
Deer, Kitty Esther, 163
Deer, Maggie (Margaret), 21, *92*, 104, 111, 126–127, 135, 163, 167, 170, 171, 173
Deer, Peter, 21, *92*, 104, 126–127, 163, 167, 170, 171
Deer, Sarah, *92*, 163, 167, 170
Deer, Thomas (Tom/Tommie), 21, 99, 107, 139, 163, 167, 170, 174
Deers, the, 162
Degouluk, 47, 112–113, 165, 168, 171
Double Island, 146; *see* Uviluktuk
Double Mer, 21
England, 16, 19, 69
England, Church of, 161–162
Esther (Eneutseak), 33, 85, *91*, 129, 130–131, 133, 138–139, 149, 160, 166, 168, 172, 174
Evelena (schooner), xv–xvi, 11, 17–18, 20–21, 23, 25, 32–34, 37, 46–48, 77– 80, 104, 165, 168
Evelina, *see* Kotuktooka
Evening Telegram, The, 133
Ford, George, 32, 136
Ford, John, 32
Ford, Mary, 33, 165, 168, 171
Ford, Robert, 32–33, 80, 98–99, 101–102, 104–106, 111, 126, 160, 165, 168, 171, 173
Ford, Susan, 33, 126, 160, 165, 168, 171, 173
Ford, William (Wm), 33, 165, 168, 171
Fort Chimo, 39, 40–42
Frobisher, Martin, 69
Germany, 75, 150
Golden Gate Park, 120
Grenfell, Wilfred (Dr.), 136, 144–147, 149, 151, 153–154, 157
Hagenbeck, Carl, 25, 57, 71–72, 75
Halifax, 11, 13, 15
Hallock, Charles, 18–20
Hamilton Inlet, 15, 146; *see* Aiviktok, Baie St. Louis, Baye Esquimaux, Baye Kessessakiou
Haven, Jens, 38, 41
Hebron, 25, 27–28, 31–32, 34, 37, 39, 40–43, 46, 47–48, 135–137, 144–145, 146, 150–151, 153, 155, 158, 160, 169
Helene, xv, 32–33, 85, *91*, 111, 129, 130–131, 133, 138–139, 149, 160, 168, 172, 174

Hopedale, 8, 15–17, 23, 25, 27–28, 29, 32–33, 146, 147, 149, 151, 155, 160
Hudson's Bay Company, xv, 7, 11, 12, 15, 17–21, 23–25, 29, 32, 39–44, 47, 49, 55, 78, 132, 135–136, 147, 161–162
Hutton, Samuel King (Dr.), 151, 153
J.W. Skiles & Co., 11–13, 98
Jackson Park, 56–57, 61, 74, 77, 81, 84–85, 97, 105
Justina (Zacharias), 34, 137, 160, 166, 169, 172, 173
Kaipokok, 17, 23–24
Kamialuit, 47, 79, 126, 132, 136, 165, 168, 171
Kangerarsuk, 47, 81, 111, 112, 132, 159, 168, 171
Kenemish, 17, 162
Killinek, 46, 162
Kitsimagvik, 41, 42
Komaktorvik, 159
Kotuktooka (Evelina), 84, 132, 136, 171
Kupper, 47, 79, 84, 111–112, 132, 136, 159, 168, 171
Kuttukitok, 47, 84, 111, 132, 136, 159, 168, 171
Labrador, xv–xvi, 1–5, 11–17, 19, 21, 23, 25–27, 33–34, 38, 40, 42, 45–50, 55, 58, 69, 72, 76, 77–78, 80, 81, 85, 94, 97, 102–103, 104, 106, 108–109, 112, 114, 119, 126, 128, 129, 131, 132, 134, 136–139, 141, 142, 144–154, 156–157, 159–163, 171, 173–174
Labrador (vessel), 41
London, 25, 27, 32, 41, 71–72, 149–150
Long Tickle, 23
Lucy, Abraha, 25, 102, 161, 166, 169, 172
Lucy, Charlotte, 25, 111, 126, 135, 161, 166, 169, 171, 173
Lucy, John, 24–25, 48, 79, 100, 102, 105, 111, 132, 139, 160, 166, 169, 172, 173–174
Lucy, Jonas (Janasik), 25, 161, 166, 169, 172
Lucy, Joseph, 24–25, 111, 126, 128, 135, 161, 166, 169, 171, 173
Lucy, Julia Hedwig, 25, 160–161, 166, 169, 172
Lucy, Katerina, 24–25, 79, 111, 132, 139, 160, 166, 169, 172
Lucy, Simon, 25, 161, 166, 169, 172
Lucy, Tomasi, 25, 139, 163, 166, 169, 174
Lucys, the, 132
MacGregor, William, 151–154, 157
Madrid, 149
Mali, 47, 132, 165, 168, 171
Manak, (Columbia) Susan, 84, 85, 113
Manak, Abraha, 25, 161, 166, 169, 171, 173
Manak, Jacobus Marcus, 25, 161, 166, 169, 171, 173
Manak, Maria, 25, 161, 166, 169, 171, 173
Manak, Peterusi, 25, 161, 166, 169, 171, 173
Manak, Sarah, 25, 84, 111, 126, 128, 135, 161, 166, 169, 171, 173
Manak, Sarah (Jr.), 25, 161, 167, 169, 171, 173
Manak, Simon, 24–25, 84, 111, 126, 128, 135, 161, 166, 169, 171, 173
Manasse, Clara, 138
Manasse, Will, 138
Mason's Point, 21

McConnell, William, 13, 15, 32, 80, 104
McKenzie, Keith, 20, 45
Memorial University of Newfoundland, 3
Mesher, Peter, 21, 99–103, 105, 107, 109, 139, 162–163, 167, 170, 172, 174
Mikak, 19
Milwaukee, 71
Montreal, 132
Moravian(s), xv–xvi, 3, 7, 11, 12, 14–19, 23–32, 34, 38–47, 49, 55, 58, 78, 113, 125, 135, 137, 141–146, 148–154, 157–158, 159–162
Morris, Edward, 153–154
Nachvak, 9, 25, 32, 35, 37–47, 94, 111, 132–136, 144–145, 147, 159, 168, 173
Naemi, 34, 111, 126, 160, 166, 169, 172, 173
Nain, 4, 14, 19, 27–29, 32–33, 38, 46, 133, 135, 137, 141–146, 148, 149, 151, 153, 155, 158, 160
Nancy Columbia, 85, *91*, 129–131, 133, 138–139, 149, 160, 172, 174
Naples, 149
New York, 59, 70–71, 75, 128, 129, 131, 134, 138–139, 149, 160, 174
New York Times, The, 104
Newfoundland, 4, 14, 16, 19, 23–25, 45, 49, 69, 102, 132–133, 136, 138, 142, 144–147, 149–152, 154–157, 163
North West River, 17–18
Nullatatok Bay, 42–43
Nunatsiavut, 3
Okkak, 18, 25, 27, 33, 38–39, 41, 42, 47, 143–144, 146, 149, 151–152
Opatik (Bay), 32–33, 138, 160
Palliser, Christopher Columbus, 85, 126–127, 172, 173
Palliser, Esther, 21, 111, 126, 135, 167, 170, 172, 173
Palliser, Hugh, 19, 69
Palliser, John, 21, 162, 166, 169, 172, 173
Palliser, Jonas, 19, 21, 85, 100–101, 105, 111, 126–127, 135, 162, 166, 169, 170, 172, 173–174
Palliser, Joseph, 18–19
Palliser, Lucy, 21, 85, 139, 162–163, 166, 169, 172, 173
Palliser, Mark, 158, 162
Palliser, Mary (Magdaline), 21, 79, 126, 138, 158, 162, 166, 167, 170, 172, 173–174
Palliser, Peter, 19, 21, 79, *93*, 100, 102, 105, 111, 126, 137–138, 162, 167, 170, 172, 174
Palliser, Sam, 21, 102, 162, 166, 169, 172, 173
Palliser, Susan (Susie; wife of Jonas), 21, 85, 111, 126–127, 135, 162, 166, 169, 172, 173
Palliser, Susie (Susan; daughter of Tom and Esther), 21, 85, 167, 170, 172, 173
Palliser, Tom (Thomas), 21, 79, 100, 102, 111, 126, 135, 162, 166, 170, 172, 173
Palliser's Point, 21
Pallisers, the, 21, 100, 162
Palmer, Thomas, 113
Paris, 63–64, 72, 138, 149, 160
Paul's Island, 29, 32
Pomiuk, 13, 47, 79, 81, 112, 126, 132, 136, 165, 168, 171

Porter, V.R., 99–100, 102–103, 105–107, 139, 163

Putnam, Frederic, xii, 12, 62, 63–65, 68, 72–76, 77, 94, 131

Ramah, 25, 27, 34–35, 42–47, 135–136, 146, 159

Rigolet, 15–21, 23–24, 33, 48, 77, 132–133, 135–136, 138, 147, 158, 161–163

Robinson, Frederick Augustine (Dr.), 147–148

Saglek, 39, 40–41, 43

San Francisco, xvi, 119–121, 125–129, 132, 133–134, 137, 156, 163, 173–174

San Francisco Chronicle, The, 108, 120

San Francisco Morning Call, The, 128

Sandwich Bay, 16, 18

Schneider, Johann, 41

Scott, Thomas G., 110, 119–120, 129, 132, 173

Seattle, 139

Semigak, 43, 159

Shugalough (sic), 18–19

Shuglawina, 18

Shuglo, Augustina (Augustinuk), 21, 129, 163, 167, 170, 171, 174

Shuglo, Jim (James; Jimmie), 18, 20–21, 100, 102, 104–105, 111, 129, 133, 162–163, 170, 171, 174

Shuglo, Liza (Eliza?), 21, 129, 163, 167, 170, 171, 174

Shuglo, Maggie (Margaret), 21, 129, 163, 167, 170, 171, 174

Shuglo, Salome (Salomie), 21, 111, 129, 162–163, 167, 170, 171, 174

Shuglo, Tom, 21, 129, 163, 167, 170, 171, 174

Shuglos, the, 129, 133, 162–163

Sikepa, 47, 132, 159, 168, 171

Smith, Donald, 40–42

Smith, J.C., 153

Snook's Cove, 21

Society for the Furtherance of the Gospel (SFG), 27–28, 30, 32, 40, 150

Spencer, Herbert, 67–68

St. John's, 132, 133, 134, 138, 146, 156, 163

St. John's Daily News, The, 141, 147

St. Lawrence River, 14

St. Louis, 139

St. Louis Post-Dispatch, The, 81, 108,

Stecker, Adolf (Br.), 135, 159

Strait of Belle Isle, 14, 144

Tabea, 34, 169, 172, 173

Taber, Ralph Graham, 11, 13, 21, 24– 26, 32, 33–35, 38, 46–47, 49–50, 63, 76, 78–80, 101, 133–134, 137–138, 144, 149, 160, 165

Tiguja(k), 47,132, 159, 165, 168, 171

Treaty of Paris, 14

Tuglavina (AngajukKâk at Nachvak), 41, 42–44, 47

Tuglavina (wife of Kangerarsuk), 47, 111–112, 132, 159, 168, 171

Tuktashina, Abraha, 25, 126, 135, 161, 167, 169, 171, 173

Tunis, 149

Tutauk, 19

Ukkusiksalik, 9, 29, 32–33, 48, 138; *see* Davis Inlet

Ulrikab, Abraham, 25

Ungava (Bay), 11, 39, 40–41, 45, 47, 78, 159

Uviluktuk, 146; *see* Double Island

Vincent, William David, 11, 13, 21, 24–25, 32, 33–35, 37–38, 46–50, 63, 76, 79–80, 101, 119, 129, 133, 173
Webeck Harbour, 23
Weiz, Samuel (Br.), 41–43
West Turnavik Island, 23
"White City", 56–57, 61–62, 74–76, 125
Winser, John, 138
Zacharias (Naemiup), 34, 98–99, 105, 111, 126–127, 136–137, 158, 160, 166, 169, 172, 173
Zoar, 9, 27, 28–30, 32–33, 138, 160, 168